CRY SABOTAGE!

By Burke Wilkinson

NOVELS

The Adventures of Geoffrey Mildmay
   Proceed at Will
   Run, Mongoose
   Last Clear Chance
Night of the Short Knives

NAVY STORIES

By Sea and by Stealth

BIOGRAPHIES FOR ALL AGES

The Helmet of Navarre
Cardinal in Armor
Young Louis XIV
Francis in All His Glory

ANTHOLOGIES

Cry Spy!
Cry Sabotage!

Bradbury Press · Scarsdale, New York

SABOTAGE!

True Stories of 20th Century Saboteurs

Edited by BURKE WILKINSON

Acknowledgments

The author and publisher wish to acknowledge and express their gratitude to the following for permission to reprint selections included in this anthology:

"The Destruction of the *Maine*" from *The* Maine: *An Account of Her Destruction in Havana Harbor* by Capt. Charles D. Sigsbee. Copyright © 1899 by The Century Company.

"The Dark Invader" from *The Dark Invader* by Capt. Franz von Rintelen von Kleist. Copyright © 1933 by The Macmillan Company. Reprinted by permission of Peter Davies Limited.

"Black Tom Blows Up" from *The Enemy Within* by Capt. Henry Landau. Copyright © 1937 by Henry Landau. Reprinted by permission of G. P. Putnam's Sons.

"A Railway Diversion" from *The Seven Pillars of Wisdom* by T. E. Lawrence. Copyright © 1926, 1935 by Doubleday, Doran and Company; 1966 by Doubleday & Company. Reprinted by permission of Raymond Savage Limited.

"The Fatal Ambush at Bal na mBlath" by Emmet Dalton reprinted by permission of the *Irish Independent,* Dublin.

"The Reichstag Is Burning" from *Reichstag Fire: Ashes of Democracy* by R. John Pritchard. Copyright © 1972 by R. John Pritchard. Reprinted by permission of Ballantine Books, Inc. and the author.

"Norway Goes Underground" from *Two Eggs on My Plate* by Oluf Reed Olsen. Copyright © 1953 by George Allen & Unwin Limited. Reprinted by permission of George Allen & Unwin Limited.

"A Stroke at the Brain" from *Combined Operations: The Official Story of the Commandos.* Copyright © 1943 by His Britannic Majesty's Stationery Office. Reprinted by permission of the Controller of Her Britannic Majesty's Stationery Office.

"De La Penne and the Dreadnought" by a *Collier's* correspondent from the February, 1949, issue of *Collier's.* Reprinted by permission of the author.

"The Secret Army" from *The Secret Army* by Tadeusz Bor-Komorowski. Copyright © 1950 by T. Bor-Komorowski. Reprinted by permission of Laurence Pollinger Limited.

"Long Island Landfall" from *Eight Spies Against America* by George J. Dasch. Copyright © 1949 by Robert M. McBride Company. Reprinted by permission of Robert M. McBride Company.

"Department of Dirty Tricks" from *Donovan of OSS* by Corey Ford. Copyright © 1970 by Hugh Grey and S. John Stebbins, executors of the estate of the late Corey Ford. Reprinted by permission of Little, Brown and Company.

"For the Glory of France" from *For the Glory of France* by Maria Wilhelm. Copyright © 1968 by Maria Wilhelm. Reprinted by permission of Julian Messner, A Division of Simon & Schuster, Inc.

"A Passage to Persia" from *Escape to Adventure* by Fitzroy MacLean. Copyright © 1949, 1950 by Fitzroy MacLean. Reprinted by permission of Little, Brown and Company.

"Cockles and Muscles: Operation Frankton" from *By Sea and By Stealth* by Burke Wilkinson. Copyright © 1956 by Coward-McCann, Inc. Reprinted by permission of the author.

"The Foxes Go to War" from *The Game of the Foxes* by Ladislas Farago. Copyright © 1971 by Ladislas Farago. Reprinted by permission of David McKay Company, Inc.

"The Labyrinth" from *The Labyrinth* by Walter Schellenberg. (translated by Louis Hagen). Copyright © 1956 by Harper & Row, Publishers, Inc. Reprinted by permission of Harper & Row, Publishers, Inc.

"The Monastery" from *The OSS and I* by William J. Morgan. Copyright © 1957 by William J. Morgan. Reprinted by permission of W. W. Norton and Company, Inc.

"Sabotage by Assassination" from *The Secret War Against Hitler* by Fabian von Schlabrendorff (translated by Hilda Simon). Copyright © 1965 by Pitman Publishing Corporation. Reprinted by permission of Pitman Publishing Corporation.

"Pin-stripe Saboteur" from *Pin-stripe Saboteur* by Charles Wighton. Copyright © 1959 by Charles Wighton. Reprinted by permission of Odhams Press Limited.

"Parachuting into Norway" from *Report from No. 24* by Gunnar Sonsteby. Copyright by Gunnar Sonsteby. Reprinted by permission of Lyle Stuart, Inc.

"Skorzeny's Secret Missions" from *Skorzeny's Secret Missions* by Otto Skorzeny (translated by Jacques LeClerq). Copyright © 1950 by E. P. Dutton and Company, Inc. Reprinted by permission of E. P. Dutton and Company, Inc.

"An Exploit of the Battling *Barb*" by John L. Steele. Published originally in this anthology by permission of the author.

"The Mission of the Pregnant *Perch*" by Clay Blair, Jr. from the November 5, 1951 issue of *Life* Magazine. Copyright © 1951 by Clay Blair, Jr. and Time, Inc. Reprinted by permission of *Life* Magazine and the author.

"Sabotage in Vietnam: Glimpses Behind the Bamboo Curtain" from *The Pentagon Papers* (*The New York Times* edition) and *The Washington Post*. *The New York Times* edition of *The Pentagon Papers* states: "no copyright is claimed in official government documents contained in this volume"; copyright © 1972 by *The Washington Post*.

"This Is a Hijacking!" from *The Hijacking* by Jörg Andreas Elten as condensed in the July, 1971, *Reader's Digest*. Copyright © 1971 by Gruner & Jahr GMBH & Company, Presshaus, Hamburg, West Germany. Reprinted by permission of *The Reader's Digest* and *Stern* Magazine.

"Patrolling the Deadly Streets of Belfast" by Peter Lennon from the February, 1972, issue of *True* Magazine. Copyright © 1972 by Fawcett Publications, Inc. and Peter Lennon. Reprinted by permission of *True* Magazine and the author.

"First Patrol" by J. Bryan III from *Esquire* Magazine. Reprinted by permission of the author.

Contents

PART TWO: WORLD WAR II

CRY SABOTAGE!

Foreword

SABOTAGE is as old as history and as new as tomorrow's head-lines. Long before the word itself came into use, it was a favorite weapon of the bold and resourceful in war.

A famous example can be found in the tale of the Trojan Horse, the huge wooden effigy the Greeks left behind them when they pretended to abandon the siege of Troy. Ostensibly, the horse was an offering to the goddess Athena. It was so big that it could not be carried into the city without great effort. The Tro-jans were eager to carry it in, despite the frantic warnings of a priest named Laocoön. He went so far as to hurl a spear against the side of the horse, where it struck with a hollow sound. Min-utes later, Laocoön and his two sons were dead, strangled by a pair of serpents who came twisting out of the sea.

The Trojans considered the death of the three fair warning of what would happen if they did *not* take the horse into the city. They proceeded to do so. After nightfall, Sinon the traitor re-leased a squad of Greek soldiers concealed in the belly of the horse. With his help, they found the city gates and threw them open. Then the men from the Greek fleet, which had sailed back under cover of darkness, surged in.

So Troy was captured and sacked, and the bitter ten-year siege ended in triumph for the Greeks. That was in the 12th century B.C., as near as can be determined. At about the same semi-mythical time there was another classic example of sabotage. The children of Israel were besieging Jericho. The account of the climactic moment is given in the Old Testament Book of Joshua: "So the people shouted when the priests blew with the trumpets, and it came to pass . . . that the wall fell down flat, so that the people went up into the city, every man straight before him, and they took the city."

This is all very mysterious until we read on. The city was destroyed and the population massacred, but Rahab the harlot, her father and mother and brethren, were spared "because she hid the messengers, which Joshua sent to spy on Jericho."

Even across the centuries, it looks very much as if the spies did more than spy. It looks as if they also managed to undermine a good section of the wall so that the children of Israel could swiftly go "up into the city."

Sabotage, as we shall see, involves some physical act of destruction, done with an element of deception and with the purpose of weakening or humiliating the enemy or enemy-to-be. (The verb *sabotage* now means to wreck or undermine anything from a trestle to a tea party to a football team "sabotaged" by the clever play of a rival quarterback.)

In almost every war in history there has been some act of sabotage or attempted sabotage, by sea and land.

Midget submarines have for a surprising length of time been a favorite means of delivery of bomb or mine. As far back as 1776, David Bushnell scored several near-misses against a British ship of the line in New York harbor. His craft: an ingenious pedal-driven submersible, strictly homemade.

Ashore, one of the favorite targets of sabotage has been the railway train. In one famous episode the tables were turned and a train was the intended means of delivery. On April 12, 1862, the crew of a small Confederate locomotive called The General, hauling three box cars, stopped for breakfast at the Kennesaw, Georgia, railway station. A Union spy named James Andrews and nineteen Union soldiers who had infiltrated deep into enemy territory commandeered the locomotive. They headed for Chattanooga, which was under Union siege. Their object was to burn and blow up bridges as they went along, thus cutting off the Tennessee city from any possible Confederate relief by rail. The legitimate crew, quickly firing up another locomotive, gave chase. At last The General ran out of fuel and steam. Andrews and his troopers took to the woods. Within a week all were rounded up. Andrews and seven of the men were executed, the usual harsh fate for the failed saboteur.

Sabotage as a form of human endeavor had no name until the 19th century. One day, it seems, an angry French worker threw his wooden shoe or *sabot* into a steam-driven engine and it came to a hissing, grinding halt. So the word *sabotage* was born, the taking of destructive action with a wooden shoe.

This may be folklore only. There is another explanation from a later date. In 1910 French railway workers were staging a massive strike. One of their favorite methods of protest was to tear up the cross ties supporting the rails. These wooded supports were also called *sabots,* and still are.

The word sabotage has, in the stormy course of the present century, been expanded to include a whole range of devious and destructive activities. From the year 1910 when the French workers tore up the cross ties until the Russian Revolution seven years later, the International Workers of the World (IWW) recognized sabotage as a legitimate form of slowdown. Then the violence of the upheaval against tsarist rule caused it to be outlawed as a weapon of labor protest.

In World War II and the Korean War, sabotage as a form of subversive action came into its own. More recently, the whole sad Vietnam War has been in a sense one panoramic act of sabotage.

With lines of battle ill-defined, destruction of men and matériel behind them became routine. Ironically the Green Berets, when created in the early 1960s to wage irregular warfare there, took a small metal reproduction of the Trojan Horse as their first insignia.

The curtain-raiser to this anthology is an account of the destruction of the *Maine* in Havana harbor in 1898. All the other exploits or near-exploits described date from 1900 on. They divide quite naturally into two categories:

(a) *Peacetime sabotage*. Underhand attempts to weaken a potential enemy by hurting his economy, reducing his war-making potential or kidnapping his political leaders.

(b) *Wartime sabotage*. Behind-the-lines activities against enemy matériel and personnel, involving some element of stealth or deception.

My own running comments put the various chapters in some historical context and give my reasons for their selection. For instance, the hijacking of a plane for private purposes does not qualify. But a hijacking for political purposes, such as the plane-burning in the Jordanian desert in 1970, does.

Whenever possible, the accounts are told by the operators themselves. The magnificent desert forays of Lawrence of Arabia and the shadowy World War II swashbuckling of Otto Skorzeny are good examples. They reveal as much about the men as about their methods.

In this time of violence we must know the mentality of the saboteur. If we do not, we will never be able to catch or to contain these most dangerous—often most dedicated—of "dark invaders."

PART ONE:
THE EARLY YEARS

1

The Destruction of the *Maine*

Capt. Charles D. Sigsbee

In 1895, Cuba was in open revolt against the aging Spanish empire. Bands of marauders were burning the vast fields of sugar cane, blowing up railway trains, making hit-and-run attacks on outlying villages. These rebels understood the uses of sabotage. Their aim was to make life in Cuba so miserable that total independence from Spain would be inevitable. They also hoped to enlist the sympathy of the United States by clever propaganda, and they succeeded very well in doing so.

The United States was in the mood to flex its muscles. With Alaska already ours by purchase, there was nowhere else to go for adventure on the continent itself. Poor, oppressed Cuba was ready-at-hand.

President Grover Cleveland was able to control the growing public wish to have a "splendid little war" against Spain. But his successor, William McKinley, a less forceful man, came under heavy pressure from the day he took office in 1897. William Randolph Hearst's pro-rebel New York Journal *stirred up a citizenry that was quite ready to be stirred. "Is it possible that the United*

*States is spoiling for a war?" one newspaper editor asked. It was
indeed.*

In December, 1897, McKinley ordered the USS Maine *to Havana. The visit was ostensibly a friendly one at a time when the
Spanish, under General Blanco, were doing their best to improve
conditions in Cuba and to grant some measure of self-rule. The
battleship also was sent there to safeguard American lives and
property.*

The Maine, *Capt. Charles D. Sigsbee commanding, arrived in
Havana harbor on January 25, 1898. With her mahogany pilot's
house and gleaming white hull she was a fine and imposing sight.
Her armament included four ten-inch guns and six six-inch rifles.
The ship's complement was 26 officers and 328 men. She was
324 feet long and displaced 6,650 tons.*

*Some weeks after her arrival, fate took a hand in a way that
made war inevitable. Here is Captain Sigsbee's own account of
the tragic events of the night of February 15:*

ON the night of the explosion, the *Maine,* lying in the harbor
of Havana at the buoy where she was moored by the Spanish
pilot on her entrance into the port, was heading in a direction
quite unusual—at least, for the *Maine.* In this connection it
should be explained that Havana is in the region of the trade-
wind, which, however, is not so stable there as farther to the
eastward, especially in the winter months. During the day the
wind is commonly from the eastward, and about sundown it is
likely to die down. During the night there may be no wind at all,
and a ship swinging at her buoy may head in any direction. On
the night of the explosion, the *Maine* was heading to the northward and westward. . . . Some of the watch officers said afterward that they had not before known her to head in that direction at Havana. I myself did not remark any peculiarity of
heading, because I had not been on deck much during the night
watches. Stated simply as a fact, the *Maine* was lying in position
to open her batteries on the shore fortifications. If an expert had
been charged with mining the *Maine*'s mooring–berth, purely as

a measure of harbor defense, and having only one mine available, it is believed that he would have placed it under the position that the *Maine* occupied that night.

A short distance astern, or nearly astern, was the American steamer *City of Washington,* Capt. Frank Stevens, of the Ward line. The Spanish cruiser *Alfonso XII* and the *Legazpi* occupied berths on the starboard side of the *Maine*. There were other vessels in the harbor, but they were more remote from the *Maine*'s berth. It was a dark, overcast night. The atmosphere was heavy, and the weather unusually hot and sultry. All of the twenty-six officers were aboard excepting Passed Assistant Engineer F. C. Bowers, Naval Cadet (Engineer) Pope Washington, Paymaster's Clerk Brent McCarthy, and Gunner Joseph Hill.

The members of the crew, 328 in number, were on board as usual. One of the steam-launches was in the water and riding at the starboard boom. The crew, excepting those on watch or on post, were turned in. The men of the quarter-watch were distributed about the deck in various places, wherever they could make themselves comfortable within permissible limits as to locality. Some of the officers were in their staterooms or in the mess-rooms below; others were on the main or upper deck, in or about the officers' smoking quarters, which were abaft the after-turret, on the port side, abreast the after-superstructure.

I was in my quarters, sitting on the after-side of the table in the port or admiral's cabin. . . . The *Maine* had been arranged to accomodate both an admiral and a captain. For this purpose her cabin space in the after-superstructure had been divided into two parts, starboard and port, which were perfectly symmetrical in arrangement and fittings. Looking from one cabin into the other through the large communicating doorway, one cabin was like the reflection of the other seen in a mirror. The two cabins were alike even in furniture. . . . At the time of the explosion I was sitting in the port cabin. . . .

About an hour before the explosion I had completed a report called for by Mr. Theodore Roosevelt, Assistant Secretary of the Navy, on the advisability of continuing to place torpedo-tubes on board cruisers and battleships. I then wrote a letter home, in which I struggled to apologize for having carried in my pocket for ten months a letter to my wife from one of her friends of long standing. The cabin mess-attendant, James Pinckney, had brought me, about an hour before, a civilian's thin coat, because of the prevailing heat; I had taken off my shirt, and was wearing this coat for the only time during the cruise. In the pocket I had found the unopened and undelivered letter. Pinckney was for some reason in an especially happy frame of mind that night. Poor fellow! He was killed, as was also good old John R. Bell, the cabin steward, who had been in the navy, in various ratings, for twenty-seven years.

At taps ("turn in and keep quiet"), ten minutes after nine o'clock, I laid down my pen to listen to the notes of the bugle, which were singularly beautiful in the oppressive stillness of the night. The marine bugler, Newton, who was rather given to fanciful effects, was evidently doing his best. During his pauses the echoes floated back to the ship with singular distinctness, repeating the strains of the bugle fully and exactly. A half hour later, Newton was dead.

I was enclosing my letter in its envelop when the explosion came. The impression made on different people on board the *Maine* varied somewhat. To me, in my position, well aft and within the superstructure, it was a bursting, rending, and crashing sound or roar of immense volume, largely metallic in character. It was followed by a succession of heavy, ominous, metallic sounds, probably caused by the overturning of the central superstructure and by falling debris. There was a trembling and lurching motion of the vessel, a list to port, and a movement of subsidence. The electric lights, of which there were eight in the cabin where I was sitting, went out. Then there was intense blackness and smoke.

The situation could not be mistaken: the *Maine* had been blown up and was sinking. For a moment the instinct of self-preservation took charge of me, but this was immediately dominated by the habit of command. I went up the inclined deck into the starboard cabin, toward the starboard air-ports, which were faintly outlined against the background of the sky. The sashes were out, and the openings were large. My first intention was to escape through an air-port, but this was abandoned in favor of the more dignified way of making an exit through the passage-way leading forward through the superstructure. I groped my way through the cabin into the passage, and along the passage to the outer door. The passage turned to the right, or starboard, near the forward part of the superstructure.

At the turning, someone ran into me violently. I asked who it was. It was Pvt. William Anthony, the orderly at the cabin door. He said something apologetic, and reported that the ship was sinking. He was directed to go out on the quarter-deck, and I followed him. Anthony has been pictured as making an exceedingly formal salute on that occasion. The dramatic effect of a salute cannot add to his heroism. If he had made a salute it could not have been seen in the blackness of that compartment. Anthony did his whole duty, at great personal risk, at a time when he might have evaded the danger without question, and deserved all the commendation that he received for his act. He hung near me with unflagging zeal and watchfulness that night until the ship was abandoned.

I stood for a moment on the starboard side of the main deck, forward of the after-superstructure, looking toward the immense dark mass that loomed up amidships, but could see nothing distinctly. There I remained for a few seconds in an effort to grasp the situation and then asked Anthony for the exact time. He replied: "The explosion took place at nine forty, sir." It was soon necessary to retire from the main deck, for the after-part of the ship was sinking rapidly. I then went up on the poop deck. By this time Lieutenant-Commander Wainwright and others were near me. Everybody was impressed by the solemnity of the disaster, but there was no excitement apparent; perfect discipline prevailed.

The question has been asked many times if I believed then

that the *Maine* was blown up from the outside. My answer to this has been that my first order on reaching the deck was to post sentries about the ship. I knew that the *Maine* had been blown up, and believed that she had been blown up from the outside. Therefore I ordered a measure which was intended to guard against attack. . . . There was the sound of many voices from the shore, suggestive of cheers.

I stood on the starboard side-rail of the poop and held on to the main-rigging in order to see over the poop-awning, which was bagged and covered with debris. I was still trying to take in the situation more completely. The officers were near me and showing a courteous recognition of my authority and responsibility. Directions were given in a low tone to Executive Officer Wainwright, who himself gave orders quietly and directed operations. Fire broke out in the mass amidships. Orders were given to flood the forward magazine, but the forward part of the ship was found to be under water. Inquiry as to the after-magazines and the guncotton magazine in the after-part of the ship showed a like condition of those compartments, as reported by those who had escaped from the wardroom and junior officers' quarters. In the captain's spare pantry in the after-superstructure there was spare ammunition. It was seen that this would soon be submerged, and that precautions in respect to the magazines were unnecessary.

The great loss of life was not then fully realized. Our eyes were not yet accustomed to the darkness. Most of us had come from the glare of the electric lights. The flames increased in the central superstructure, and I directed Lieutenant-Commander Wainwright to make an effort to play streams on the fire if practicable. He went forward on the poop-awning, accompanied by Lieutenant Hood and naval cadets Boyd and Cluverius, making a gallant inspection in the region of the fire, but was soon obliged to report that nothing could be done. The fire-mains and all other facilities were destroyed, and men were not available for the service.

We then began to realize more clearly the full extent of the damage. One of the smokestacks was lying in the water on the starboard side. Although it was almost directly under me, I had not at first identified it. As my eyes became more accustomed to the darkness, I could see, dimly, white forms on the water and hear faint cries for help. Realizing that the white forms were our own men, boats were lowered at once and sent to the assistance of the injured and drowning men. Orders were given, but they were hardly necessary: the resourceful intelligence of the officers suggested correct measures in the emergency. Only three of our fifteen boats were available—the barge, the captain's gig, and the whale boat. The barge was badly injured. Two of these were manned by officers and men jointly. How long they were gone from the ship I cannot recall, but probably fifteen minutes. Those of us who were left on board remained quietly on the poop deck.

Nothing further could be done; the ship was settling rapidly. There was one wounded man on the poop; he had been hauled from under a ventilator on the main deck by Lieutenants Hood and Blandin just as the water was rising over him. Other boats, too, were rescuing the wounded and drowning men. Chief among them were the boats from the *Alfonso XII*, and from the steamer *City of Washington*. The visiting boats had arrived promptly and were unsparing of effort in saving the wounded. The Spanish officers and crews did all that humanity and gallantry could compass. During the absence of our boats the fire in the wreck of the central-superstructure became fiercer. The spare ammunition that had been stowed in the pilothouse or thrown up from the magazines below was exploding in detail. It continued to explode at intervals until nearly two o'clock in the morning.

At night it was the custom on board the *Maine* to close all watertight compartments except the few needed to afford passageway for the crew. They had been reported closed as usual that night. Down the cabin skylights the air could be heard whistling through the seams of the doors and hatches, indicating that even the after-bulkheads had been so strained as to admit the water into the compartments. Presently Lieutenant-Commander

Wainwright came to me and reported that our boats had returned alongside the ship at the stern, and that all the wounded that could be found had been gathered in and sent to the Spanish cruiser and the *City of Washington* and elsewhere. The afterpart of the poop deck of the *Maine,* the highest intact point above water, was then level with the gig's gunwale, while that boat was in the water alongside. We had done everything that could be done, so far as could be seen.

It was a hard blow to be obliged to leave the *Maine;* none of us desired to leave while any part of her poop remained above water. We waited until satisfied that she was resting on the bottom of the harbor. Lieutenant-Commander Wainwright then whispered to me that he thought the forward ten-inch magazine had been thrown up into the burning material amidships and might explode at any time, with further disastrous effects. He was then directed to get everybody into the boats, which was done. It was an easy operation; one had only to step directly from the deck into the boat. There was still some delay to make sure that the ship's stern had grounded, and still more because of the extreme politeness of the officers, who considerately offered me a steadying hand to step into the boat. Lieutenant-Commander Wainwright stood on one side and Lieutenant Holman on the other; each offered me a hand. I suggested the propriety of my being the last to leave, and requested them to precede me, which they did. There was favorable comment later in the press because I left last. It is a fact that I was the last to leave, which was only proper; that is to say, it would have been improper otherwise; but virtually all left last. The fine conduct of those who came under my observation that night was conspicuous and touching. The heroism of the wounded men I did not see at the time, but afterward good reports of their behavior were very common. The patient way in which they bore themselves left no doubt that they added new honors to the service when the *Maine* went down.

Our boats pulled to the *City of Washington.* On the trip I called to the rescuing boats, requesting them to leave the vicinity of the wreck and informing them that there might be another explosion. Mr. Sylvester Scovel, the newspaper correspondent, was asked to translate my request to the Spanish boats, which he did.

On arriving on board the *City of Washington,* I found there a number of our wounded men. They had been carried below into the dining-saloon, where they had been placed on mattresses. They were carefully tended by both officers and crew of the vessel. Every attention that the resources of the vessel admitted had been brought to bear in their favor. The *City of Washington,* then under command of Captain Stevens, did great service. The same was true of the *Alfonso XII,* and, it may be, of the other Spanish vessels also. One or more wounded men were cared for on board the Spanish transport *Colon.*

I walked among the wounded some minutes, and spent a few more in watching the fitful explosion of ammunition on board the *Maine.* Then I went to the captain's cabin and composed my first telegram to the Navy Department. I had already directed that a muster be taken of the survivors and had sent a request to the captain of the *Alfonso XII* that he keep one or more patrol boats about the wreck. The relations between the United States and Spain had reached a condition of such extreme tension that the patience of the people of the United States was about exhausted. Realizing this fully that night, I feared the result of first impressions of the great disaster on our people, for I found it necessary to repress my own suspicions. I wished them, as a matter of national pride and duty, to take time for consideration. . . . It seemed also to be a duty of my position to sustain the government during the period of excitement or indignation that was likely to follow the reception of the first report; therefore I took the course of giving to my telegram an uncommonly strong advisory character. . . . After my name had been signed in the first instance, I was informed that a number of Spanish officers —civil, military, and naval—had arrived on board to express sympathy. I went out on deck, greeted these gentlemen, and thanked them for their visit. Returning to the draft of the telegram, I erased my name and added a few more words relative to the visit and sympathy of the Spanish officers. I added these additional words to strengthen the quieting effect of the telegram.

Here is the historic telegram:

SECNAV WASHINGTON DC

MAINE BLOWN UP IN HAVANA HARBOR AT 9:40 TONIGHT AND DE-STROYED X MANY WOUNDED AND DOUBTLESS MORE KILLED AND DROWNED X WOUNDED AND OTHERS ABOARD SPANISH MAN OF WAR AND WARD LINE STEAMER X SEND LIGHTHOUSE TENDERS FROM KEY WEST FOR CREW AND THE FEW PIECES OF EQUIPMENT ABOVE WATER X NO ONE HAS CLOTHING OTHER THAN THAT UPON HIM X PUBLIC OPINION SHOULD BE SUSPENDED UNTIL FURTHER REPORT X ALL OFFICERS BELIEVED TO BE SAVED X JENKINS AND MERRITT NOT YET ACCOUNTED FOR X MANY SPANISH OFFICERS INCLUDING REPRESENTATIVES OF GENERAL BLANCO NOW WITH ME TO EXPRESS SYMPATHY X

SIGSBEE

The burning question was whether the Maine *had been sunk by an internal or external explosion. The United States sent a three-man naval team to look into the disaster. Their report was made public on March 28: the explosion of a submarine mine by persons unknown was ruled to be the cause of the accident.*

This was quite enough for the American public, already at fever pitch. Since a submarine mine meant an external explosion, the report confirmed the suspicion that the Spanish—but not the rebels!—were guilty. Remember the Maine! *was the battlecry of the nation.*

On Thursday, April 21, 1898, President McKinley signed the war resolution, which had been passed by the Senate and House the day before. Two days later an American squadron was blockading Havana, and the war was on.

There is a postscript to the story of the Maine. *Long after the swift defeat of Spain in the Spanish-American War, the* Maine *was raised. This was in 1911. A much fuller study of the wreck than had been possible when she was submerged tended to scout the external-explosion theory rather than to confirm it.*

The Maine, *without any undue delay, was towed into deep water and scuttled, so that her drowned and shattered hull, lying many fathoms deep, holds all her secrets now.*

2

The Dark Invader

Franz von Rintelen

Externally, there was nothing of the dark invader about Franz von Rintelen von Kleist. He was a handsome man with intelligent eyes and a scholar's broad forehead. He carried himself with the ease of his aristocratic background. With his confident charm and command of languages, he could easily pass as an English or Italian gentleman, and often did.

The title of his famous book refers to his deeds rather than to his looks. Written long after his shadowy activities in America, The Dark Invader *is a classic account of sabotage and spying.*

Von Rintelen had been a banker in London, New York and Latin America, but the outbreak of World War I found him back in Berlin on the staff of Admiral von Tirpitz. By early 1915 it was clear that the still-neutral United States was already beginning to supply the Allies with munitions at an alarming rate. Von Rintelen asked to be assigned to New York. "I'll buy what I can and blow up what I can't," said the dashing young naval officer. His seniors were impressed and the secret orders were cut.

Here he is leaving Berlin for his new assignment under the name of Swiss citizen Emile Gaché:

I STARTED from the Stettiner Bahnhof, on which the German flag was flying in honor of the birthday of the Emperor William I, on March 22, 1915. As soon as I was settled in the train I began a task which looked very funny but which had a serious purpose. I wrote post cards to all my acquaintances, dozens of picture post cards to my friends, particularly the military and naval attachés of neutral states. These cards I sent to other friends, in envelopes, with the request that they should post them, so that the attachés and all the people from whom I wanted to hide my tracks received cards from "Somewhere in Flanders," from Upper Bavaria and from Silesia. Upon my arrival at Christiania I succeeded in obtaining at the British and American consulates magnificent genuine visas for my Swiss passport, and I felt safe.

When the steamer was on the high seas, a British cruiser sent a lieutenant and a couple of sailors on board to see if the ship was harboring any Germans. The lieutenant ascertained that there were no Germans on board. As we approached the American coast I grew a little uneasy, for the British cruiser *Essex* was stationed off New York—three miles and two inches off. She was commanded by Captain Watson, who had been naval attaché in Berlin until shortly before the outbreak of war. We had been friends, and he had been kind enough to give me occasionally a few hints on English naval expressions. This would have been a fine *rencontre!* I was lucky, however, for the *Essex* was not inspecting the passenger boats on that day but, as I could see through field glasses, was engaged in target practice.

Once around these "dangerous corners," I at last landed, safe and sound, on the pier in New York. . . .

Hardly a week after my arrival in the United States I received a letter from Captain Boy-Ed, the Naval Attaché, conveying the wish of Count Bernstorff, the Ambassador, to have a conference with me. After some hesitation, in view of the nature of my mission, I decided to go, and duly appeared at the Ritz-Carlton on Madison Avenue. Bernstorff at once asked me the object of my presence in America. In reply, I politely suggested he should not ask that question, since my answer might complicate his diplomatic duties. At that he drew his chair up to the sofa on which I was sitting and almost whispered: "Now, Captain, please understand that although I am here as an ambassador, I am an old soldier as well. You may tell me anything in confidence."

These words appealed to the officer in me; and I not only gave a full account of how my mission had originated in Berlin, but also made it clear that it had a purely military character which lay in the general direction of sabotage. I told him that, as an officer, I cared nothing for America's so-called neutrality, that the whole of Germany thought as I did and considered America "the unseen enemy." I had come, I told him, to do what I could to save the German *Landwehrleute*—our territorials—from American shells. Though I proposed to act with energy, I promised I would do so cautiously. . . .

I moved into a modest but good hotel, the Great Northern on Fifty-seventh Street, and began to make inquiries with a view to discovering whether it was really possible to buy sufficient explosives to damage seriously the manufacture of munitions for the Allies. I went to several firms and told them that I was a German agent anxious to purchase powder, but within a few days I was satisfied that it would be quite impossible to buy up the vast quantities of explosives that were by now available on the American market. The daily production was so great that if I had bought up the market on Tuesday, there would still have been an enormous fresh supply on Wednesday. . . .

From Italian activities in the New York area it became obvious to Captain von Rintelen that Italy intended to enter the war against Germany:

I became obsessed with one idea. If Italy came into the war, and American shells were to be hurled against the German trenches from Italian guns as well, it was high time that something was *really* done, and I could no longer content myself with running about and discovering that there was too much explosive material in America for us ever to buy up.

I began to lead a dual existence. In the evening I went about as "myself" in dress suit and white tie; I had decided that it was much more dangerous to go about New York under a false name. For if one of the numerous English agents should find out anyhow who I actually was, he would know instantly that I had something nefarious up my sleeve. If, however, I did not conceal my identity, it would be assumed that I was in America on some peaceful economic mission. Otherwise, it would be argued, I should have kept behind the scenes. I appeared openly in the evening, and on one occasion I had the great pleasure of speaking at a lecture organized by a distinguished scientific club in New York, the Century Club. . . .

During the day I dressed unobtrusively and went first of all through the whole of the dock district, where I saw numerous English, French and Russian transports waiting to take munitions on board. I watched them being loaded and saw them steam out of the harbor and make for the East, their holds full of shells. I wished them at the bottom of the sea. . . .

Systematically I studied the conditions in the New York docks, and I soon became aware that a large number of German sailors, mates and captains were hanging about the harbor with nothing to do. The merchantmen in which they would otherwise be serving lay in dock and were unable to leave, since they would be captured by the British on the high seas. . . .

For some months Von Rintelen enjoyed spectacular success as a saboteur. He found a pro-German expert who designed a small incendiary bomb or "cigar." With an interned German ship, S. S. Frederick the Great, serving as workshop, Von Rintelen's men were soon able to turn out fifty bombs a day. Placed unobtrusively in the holds of Allied shipping, they went off many hours later at sea. No one knows the exact number of ships that were lost in this way, but there were many.

After some months of success it became apparent that American and English detectives had picked up Von Rintelen's trail. They were helped in their work by the New York police and encouraged by the British naval attaché, a certain Captain G———.

*Von Rintelen went under cover at a New England resort to do
a little serious thinking about what next:*

If the police really had found something out, it was too risky
to deposit any more of our incendiary bombs. We should have to
liquidate our whole scheme, and others would have to finish
what we had begun. The English detectives would be waiting for
our next move in order to catch us, though if they were not
really on our track, we could continue with our work in spite of
Captain G—— and his men from Scotland Yard.

That afternoon I drove along the coast to another watering
place a little distance away. It was more fashionable and elegant
and slightly less sleepy than the retreat in which I had hidden
myself. I walked up and down in deep thought and finally
landed on a terrace of a small hotel. A jazz band was playing,
and I drank iced coffee while I racked my brains to find a means
of discovering what Captain G—— did and did not know of our
activities.

I suddenly looked up and saw two ladies who knew me standing nearby. They were ignorant of my name and who I was, and
their knowledge of me rested only on a chance meeting at a society function in New York. We had met at a late hour in the evening, and I remembered that only the host had known who I
was, none of the guests having had any inkling of my real identity. The two ladies recognized me and came up to my table.
They were Mrs. James B—— and Miss Mabel L——. Mrs.
B——, who was the older of the two, was the wife of a coal merchant in New York, and Miss L——, who was young and very
pretty, was "her best friend." They told me that they were very
glad to see me, for there were many more ladies than men in the
place, and I gathered that they did not have any accurate re-
membrance of my name. I hastened to inform them that it was
Brannon, and they remembered immediately that it was.

We discussed a variety of things: water sports, the war, the new
dances, the stock exchange and religion; and I then learned that
they were staying at the hotel on whose terrace we were sitting.
They told me that a large party was being given in the hotel on

the following evening for which invitations had already been sent out, and they asked me to come along. It appeared to be difficult to round up enough dancing men, and the ladies reckoned on my cooperation in the entertainment. I had no desire to go, for I had other things on my mind, until Miss L—— surprised me by saying:

"Some nice people are coming. You are English, aren't you? You will be interested. Captain G——, the attaché at your Embassy, will be there. He is a charming person. Do you know him? No? Well, *do* come. You will find him easy to get on with."

I looked out over the sea. The orchestra was playing softly. My two companions began to devour pastries in large quantities. On the spur of the moment I decided to take a great risk in order to find out what I wanted to know.

"Yes," I said, "I shall be very glad to come."

They told me that the hotel was small but very fashionable, and that you could only be accepted as a guest if you were recommended by a member of New York society. Most of the apartments were already booked for a long time ahead. All the visitors knew each other and they formed, so to speak, a private club.

I moved into this fashionable hotel on the following morning, having been recommended by both the ladies. We sat on the beach together and went for walks, and I may repeat that Miss L—— was really very young and very pretty, while Mrs. B—— manifested a tact which appeared to have been acquired from a familiarity with difficult situations. We passed the day in complete harmony.

In the evening, when the ladies were wearing their best gowns and the gentlemen appeared in all the elegance and dignity of swallowtails, the moment arrived for which I had waited. Mrs. B—— introduced me to the British naval attaché. I was informed that I had the pleasure of meeting Captain G——, and the attaché was informed that he had the pleasure of meeting Mr. Brannon.

After Mrs. B—— had left us, we stood at one of the large

windows that opened on to the sea. The attaché was obviously trying to think of some pleasant remark to make to his countryman. He was tall, broadshouldered, with a clever face expressive of great energy, and was leaning out of the window a little to breathe in the sea air.

I began to put my plan into action.

"I am Commander Brannon, sir, and have been sent to the United States to study a new torpedo invention. I heard something yesterday in New York that I wished to communicate to you personally, but you had already left, and I thought that it might wait until your return."

"Oh," said the attaché, "I am glad to meet you out here, then!"

"They only know here that I am an Englishman," I put in hastily; "but they have no idea that I am in the Navy, and it is not necessary for them to discover it."

"You are right," said the attaché; "but tell me, Commander, what was it you wished to report to me?"

I pulled myself together. Now was the moment.

"A certain Captain Johnson, in charge of an English transport, has informed me of the strange incident of which he was a witness. He saw five men carrying heavy cases through the docks a few days ago, and as their behavior looked rather odd he followed them for a couple of hundred yards. They loaded their mysterious cases into a motorboat and shot off into the harbor. It was a clear night and he saw them draw alongside a vessel which had been loading munitions, in order presumably to go out to sea next day. The strange thing was that these men, together with their cases, were taken on board by means of a crane. The vessel sailed, but in the morning, before it left the harbor, Johnson called on the captain to tell him what he had seen. And what do you think happened? Not a soul on the whole ship admitted having seen the five men—neither the officer of the watch, nor any of the crew, nor our detectives. Don't you think there was something queer about it?"

Captain G—— had listened very attentively. "Tell me," he

said, "did your confidant see any of these five fellows sufficiently clearly to recognize him again? Was he close enough to notice how they were dressed, and did he describe to you what they looked like?"

I regretted that Captain Johnson, who had already gone off to sea again, had told me no more than I had imparted to the attaché, and that I had no more helpful information to divulge.

"I thought it would interest you," I said. "We have heard so much in the last few weeks about acts of sabotage against our ships."

"Yes, of course," replied Captain G——, "of course it interests me. I suppose you have read that we have definite suspicions. There is a gang working in New York harbor under the direction of a German officer. We even know his name. He is called Rintelen, and has been mentioned a number of times in wireless messages by the German Embassy. The strange thing is, however, that the American police stick to their statement that he is a gentleman who is not doing anything criminal, and yet my men have often seen him hanging about the docks. He even admitted his identity once in a tavern, when he was drunk and hadn't a hold on his tongue. He did not give away any details concerning his activities, but it is certain that he owns a motorboat, and runs about in it for days together selling goods of all kinds to the ships in the harbor. I cannot tell you any more, Commander, but I can promise you that he will soon be in our hands."

"Yes, that's not likely to be a difficult job," I said, laughing internally till it hurt. "A fellow who gets drunk and lets his tongue run away with him, and sails about the harbor openly in a motorboat, must be easy to trap."

The jazz band broke into our conversation, and I had to dance with Miss L——. She found me a delightful companion, for I was very elated, and I had good reason to be.

It is true that I knew the English suspected me, though I had no idea how they came to believe that I was accustomed to getting drunk in waterside taverns, and that I was doing business in a motorboat. Naturally I did not like being under suspicion, but it was inevitable sooner or later, and it did not matter so much, since at the same time they believed such glorious nonsense about my character. It was obvious that they were not aware of the identity of either the instigators or the tools concerned in our plot; in other words, that they were on the wrong track, chasing a phantom which they believed, for heaven knows what reasons, to be identical with myself. The ground began to burn under my feet: I could now return to New York and resume my activities.

Suddenly I saw the attaché talking to a man who looked like a servant and must have just handed him a letter. The dancing continued, and when G—— and I met a little later on at the buffet, he drew me into a quiet corner to consume a dish of herring salad. He asked me about a number of fellow officers, and as I had been employed in the Department of the Admiralty at Berlin, which was concerned with British matters, and had met British naval officers in the course of numerous journeys and social functions, having indeed written a dissertation on the British Navy for the staff examination, I was able to relate a variety of stories about officers whom we both knew. We sat in our corner and talked shop to the great displeasure of the ladies. Captain G—— soon became more confidential and told me that he had just received a letter that would necessitate his doing a little work that very night. He had just heard that the captain of a small freighter had reported in New York having sighted the German cruiser *Karlsruhe* in the Atlantic. He gave the degrees of latitude and longitude, and it was evident that the *Karlsruhe* had some definite plan in view since she had not bothered the freighter at all.

The *Karlsruhe!* I had had no news of her since leaving Berlin, and now she, or a raider of the same name, to mislead the British, was apparently cruising about the Atlantic in order to molest English merchantmen on their way from America to Europe. This was what I thought to myself, but I only said: "The *Karlsruhe!* Really, the *Karlsruhe!* What are you going to do?"

"It's very simple," replied Captain G——. "You can probably imagine. In an hour's time I am going to cable to the Admiralty in London, and at the same time I shall inform the Bermuda Squadron, on my own initiative, that this impudent little cruiser is sailing about our seas. The Bermuda Squadron will send the cruiser *Princess Royal* to put a stop to it. We shall see."

If the powerful cruisers of the Bermuda Squadron should come upon the little *Karlsruhe,* there was no doubt what the end would be. This realization was accompanied by the immediate resolution to try to provide something else for the Bermuda Squadron to do instead of going in chase of the *Karlsruhe.* If I could succeed in holding up action for a few days, it might be possible to warn the German vessel by wireless. I did not yet know how this could be done, but hoped for a lucky idea.

"I think," I said, "that the Bermuda Squadron ought to keep an eye on the German auxiliary cruisers."

"The German auxiliary cruisers? *What* cruisers? What do you mean?"

"I mean, sir, that the Bermuda Squadron ought to prevent the large German steamers, which are lying in the North American harbors, from breaking through. There are about thirty or forty of them and they are very swift. It is rumored that they would try to avoid being interned if the United States broke off diplomatic relations with Germany, and they are said to have guns on board which the confounded Boches have managed to get hold of."

The attaché bit his lip.

"Yes, yes, of course," he said. "Yes, of course."

I could see that this information had startled him. There was not a word of truth in it, though the idea had once been *on the tapis.* Attachés resemble one another all over the world. They would rather let their ears be cut off than admit that there is anything connected with their job that they do not know.

At last he said, "I thought this affair of the German steamers had been kept pretty quiet. How did you hear about it?"

"I got it from the American engineer whose invention I am testing, and also—now, who was it who told me? —yes, I remember, it was an oil merchant."

The attaché grew distinctly pensive. "Yes," he said, "I must reconsider the matter. It would of course be more useful to catch the steamers than send our battleships chasing after the *Karlsruhe*."

I was called to take part in a game which the ladies had organized, and I was unable to get out of it. I then had to dance, but my eyes sought G——, who had disappeared. Shortly afterwards I was accompanying Miss L—— on a walk along the beach under a very romantic moon, when I saw a man in evening dress crossing the promenade. It was G——. When he came up he took Miss L——'s other arm and we all three went back to the hotel. I contemplated as we walked how I could find out what G—— had been doing in the meantime. I decided to base my action on my "special" knowledge of the *genus* attaché, and began to say flattering things to him. I gave vent to my regret that I should probably never become an attaché myself, which, I said, had always been my ambition, though it was likely never to be achieved.

"You, sir, are a factor in the history of this great war. People will always say of you, 'Yes, he was naval attaché in Washington.' London acts on your advice, and things are done at your bidding."

Captain G—— listened attentively and was visibly pleased. He said something patronizing, and as we stepped aside to let Miss L—— enter the hotel he held me back and whispered:

"Commander, you are an understanding sort of person and will know how to keep a secret. The telegrams I am about to dispatch will prepare a surprise for the German steamers if they try to leave dock. So we will let the *Karlsruhe* alone for a bit. . . ."

Every ball comes to an end eventually, and when I was back in my room I felt very happy. I had achieved more than I dared to hope, for I knew that the English had no inkling of the shady paths that my agents and I had been pursuing in New York, and I believed that I had saved the *Karlsruhe* from the guns of the British battleships.

It had been a good evening. . . .

Shortly afterward, the Karlsruhe *was destroyed at sea in an accidental explosion. This was a source of great chagrin to Von Rintelen. However, his own nerve and wits continued to serve him well in many delicate situations.*

Predictably, his continuing success aroused the jealousy of Captain von Papen, the slightly ridiculous military attaché. Von Papen managed to have Von Rintelen ordered home, still under his Swiss alias and passport. The Dutch ship on which he sailed put in at an English port. Admiral Sir Reginald Hall, British Chief of Naval Intelligence, had Von Rintelen taken off and brought to London. Under the sharp questioning and hypnotic glance of Admiral Hall, Von Rintelen continued to assert his Swiss identity. Suddenly, the Admiral snapped a quick order in German and Von Rintelen instantly responded by clicking his heels.

"All right, sir, I am Captain Franz von Rintelen of the German Navy," he then confessed, "and I demand treatment as an officer." Von Rintelen's treatment was two years in a British prison. Then Admiral Hall sent him back to the United States, where he was tried, convicted and sentenced to four years at the Federal penitentiary in Atlanta.

He lived in England in the 1930s and became a close friend of Admiral Hall's, despite all that had gone before. It was during this period that he wrote his celebrated book.

3

Black Tom Blows Up

Capt. Henry Landau

No one has ever linked the debonair Franz von Rintelen with the disaster described in this chapter. Even though he was active in New York at the time (1916), he was quite incapable of planning or carrying out this most terrifying act of sabotage. But the German origins of the explosion were finally established after many years of investigation.

This account of Black Tom and its aftermath are from The Enemy Within *by Capt. Henry Landau.*

AT 2:08 A.M. on the night of July 30, 1916, New York City was rocked by the greatest explosion in her history. Over two million pounds of munitions stored on Black Tom Island in New York harbor blew up in a series of explosions. Two of the blasts were distinctly heard in Camden and Philadelphia, nearly a hundred miles away. The tremendous concussion shattered practically every window in Jersey City, and in Manhattan and Brooklyn thousands of heavy plate-glass windows fell from office buildings and skyscrapers into the streets. Buildings trembled; some of the inhabitants were thrown from their beds; and the population, panic-stricken, emptied itself out into the streets.

For hours the sky was lit up by the fierce fire which raged on Black Tom Island, and for three hours a steady stream of high explosives and shrapnel shells were hurled from the conflagration as they exploded, some of them landing as far off as Governors Island. Buildings on Ellis Island were wrecked, and all immigrants there had to be evacuated. During these terrifying hours, Black Tom and its vicinity might well have been part of the western front during a gigantic battle. The residents of Greater New York and northern New Jersey were shaken badly by the blast, but fortunately the terminal was just far enough away to prevent the metropolitan area's being razed.

To follow intelligently the tragic events which happened on that night, it is necessary to understand the layout of the terminal and also the conditions which prevailed there at the time of the explosion.

Black Tom is a promontory nearly one mile long which juts out into the Upper Bay from the New Jersey shore, about opposite the Statue of Liberty. It was originally an island, but at the time of the explosion was joined to the shore by a fill about 150 feet wide.

On Black Tom the Lehigh Valley Railroad Company had built large warehouses, numerous piers, and a network of tracks. Within a short time after the commencement of World War I, Black Tom became the most important point in America for the transfer of munitions and supplies to Allied vessels. Loaded freight cars were run into the northern part of the terminal, and from there the munitions were loaded into barges hired by the consignees and tied up at the adjoining piers.

As it was not always possible for the representatives of the Allied governments to determine beforehand the exact time steamers would be ready to receive the loads of munitions, it was quite usual for the munitions cars to be kept there for several days, sometimes a week, waiting to be unloaded. Thus, on the night of the explosion there were thirty-four carloads of munitions on

Black Tom, consisting of eleven cars of high explosives, seventeen of shells, three of nitro-cellulose, one of TNT, and two of combination fuses; in all a total of approximately 2,132,000 pounds of explosives.

At the north pier, bordering on the tracks, ten barges were tied up, most of them loaded with explosives which they had taken on at other terminals and piers in New York harbor. They had tied up at Black Tom, some to take on additional explosives, others to stay there during the night and over the following Sunday until their loads could be shifted to steamers. One of these barges, the *Johnson 17,* was loaded with 100,000 pounds of TNT and 417 cases of detonating fuses—a veritable floating bomb.

During July, 1916, Black Tom Terminal was guarded at night by watchmen (Leyden, Kane, Groat, Kelly, Sloane, and Garrity) provided by the Lehigh Valley Railroad Company, and by private detectives (Burns, Scott, Bryan, and Gibson) furnished by the Dougherty Detective Agency and paid for by the Allied governments, owners of the munitions. These men went on duty at 5:00 P.M. and remained until 6:00 A.M.

There was no gate on the tongue of land connecting Black Tom to the mainland. Consequently it was an easy matter for a person to reach the terminal; and, unless of a suspicious appearance, he would not have been stopped by the guards, as this passageway was also commonly used by the barge men whose boats were tied up at the pier. Furthermore, the terminal was in an isolated spot and unlighted, thus making it difficult to see a person prowling about. In addition anyone could reach it at night in a boat with little danger of being observed.

On Saturday evening, July 29, at five o'clock, all work stopped on Black Tom; the workmen departed for their usual Sunday holiday; and all locomotive engines were sent to the mainland. The terminal was a dead yard.

A gentle wind was blowing from the southwest. The night was quiet, and the guards placidly made their periodical rounds.

At 1:45 A.M. a fire was suddenly noticed in one of the munitions cars. At the first sight of it the guards turned in a fire alarm and fled in a panic.

Five independent witnesses on Black Tom Island at the time gave affidavits that the fire started inside the car and that the fire burned for about twenty minutes before the first explosion. A witness on Bedloe's Island, who had a view of the pier as well, later stated that another fire appeared almost simultaneously in a barge about three hundred yards away, presumably the *Johnson 17*.

At 2:08 A.M. the first explosion occurred, and this was followed by a second terrific blast at 2:40. In the confusion no one was able to tell whether the barge or the munitions near the car blew up first. However this fact is established: the *Johnson 17* was 325 feet away from the pier when it exploded. This was determined by the crater, which soundings of the river bed disclosed. The depth of the river at that point was found to be 21 feet; whereas a geodetic survey made a few days before the explosion had established a depth of 7 feet at the same spot. How the barge drifted so far away from the pier is not known. Only Johnson, the captain of the barge and the only man on board at the time, could tell whether its moorings had been burned away, or whether he had cast it loose. Both he and his barge had disappeared, however. Three months later his body drifted up on Bedloe's Island.

Another huge crater was found at a spot near where the burning car had stood. Thus it appeared that the two major explosions had been caused by the detonation of the munitions near the car and on the barge, the two places where the fires had been observed.

The two explosions and the conflagration which broke loose destroyed the entire Black Tom Terminal together with all the munitions and rolling stock which happened to be there that night. The damage was estimated at $14,000,000, and three men and a child were killed. These included Leyden, one of the night watchmen, and a policeman named James Doherty.

The immediate outcome of the Black Tom disaster was that

several suits were filed against the Lehigh Valley Railroad Company by the Russian government, which owned most of the munitions that had exploded, and by the property owners in the neighborhood. The plaintiffs maintained that the railroad had been negligent in not providing better protection for the property in view of the fact that it was known that German sabotage agents were at work in this country.

The Lehigh Valley based its defense on the theory that the explosions had been caused by spontaneous combustion, a defense which seemed the most expedient at the time, but one which rose to plague it later; for this was the very defense which the Germans raised when, after the war, the railroad and other American claimants in the Black Tom case filed their claims against Germany for damages with the Mixed Claims Commission. At these early trials, however, experts proved to the satisfaction of the jury that spontaneous combustion was impossible. It was established that the smokeless powder contained in the shells was manufactured in accordance with the specifications of the United States Army and Navy; that it was all new powder, treated with a stabilizer known as diphenylamine, which prevented spontaneous combustion. Dr. Free, United States government expert, testified that he had examined nearly two billion pounds of powder manufactured in this way and that it was inconceivable that spontaneous combustion could have occurred. It was further shown that even untreated smokeless powder would require a temperature of 356° Fahrenheit before it would ignite.

As regards TNT, experts testified that it was impossible for it to ignite spontaneously. Finally, it was pointed out that if the shells had gone off by spontaneous combustion, the guards would not have seen flames destroying the freight car for twenty-three minutes before the first explosion at 2:08 A.M. Besides all this there was evidence to show that before either of the explosions occurred another fire had broken out almost simultaneously with the first at a point nearly three hundred yards away from the car—the distance between it and the barge *Johnson 17*. This fact alone indicated that the origin of the explosions was incendiary. In most of these cases the jury found that the Lehigh Valley Railroad Company had been negligent in not having sufficient guards to protect the property.

But there were other developments. The local police were busily searching for leads. A Mrs. Chapman, a resident of Bayonne, New Jersey, who since her childhood had known Capt. John J. Rigney of the Bayonne Police Department, reported to him her suspicions that a cousin, Michael Kristoff, was responsible for the destruction of Black Tom. She related that Kristoff, who had formerly lodged with her and at the time lodged with her mother, Mrs. Anna Rushnak, at 76 East 25th Street, Bayonne, did not return home until four o'clock in the morning on the night of the explosion. Hearing him pace the floor, her mother went to his room. She found him in a state of great excitement and near nervous prostration. To her anxious query as to what had happened, the only reply she could get out of him was, "What I do! What I do!" This he kept repeating over and over again as he ran his hands through his hair.

According to Captain Rigney, Mrs. Chapman also told him that "Kristoff had been in the habit of going away from time to time and that everywhere he went there was an explosion." She referred to some place in Columbus, Ohio, where he had gone, and she said that whenever he came back from any of these trips he always had plenty of money. She also said that she had seen maps and charts in Kristoff's possession while he had been staying with her at her house at 114 Neptune Avenue, Jersey City, New Jersey.

The result was that after shadowing Kristoff for some time, Captain Rigney arrested him near Mrs. Rushnak's home on August 31, 1916, and turned him over to Peter Green of the Jersey City Police Department.

All that was known about Kristoff was that he was born in 1893 in Presov, then in the Slovak region of Hungary, now a part of Czechoslovakia, and had been given the surname Michael. When he was six years old, his parents emigrated to the United States, where his mother had several members of her family living. By 1916 he had grown into a tall, slimly built young man, with light reddish hair, pale blue eyes, fair complexion, and a weak receding chin. For some months prior to July he had been working for the Tidewater Oil Company at Bayonne, New Jersey, close to Black Tom.

When examined by the Bayonne police authorities, his story ran substantially as follows: On January 3, 1916, he was sitting in the waiting room of the Pennsylvania Railroad Station, 33rd Street, New York City, when he was accosted by a man who asked him the time and then inquired where he was going. Kristoff informed him that he was waiting for a train to go to Cambridge, Ohio, where he intended to visit his sister. This man, who then gave his name as Graentnor, offered him a job at twenty dollars per week, which he accepted. He went with Graentnor to the Hotel York, and on the next day they started off on a series of travels which took them in turn to Philadelphia, Bridgeport, Cleveland, Akron, Columbus, Chicago, Kansas City, St. Louis, and finally back to New York. After arranging to meet him in the lobby of the Hotel McAlpin, Graentnor disappeared, and he never saw him again. Kristoff stated that during these journeys his job was to carry Graentnor's two suitcases, which contained blueprints of bridges and factories, also money and books. He had no idea whom Graentnor saw in these towns, but ventured an opinion that the plans were "to show people how to build bridges and houses and factories."

His whole story sounded so unintelligible to the police authorities that they got the impression Kristoff was half demented, and, therefore, they called in a doctor to examine him. It was finally decided that he was not altogether sane, but not dangerously insane. Whereupon, in spite of the fact he had furnished several false alibis as to where he had been on the night of the explosion and had admitted working for the Eagle Oil Works, adjacent to Black Tom, and not returning for his pay after the explosion, he was released on September 25, 1916, after promising to look for Graentnor.

But the Lehigh Valley Railroad officials were not convinced. To them the strange story of Kristoff was not that of a crazy man but that of a man attempting to cover up his tracks. They felt that in his clumsy evasions he had admitted some truths. Factories were being blown up all over the country, and Graentnor and his two suitcases filled with blueprints sounded real.

From the payroll records of the Tidewater Oil Company in Bayonne, where Kristoff had been employed prior to his work at the Eagle Oil Works, they discovered that he had been absent for five work days in January, 1916. Subsequently he had left the employ of the company on February 29, 1916, and had not returned to work until June 19. After working there for a month he had transferred his services to the Eagle Oil Works. In addition, Mrs. Chapman later gave them an affidavit to the effect that while cleaning Kristoff's room one day shortly before the Black Tom explosion she had found an unmailed letter to a man named "Grandson" or "Graentnor," in which he had demanded a large sum of money. The Lehigh Valley Railroad, therefore, hired Alexander Kassman, an employee of the W. J. Burns Detective Agency, to shadow him.

For almost a year Kassman lived in close contact with Kristoff; they worked at the same chocolate factory and met nightly. Kassman posed as an Austrian anarchist, took Kristoff to anarchists' meetings, and thus won his confidence. At regular intervals Kassman reported to the Burns Agency. A perusal of these reports shows that Kristoff on numerous occasions admitted to Kassman that he had assisted in blowing up Black Tom.

In May, 1917, Kassman lost track of Kristoff. Records discovered long afterwards revealed, however, that Kristoff employed a well-known ruse to divert attention from himself: on May 22, 1917, he enlisted in the United States Army. A later entry in his army records shows that he was discharged on September 12, 1917, because of tuberculosis and for having enlisted under false enlistment papers.

Kristoff now vanished completely until the spring of 1921, when he was located in prison at Albany, New York, where he had been committed for larceny under the name of "John Christie."

Once again the Lehigh Valley Railroad attempted to get from

him further information about Black Tom. Through the cooperation of the county officials of Albany County, a detective of the Washington Detective Bureau was placed in a cell next to Kristoff, and together with him was assigned to work in the prison bake shop. The detective remained there nineteen days, but Kristoff was on the defensive when approached about Black Tom. He was well aware that a murder charge was involved. He repeated the same story about Graentnor and the blueprints which he had told to the Bayonne police five years previously; and, although he refused to make any admission that he had blown up Black Tom, he did admit that he had been working with a German group for several weeks and that they had promised him a large sum of money. . . .

Of the various investigations which were conducted at the time by the Department of Justice, the Interstate Commerce Commission, the local authorities, and the owners, none was successful. It was not until after 1922, when the Mixed Claims Commission was established, that the American lawyers employed by the owners gradually began by exhaustive investigations to lift the curtain of mystery which surrounded the destruction of Black Tom, and by piecing the intricate clues together began to build up their case against Germany. . . . The evidence they collected led the American investigators to the conviction that Graentnor was a known German agent called Hinsch or at least that Hinsch knew a Graentnor whose name he borrowed as an alias; that two other German agents rowed across to Black Tom from the New York side to assist Kristoff in blowing up the terminal; and that two of the Dougherty guards, Burns and Scott, were paid agents of Germany's.

The Black Tom case was the most famous international law suit of modern times. Litigation lasted seventeen years. Finally, in October, 1939, the Mixed Claims Commission ruled that Germany had destroyed both the munitions stored on Black Tom Island and the Russian supplies at King Island, New Jersey, which blew up some six months later (January 11, 1917). The Com-

mission also noted evidence of nineteen other explosions before America's entry into World War I.

The award to Russia and the United States was $55,000,000 but it was never paid. World War II had already broken out and soon both Russia and the United States would again be among the enemies of Germany.

4

A Railway Diversion

T. E. Lawrence

Col. T. E. Lawrence, known as Lawrence of Arabia, was the no-blest of saboteurs. Born in 1888, he took a First Class degree in modern history at Oxford in 1910. Then, for four years, he trav-eled in Syria and Mesopotamia, doing some archaeological work and picking up his mastery of spoken Arabic in the process. Too short a man for military service, he started his World War I career as a mapmaker in Cairo. By 1916 he was in the South-Arabian city of Jidda, working for the Foreign Office's Arab Bureau.

By then his real talents were beginning to show: a flair for leadership, skill and insight in his dealings with the Arabs, practical ability in the arts of desert warfare. At Jidda he met Emir Feisal and was able to convince him that the Arab cause against the Turks was a promising one despite some early set-backs. The Turks, linked to the Germans, had captured Medina and were planning to push on down to Mecca itself.

Lawrence persuaded Feisal to set up a command post at Wadi Ais, a valley with many springs about one hundred miles north of Medina. (Wadi is the Arabic word for stream or valley, deriving from wadaya, *to flow.) Since Wadi Ais lay near the Turkish railway, it was a good place from which to launch surprise attacks.*

At this time Lawrence came down with dysentery. While ill, he did some serious thinking about the purposes of the war that he and the Arabs were undertaking. It was, for example, perfectly clear that the Turks had overwhelming manpower and that they held human life cheap. "Our cue," Lawrence reasoned, "was to destroy not the Turk's army but his minerals. The death of a Turkish bridge or rail, machine gun or high explosive was more profitable to us than the death of a Turk." By contrast, he argued that irregulars like the Arabs were individuals: "An individual death, like a pebble dropped in water, might make but a brief role; yet rings of sorrow widened out therefrom. We could not afford casualties." Here, in terms both poetic and practical, is the essence of his philosophy as a saboteur.

The following account of Lawrence's first forays after that bout of dysentery is taken from his magnificent book, The Seven Pillars of Wisdom, *published in 1926.*

OBVIOUSLY I was well again, and I remembered the reason for my journey to Wadi Ais. The Turks meant to march out of Medina, and Sir Archibald Murray* wanted us to attack them in professional form. It was irksome that he should come butting into our show from Egypt, asking from us alien activities. Yet the British were the bigger; and the Arabs lived only by grace of their shadow. We were yoked to Sir Archibald Murray, and must work with him, to the point of sacrificing our non-essential interests for his, if they would not be reconciled. At the same time we could not possibly act alike. Feisal might be a free gas: Sir Archibald's army, probably the most cumbrous in the world, had to be laboriously pushed forward on its belly. It was ridiculous to suppose it could keep pace with ethical conceptions as nimble as

* The British commander in Cairo

the Arab Movement; doubtful even if it would understand them. However, perhaps by hindering the railway we could frighten the Turks off their plan to evacuate Medina, and give them reason to remain in the town on the defensive: a conclusion highly serviceable to both Arabs and English, though possibly neither would see it, yet.

Accordingly, I wandered into Abdulla's* tent, announcing my complete recovery and an ambition to do something to the Hejaz railway. Here were men, guns, machine guns, explosives and automatic mines: enough for a main effort. But Abdulla was apathetic. He wanted to talk about the royal families of Europe, or the Battle of the Somme; the slow march of his own war bored him. However, Sherif Shakir, his cousin and second in command, was fired to enthusiasm, and secured us license to do our worst. Shakir loved the Ateiba and swore they were the best tribe on earth; so we settled to take mostly Ateiba with us. . . .

Shakir promised to collect the force, and we agreed that I should go in front (gently, as befitted my weakness) and search for a target. The nearest and biggest was Aba el Naam Station. With me went Raho, Algerian officer in the French army and member of Bremond's mission, a very hard-working and honest fellow. Our guide was Mohammed el Kadhi. . . . Mohammed was eighteen, solid and silent natured. Sherif Fauzan el Harith, the famous warrior who had captured Eshref at Janbila, escorted us with about twenty Ateiba and five or six Juheina adventurers.

We left on March the twenty-sixth, while Sir Archibald Murray was attacking Gaza, and rode down Wadi Ais; but after three hours the heat proved too much for me, and we stopped by a great sidr tree and rested under it the midday hours . . . and then did only a short march, leaving Wadi Ais by the right, after passing in an angle of the valley a ruined terrace and cistern. . . .

The following morning we had two hours' rough riding around the spurs of Jebel Serd into Wadi Turaa, a historic valley,

* Emir Feisal's brother

linked by an easy pass to Wadi Yenbo. We spent this midday also under a tree, near some Juheina tents. . . . Then we rode on rather crookedly for two more hours, and camped after dark. By ill luck an early spring scorpion stung me severely on the left hand while I lay down to sleep. The place swelled up, and my arm became stiff and sore.

At five next morning, after a long night, we restarted and passed through the last hills, out into the Jurf, an undulating open space which ran up southward to Jebel Antar, a crater with a split and castellated top, making it a landmark. We turned half-right in the plain, to get under cover of the low hills which screened it from Wadi Hamdh, in whose bed the railway lay. Behind these hills we rode southward till opposite Aba el Naam. There we halted to camp, close to the enemy but quite in safety. The hilltop commanded them, and we climbed it before sunset for a first view of the station.

The hill was, perhaps, six hundred feet high and steep, and I made many stages of it, resting on my way up. But the sight from the top was good. The railway was some three miles off. The station had a pair of large, two-storied houses of basalt, a circular watertower, and other buildings. There were bell-tents, huts and trenches, but no sign of guns. We could see about three hundred men in all.

We had heard that the Turks patrolled their neighborhood actively at night. A bad habit this, so we sent off two men to lie by each blockhouse and fire a few shots after dark. The enemy, thinking it a prelude to attack, stood-to in their trenches all night, while we were comfortably sleeping; but the cold woke us early with a restless dawn wind blowing across the Jurf and singing in the great trees round our camp. As we climbed to our observation point the sun conquered the clouds and an hour later it grew very hot.

We lay like lizards in the long grass around the stones of the foremost cairn upon the hilltop and saw the garrison parade. Three hundred and ninety-nine infantry, little toy men, ran about when the bugle sounded and formed up in stiff lines below the black building till there was more bugling. Then they scattered, and after a few minutes the smoke of cooking fires went up. A herd of sheep and goats in charge of a little ragged boy issued out toward us. Before he reached the foot of the hills there came a loud whistling down the valley from the north, and a tiny, picture-book train rolled slowly into view across the hollow-sounding bridge and halted just outside the station, panting out white puffs of steam. . . .

Only the sun moved in our view. As it climbed we shifted our cloaks to filter its harshness and basked in luxurious warmth. The restful hilltop gave me back something of the sense interests which I had lost since I had been ill. I was able to note once more the typical hill scenery, with its hard stone crests, its sides of bare rock, and lower slopes of loose sliding screes, packed, as the base was approached, solidly with a thin dry soil. . . .

At dusk we climbed down again. Our main body would come this night, so that Fauzan and I wandered out across the darkling plain till we found a pleasant gun position in some low ridges not two thousand yards from the station. On our return, very tired, fires were burning among the trees. Shakir had just arrived, and his men and ours were roasting goat flesh contentedly.

After supper Shakir told me that he had brought only three hundred men instead of the agreed eight or nine hundred. However, it was his war, and therefore his tune, so we hastily modified the plans. We would not take the station; we would frighten it by a frontal artillery attack, while we mined the railway to the north and south in the hope of trapping that halted train. Accordingly we chose a party of dynamiters who should blow up something north of the bridge at dawn, to seal that direction, while I went off with high explosives and a machine gun with its crew to lay a mine to the south of the station, the probable direction from which the Turks would seek or send help in their emergency.

Mohammed el Khadi guided us to a deserted bit of line just before midnight. I dismounted and fingered its thrilling rails for the first time during the war. Then, in an hour's busy work, we laid the mine, which was a trigger action to fire into twenty pounds of blasting gelatine when the weight of the locomotive overhead deflected the metals. Afterwards we posted the machine-gunners in a little bush-screened watercourse, four hundred yards from and fully commanding the spot where we hoped the train would be derailed. They were to hide there, while we went on to cut the telegraph, that isolation might persuade Aba el Naam to send their train for reinforcements, as our main attack developed.

So we rode another half hour and then turned in to the line, and again were fortunate to strike an unoccupied place. Unhappily the four remaining Juheina proved unable to climb a telegraph pole, and I had to struggle up it myself. It was all I could do, after my illness; and when the third wire was cut the flimsy pole shook so that I lost grip and came slipping down the sixteen feet upon the stout shoulders of Mohammed, who ran in to break my fall and nearly got broken himself. We took a few minutes to breathe but afterwards were able to regain our camels. Eventually we arrived in camp just as the others had saddled up to go forward.

Our mine-laying had taken four hours longer than we had planned and the delay put us in the dilemma either of getting no rest or of letting the main body march without us. Finally by Shakir's will we let them go and fell down under our trees for an hour's sleep, without which I felt I should collapse utterly. The time was just before daybreak, an hour when the uneasiness of the air affected trees and animals and made even men sleepers turn over sighingly. Mohammed, who wanted to see the fight, awoke. To get me up he came over and cried the morning prayer-call in my ear, the raucous voice sounding battle, murder, and sudden death across my dreams. I sat up and rubbed the sand out of red-rimmed aching eyes, as we disputed vehemently of prayer and sleep. He pleaded that there was not a battle every day, and showed the cuts and bruises sustained during the night in helping me. By my blackness and blueness I could feel for him, and we rode off to catch the army. . . .

We arrived just as the guns opened fire. They did excellently, and crashed in all the top of one building, damaged the second, hit the pumproom, and holed the watertank. One lucky shell caught the front wagon of the train in the siding, and it took fire furiously. This alarmed the locomotive, which uncoupled and went off southward. We watched her hungrily as she approached our mine, and when she was on it there came a soft cloud of dust and a report and she stood still. The damage was to the front part, as she was reversed and the charge had exploded late; but, while the drivers got out and jacked up the front wheels and tinkered at them, we waited and waited in vain for the machine gun to open fire. Later we learned that the gunners, afraid of their loneliness, had packed up and marched to join us when we began shooting. Half an hour after, the repaired engine went away toward Jebel Antar, going at a foot pace and clanking loudly; but going nonetheless.

Our Arabs worked in toward the station, under cover of the bombardment, while we gnashed our teeth at the machine-gunners. Smoke clouds from the fire trucks screened the Arab advance, which wiped out one enemy outpost and captured another. The Turks withdrew their surviving detachments to the main position and waited rigorously in their trenches for the assault, which they were in no better spirit to repel than we were to deliver. With our advantages in ground the place would have been a gift to us, if only we had had some of Feisal's men to charge home.

Meanwhile the wood, tents and trucks in the station were burning, and the smoke was too thick for us to shoot, so we broke off the action. We had taken thirty prisoners, a mare, two camels and some more sheep and had killed and wounded seventy of the garrison, at a cost to ourselves of one man slightly hurt. Traffic was held up for three days of repair and investigation. So we did not wholly fail.

We left two parties in the neighborhood to damage the line on the next day and the next, while we rode to Abdullah's camp on April the first. Shakir, splendid in habit, held a grand parade on entry and had thousands of joy-shots fired in honor of his partial victory. The easy-going camp made carnival. . . .

In the morning we determined on another visit to the line for fuller trial of the automatic mine-action which had half-failed at Aba el Naam. Old Dakhil-Allah (hereditary lawman of the Juheina) said that he would come with me himself on this trip; the project of looting a train had tempted him. With us went some forty of the Juheina, who seemed to me stouter men than the high-bred Ateiba. However, one of the chiefs of the Ateiba, Sultan el Abbud, a boon friend of Abdulla and Shakir, refused to be left behind. This good-tempered but hare-brained fellow, sheikh of a poor section of the tribe, had had more horses killed under him in battle than any other Ateiba warrior. He was about twenty-six and a great rider, full of quips and fond of practical jokes, very noisy, tall and strong, with a big, square head, wrinkled forehead, and deep-set bright eyes. A young moustache and beard hid his ruthless jaw and the wide, straight mouth, with white teeth gleaming and locked like a wolf's.

We took a machine gun and its soldier-crew of thirteen with us to settle our train when caught. Shakir, with his grave courtesy to the Emir's guest, set us on our road for the first half hour. This time we kept to the Wadi Ais almost to its junction with Hamdh, finding it very green and full of grazing, since it had flooded twice already in this winter. At last we bore off to the right over a ditch on to a flat, and there slept in the sand, rather distressed by a shower of rain which sent little rills over the ground about midnight. But the next morning was bright and hot, and we rode into the huge plain where the three great valleys, Tubja, Ais and Jizil, flowed into and became one with Hamdh. . . . At noon we halted by a place like a wilderness garden, waist deep in juicy grass and flowers, upon which our happy camels gorged themselves for an hour and then sat down, full and astonished.

The day seemed to be hotter and hotter: the sun drew close, and scorched us without intervening air. The clean, sandy soil was so baked that my bare feet could not endure it, and I had to walk in sandals, to the amusement of the Juheina, whose thick soles were proof even against slow fire. As the afternoon passed on, the light became dim, but the heat steadily increased with an oppression and sultriness which took me by surprise. . . .

The raiders endured a violent wind storm followed by torrents of rain.

We did not reach the railway till after ten o'clock at night, in conditions of invisibility which made it futile to choose a machine-gun position. At random I pitched upon kilometer 1,121 from Damascus for the mine. It was a complicated mine, with a central trigger to fire simultaneous charges thirty yards apart, and we hoped in this way to get the locomotive whether it was going north or south. Burying the mine took four hours, for the rain had caked the surface and rotted it. Our feet made huge tracks on the flat and on the bank, as though a school of elephants had been dancing there. To hide these marks was out of the question, so we did the other thing, trampling about for hundreds of yards, even bringing up our camels to help, until it looked as though half an army had crossed the valley, and the mine-place was no better and no worse than the rest. Then we went back a safe distance, behind some miserable mounds, and cowered down in the open, waiting for day. The cold was intense. Our teeth chattered, and we trembled and hissed involuntarily, while our hands drew in like claws.

At dawn the clouds had disappeared and a red sun promised, over the very fine broken hills beyond the railway. Old Dakhil-Allah, our active guide and leader in the night, now took general charge and sent us out singly and in pairs to all the approaches of our hiding place. He himself crawled up the ridge before us to watch events upon the railway through his glasses. I was praying that there might be no events till the sun had gained power and warmed me, for the shivering fit still jerked me about. However, soon the sun was up and unveiled, and things improved. My clothes were drying. By noon it was nearly as hot as the day before, and we were gasping for shade, and thicker clothes, against the sun.

First of all, though, at six in the morning, Dakhil-Allah reported a trolley, which came from the south, and passed over the mine harmlessly—to our satisfaction, for we had not laid a beautiful compound charge for just four men and a sergeant. Then sixty men sallied out from Madahrij. This disturbed us till we saw that they were to replace five telegraph poles blown down by the storm of the afternoon before. Then at seven-thirty a patrol of eleven men went down the line: two inspecting each rail minutely, three marching each side of the bank looking for crosstracks, and one, presumably the NCO, walking grandly along the metals with nothing to do.

However, today they did find something, when they crossed our footprints about kilometer 1,121. They concentrated there upon the permanent way, stared at it, stamped, wandered up and down, scratched the ballast, and thought exhaustively. The time of their search passed slowly for us. But the mine was well hidden, so that eventually they wandered on contentedly toward the south, where they met the Hedia patrol, and both parties sat together in the cool shade of a bridge arch and rested after their labors. Meanwhile the train, a heavy train, came along from the south. Nine of its laden trucks held women and children from Medina, civil refugees being deported to Syria, with their household stuff. It ran over the charges without explosion. As artist I was furious; as commander deeply relieved: women and children were not proper spoil.

The Juheina raced to the crest where Dakhil-Allah and myself lay hidden, when they heard the train coming, to see it blown in pieces. Our stone headwork had been built for two, so that the hilltop, a bald cone conspicuously opposite the working party, became suddenly and visibly populous. This was too much for the nerves of the Turks, who fled back into Madahrij, and thence, at about five thousand yards, opened a brisk rifle fire. They must also have telephoned to Hedia, which soon came to life: but since the nearest outpost on that side was about six miles off, its garrisons held their fire and contented themselves with selections on the bugle, played all day. The distance made it grave and beautiful.

Even the rifle shooting did us no harm; but the disclosure of ourselves was unfortunate. At Madahrij were two hundred men, and at Hedia eleven hundred, and our retreat was by the plain of Hamdh on which Hedia stood. Their mounted troops might sally out and cut our rear. The Juheina had good camels, and so were safe; but the machine gun was a captured German sledge-Maxim: a heavy load for its tiny mule. The servers were on foot, or on other mules. Their top speed would be only six miles an hour, and their fighting value, with a single gun, not high. So after a council of war we rode back with them halfway through the hills, and there dismissed them, with fifteen Juheina, toward Wadi Ais.

This made us mobile, and Dakhil-Allah, Sultan, Mohammed and I rode back with the rest of our party for another look at the line. The sunlight was now terrific, with faint gusts of scorching heat blowing up at us out of the south. We took refuge about ten o'clock under some spacious trees, where we baked bread and lunched, in nice view of the line, and shaded from the worst of the sun. About us, over the gravel, circles of pale shadow from the crisping leaves ran to and fro, like gray, indeterminate bugs, as the slender branches dipped reluctantly in the wind. Our picnic annoyed the Turks, who shot or trumpeted at us incessantly through midday and till evening, while we slept in turn.

About five they grew quiet, and we mounted and rode slowly across the open valley toward the railway. Madahrij revived in a paroxysm of fire, and all the trumpets of Hedia blared again. When we reached the line we made our camels kneel down beside it, and, led by Dakhil-Allah as Imam, performed a sunset prayer quietly between the rails. It was probably the first prayer of the Juheina for a year or so, and I was a novice, but from a distance we passed muster, and the Turks stopped shooting in bewilderment. This was the first and last time I ever prayed in Arabia as a Moslem.

After the prayer it was still much too light to hide our actions: so we sat around on the embankment smoking till dusk, when I tried to go off by myself and dig up the mine, to learn, for service on the next occasion, why it had failed. However, the Juheina were as interested in that as I. Along they came in a swarm and clustered over the metals during the search. They brought my heart into my throat, for it took me an hour to find just where the mine was hidden. Laying a mine was shaky work, but scrabbling in pitch darkness up and down a hundred yards of railway, feeling for a hair-trigger buried in the ballast, seemed, at the time, an almost uninsurable occupation. The two charges connected with it were so powerful that they would have rooted out seventy yards of track; and I saw visions of suddenly blowing up, not only myself, but my whole force, every moment. To be sure, such a feat would have properly completed the bewilderment of the Turks!

At last I found it, and ascertained by touch that the lock had sunk one-sixteenth of an inch, due to bad setting by myself or because the ground had subsided after the rain. I firmed it into its place. Then, to explain ourselves plausibly to the enemy, we began blowing up things to the north of the mine. We found a little four-arch bridge and put it into the air. Afterwards we turned to rails and cut about two hundred. And while the men were laying and lighting charges I taught Mohammed to climb a splintery pole; together we cut the wires, and with their purchase dragged down other poles. All was done at speed, for we feared lest Turks come after us. And when our explosive work was finished we ran back like hares to our camels, mounted them, and trotted without interruption down the windy valley once more to the plain of Hamdh. . . .

In the morning we slept lazily long and breakfasted at Rubiaan, the first well in Wadi Ais. Afterwards we were smoking and talking, about to bring in the camels, when suddenly we felt the distant shock of a great explosion behind us on the railway. We wondered if the mine had been discovered or had done its duty. Two scouts had been left to report, and we rode slowly, for them and because the rain two days ago had brought down Wadi

Ais once more in flood, and its bed was all flecked over with shallow pools of soft, gray water, between banks of silvery mud, which the current had rippled into fish scales. The warmth of the sun made the surface like fine glue, on which our helpless camels sprawled comically or went down with a force and completeness surprising in such dignified beasts. Their tempers were roughened each time by our fit of mirth.

The sunlight, the easy march and the expectation of the scouts' news made everything gay, and we developed social virtues: but our limbs, stiff from the exertions of yesterday, and our abundant food determined us to fall short of Abu Markha for the night. So, near sunset, we chose a dry terrace in the valley to sleep upon. I rode up it first and turned and looked at the men reined in below me in a group, upon their bay camels like copper statues in the fierce light of the setting sun; they seemed to be burning with an inward flame.

Before bread was baked the scouts arrived to tell us that at dawn the Turks had been busy around our damages, and a little later a locomotive with trucks of rails and a crowded labor gang on top had come up from Hedia, and had exploded the mine fore and aft of its wheels. This was everything we had hoped, and we rode back to Abdulla's camp on a morning of perfect springtime, in a singing company. We had proved that a well-laid mine would fire, and that a well-laid mine was difficult even for its maker to discover.

Such was the beginning of a series of spectacular hit-and-run raids. Lawrence even routed the Turks in a set battle at Wadi el-Hesa. In 1918 he led his splendid irregulars into Damascus some hours ahead of the British troops under General Allenby. After the war, Feisal was elected king of Iraq but Lawrence, disappointed that so many wartime promises made to the Arabs were broken, returned to England and became more and more of an enigma and a recluse. Refusing the honors he had so richly earned, he enlisted in the Royal Air Force in 1922 and again in 1925. In 1927 he legally changed his name to Shaw. He was killed in a motorcycle accident in 1935.

The dedication of The Seven Pillars of Wisdom *did nothing to dispel the mystery of its author. Lawrence dedicates the book "To S. A.," and here is the first verse of the poem that follows:*

I loved you, so I drew these tides of men into my hands
    and wrote my will across the sky in stars
To earn you freedom, the seven-pillared worthy house,
    that your eyes might be shining for me when we came.

No one to this day has ever established who S. A. was, even though the deeds that stemmed from Lawrence's love are history.

5

The Fatal Ambush at Bal na mBlath

Emmet Dalton

The Irish Republican Army (IRA) was founded in 1919 by Michael Collins and others. Its roots go far back into the stormy history of Ireland. Three rebellions had flared in the 19th century with the same enduring purpose: total freedom from British rule. The IRA's direct ancestor was the Irish Republican Brotherhood, which played a part in the gallant but doomed rising of 1916. Then in 1919 the age-old conflict broke out again. For almost three years the IRA challenged regular British regiments, the Royal Irish Constabulary and the hated Black and Tans (soldiers of fortune who had re-enlisted in the British army at the end of World War I).

Using hit-and-run tactics, ambush and sabotage, the IRA fought the British to a standstill. They also used another long-time Irish technique: the boycott. By its tactics of denying essential services like mail and milk, and imposing a climate of silent contempt, the boycott helped to make life intolerable for pro-British landowners in outlying places.

Finally, a compromise peace was worked out, resulting in the creation of the Irish Free State. Michael Collins, the most gifted of the Irish leaders, was one of the creators of the Free State, and its staunch supporter. But some of the more violent Republicans, including many officers and men of the IRA, refused to accept it, because the ties with England were not totally severed.

In July, 1922, civil war broke out between the Free State supporters and the diehard Republicans. This was phase two of the "trouble," and it was even more bitter than the first, with brother against brother now. The big, handsome 32-year-old Collins commanded the Free State forces. On August 23, 1922, he was on an inspection tour in his native County Cork, scene of some of the sharpest fighting of the war. IRA flying columns were in the area, and there were warnings of an ambush. So General Collins drove in the middle of the armed convoy. He and Maj. Gen. Emmet Dalton were in a touring car with the top down.

Here is Dalton's account of a tragic day for Ireland:

ABOUT three miles from Clonakilty we found the road blocked with felled trees. We spent about half an hour clearing the road. General Collins, always ready for emergencies, great or small, directed the work and took a hand in carrying it out. Active and powerful in body as in mind, he handled ax and saw with the same vigor as he could exhibit in the direction of affairs of state, military or civil.

Having at last cleared a way, we went into the town of Clonakilty, which is the hometown of General Collins. Here he interviewed the garrison officer and had conversation with many of his friends. It was pleasant to see with what delight and affection they met him. We had lunch in a friend's house in the town before setting out for Roscarbery.

It may be mentioned here that, on his arrival in Clonakilty, the whole town turned out to welcome him. . . .

Just outside the town of Bandon, General Collins pointed out to me several farmhouses, which he told me were used by the lads in the old days of "the Terror." He mentioned to me the home of one particular friend of his own, remarking, "It's too bad he's on the other side now, because he is a damn good soldier." Then he added pensively, "I don't suppose I will be ambushed in my own country."

It was now about a quarter past seven, and the light was failing. We were speeding along the open road on our way to Macroom. Our motorcyclist scout was about fifty yards in front of the Crossley tender, which we followed at the same interval in the touring car. Close behind us came the armored car.

We had just reached a part of the road which was commanded by hills on all sides. The road itself was flat and open. On the right we were flanked by steep hills; on the left there was a small two-foot bank of earth skirting the road. Beyond this there was a marshy field bounded by a small stream, with another steep hill beyond it.

About halfway up this hill there was a road running parallel to the one that we were on, but screened from view by a wall and a mass of trees and bushes. We had just turned a wide corner on the road when a sudden and heavy fusillade of machine-gun and rifle fire swept the road in front of us and behind us, shattering the windscreen of our car.

I shouted to the driver, "Drive like hell!" But the commander-in-chief, placing his hand on the man's shoulder, said, "Stop! Jump out and we'll fight them."

We leaped from the car and took what cover we could behind the little mud bank on the left-hand side of the road. It seemed that the greatest volume of fire was coming from the concealed roadway on our left-hand side. The armored car now backed up the road and opened a heavy machine-gun fire at the hidden ambushers.

It may be mentioned here that the machine gun in the armored car jammed after a short time. (The machine-gunner, MacPeake, not long after this occurrence, deserted to the Irregulars, bringing an armored car with him.)

It was the Crossley tender, of which commandant O'Connell was in charge, which received the first shot. The road had been barricaded by an old cart, which the occupants of the tender promptly removed out of the way. After a few minutes the firing at them ceased, and the ambushers concentrated their fire on Collins and the other men who had occupied the touring car. Sean O'Connell then ran down the road and joined them.

General Collins and I were lying within arm's length of each other. Captain Dolan, who had been in the back of the armored car, together with our two drivers, was several yards farther down the road to my right.

General Collins and I, with Captain Dolan who was near us, opened a rapid rifle fire on our seldom visible enemies. About fifty or sixty yards farther down the road, and around the bend, we could hear that our machine-gunners and riflemen were also heavily engaged.

We continued this fire fight for about twenty minutes without suffering any casualties, when a lull in the enemy's attack became noticeable. General Collins now jumped up to his feet and walked over behind the armored car, obviously to obtain a better view of the enemy's position.

He remained there, firing occasional shots and using the car as cover. Suddenly I heard him shout, "Come on, boys! There they are, running up the road." I immediately opened fire upon two figures that came in view on the opposite road.

When I next turned around, the commander-in-chief had left the car position and had run about fifteen yards back up the road. Here he dropped into the prone firing position and opened up on our retreating enemies.

Dolan and O'Connell and I took up positions on the road farther down. Presently the firing of Collins ceased, and I heard, or fancied I heard, a faint cry of "Emmet!" Sean O'Connell and I rushed to the spot with a dreadful fear clutching our hearts. We found our beloved chief and friend lying motionless in a firing position, firmly gripping his rifle, across which his head was resting.

There was a fearful gaping wound at the base of the skull behind the right ear. We immediately saw that General Collins was almost beyond human aid. He could not speak to us.

The enemy must have seen that something had occurred to cause a sudden cessation of our fire, because they intensified their own.

O'Connell now knelt beside the dying but still conscious chief, whose eyes were wide-open and normal, and he whispered into the ear of the fast-sinking man the words of the Act of Contrition. For this, he was rewarded by a slight pressure of the hand.

Meanwhile I knelt beside them both and kept up bursts of rapid fire, which I continued while O'Connell dragged the chief across the road and behind the armored car. Then, with my heart torn with sorrow and despair, I ran to the chief's side. Very gently I raised his head on my knee and tried to bandage his wound, but, owing to the awful size of it, this proved very difficult.

I had not completed my grievous task when the big eyes closed, and the cold pallor of death overspread the general's face. How can I describe the feelings that were mine at that bleak hour, kneeling in the mud of a country road not twelve miles from Clonakilty, with the still bleeding head of the idol of Ireland resting on my arm.

My heart was broken, my mind was numbed. I was all unconscious of the bullets that still whistled and ripped the ground beside me. I think that the weight of the blow would have caused the loss of my reason had I not abruptly observed the tear-stained face of O'Connell, now distorted with anguish, and calling also for my sympathy and support.

We paused for a moment in silent prayer, and then, noting that the fire of our enemies had greatly abated and that they had practically all retreated, we two, with the assistance of Lieutenant Smith, the motorcyclist scout officer, who had come on the scene, endeavored to lift the stalwart body of Michael Collins into the back of the armored car.

It was then that we suffered our second casualty—Lieutenant Smith was shot in the neck. He remained on his feet, however, and helped us to carry our precious burden around a turn in the road and under cover of the armored car.

Having transferred the body of our chief to the touring car, where I sat with his head resting on my shoulder, our awe-stricken little party set out for Cork.

By May, 1923, the Republican cause was a lost one. The Republican leaders surrendered to the Free State, and this violent, two-part phase of Ireland's woe was over at last. In character, the IRA went underground.

To this day there is controversy over who killed Collins. By the nature of the wound, the shot seemed to have come from behind. The fact that MacPeake, the machine-gunner, went over to the Republican cause soon after was in itself most suspicious. On the other hand, Oliver St. John Gogarty, the doctor-author who examined the body of Collins, stated that the shot could well have been a ricochet. But nothing was ever proved. As in so much of Irish history, the truth remains shrouded in the eternal mists and rain of the fair but troubled land.

6

"The Reichstag Is Burning!"

R. John Pritchard

ON *January 30, 1933, Adolf Hitler became Chancellor of Germany. But the leader of the Nazi party was by no means in full command of the destiny of the Republic. His twelve-man Cabinet was a coalition, with only two other members who were Nazis (one was Hermann Göring, acting Prussian Minister of the Interior). Paul von Hindenburg, the ancient and reactionary Army chieftain, was titular President of the Republic and his lackey, Franz von Papen, was Vice Chancellor.*

Another obstacle to Hitler's towering ambition to control Germany was the Communist Party. It was not particularly strong or effective. Out of a total of some 650 seats in the German Reischstag, or parliament, it held eighty-one. The Reichstag was in fact so fragmented that no one party held a majority. . . .

Less than a month after Hitler became Chancellor, certain events took place behind the vast, ornate facade of the Reichstag building which would profoundly affect the history of Germany and the world. This selection is historian John Pritchard's account of what happened there on the night of Monday, February 27, 1933.

A cast of the principal characters will help keep the sequence of events in focus, as it was an evening that was as confused as it was spectacular:

Rudolf Scholz	Night watchman of the Reichstag
Albert Wendt	Night porter there
Ernst Torgler Wilhelm Koenen }	Communist deputies
Hans Flöter	A student of theology
Karl Buwert	A sergeant of police
Werner Thaler	A typesetter
Alexander Scranowitz	Chief House Inspector of the Reichstag
Emil Lateit	Duty Officer at the Brandenburg Gate Police Station
Marinus Van der Lubbe	Arsonist and saboteur

(also Police Constables Poeschel, Losigkeit and Graining)

ON Monday, February 27, 1933, Rudolf Scholz is the night watchman at the German Reichstag building, which houses the German Parliament. Like many other employees at the Reichstag, he has worked there faithfully for many years and is a virtual fixture of the place. As he begins his nightly rounds in the enormous building, he punches his time clock. It registers 8:10 P.M. At this time every entrance except the north, Portal Five, is supposed to be closed, since the Reichstag is not in session.

Scholz takes his duties seriously this night, as any other. Like many men who have become accustomed to a lifetime of dull, tedious occupations, he prides himself on his attention to details. His appointed task is to turn off all lights and to make sure that every door and window is securely latched after the deputies have gone home. Such is his usual care that he generally takes about half an hour to finish his nightly circuit of inspection.

While Inspector Scholz makes the rounds, Albert Wendt, a lugubrious-looking individual with an enormous walrus moustache, is night porter at Portal Five. Wendt receives a request to put through a telephone call from Erich Birkenhauer, a Communist journalist from Essen, to Ernst Torgler, the chairman of the Reichstag Communist faction. Because the outside switchboard closed at 8:00 P.M., Torgler comes down to take the call in Wendt's presence. Later Wendt would recall that Torgler promised to meet someone at a restaurant. It is still a very dull evening. The time is 8:20.

In the meantime, Rudolf Scholz has found nothing unusual. Security precautions at the Reichstag were always vigilantly maintained, but the Reichstag staff has been especially careful in observing them in the last several months owing to a recent investigation of all security regulations when someone stole a valuable document from the archives. Besides, Rudolf Scholz is aware of the political tensions in the air; while he is preoccupied with private thoughts tonight, he overlooks nothing—especially anything which appears out of the ordinary.

At approximately 8:30, Scholz arrives at the Plenary, or Parliamentary Sessions Chamber. Making sure that everything is correctly in order, he starts to continue. But as he leaves his sharp ears pick up the sound of footsteps on the rich carpeting. He snaps on the lights to see who is there. It is only Miss Anna Rehme, the group secretary for the Communists. Answering Scholz's questions, Miss Rehme explains that one of the Communist deputies, Wilhelm Koenen, who is also the secretary-general of the German Communist Party, has requested that she bring some election materials to the Communist Party chambers upstairs. After exchanging a few additional pleasantries, Scholz continues on with his inspections, but he takes note of the time: 8:32. He completes his rounds a few minutes later, at 8:35, finishing at the north entrance, Portal Five. While he prepares himself to go home, he chats idly with Wendt.

Soon Torgler, Koenen, and Miss Rehme join them. Torgler gives his keys to Scholz, and they indulge in some light conversation. Torgler and his companions leave at 8:38. They are the last deputies to leave the Reichstag, and there is absolutely nothing unusual in the way they leave; they certainly give no sign of being in flight. Anna Rehme is obese and suffers from varicose veins, so they make their way very slowly. Talking quietly, the trio walk along the River Spree embankment to the Friedrichstrasse Station, where Anna Rehme leaves them. Torgler and Koenen continue on to the Friedrichstrasse branch of Aschinger's Restaurant, a respectable place where Torgler and Koenen are well known. There they join Birkenhauer for dinner as arranged earlier. The three sit together in a quiet corner, and Torgler orders beef broth, stewed kidneys, raw hamburger, and beer. They talk until around 10:00 when an obviously excited head waiter comes over to their table and asks whether they have already heard that the Reichstag is on fire. They look at each other in astonishment and rise to their feet. "Are you crazy?" says Torgler. "That's impossible!"

Meanwhile, at the Reichstag, Rudolf Scholz finally leaves for home at around 8:40, and Albert Wendt remains alone by the door. At 8:45 he records the arrival of Willi Otto, the Reichstag postman, who empties the letter boxes at the Reichstag Post Office in the gallery every night. By 8:55 Willi Otto, too, leaves the Reichstag, again passing through Portal Five. The entire building is bathed in complete silence; a whisper would echo the length of the house.

Outside the Reichstag Berlin is freezing cold; the thermometer reads 22 degrees Fahrenheit. An icy wind blows briskly out of the east throwing up whitecaps on the River Spree which curves along closely under the Reichstag's northeast tower. Because the Reichstag is not in session, the streets nearby are lighted very dimly, and dark shadows consequently mantle the exterior walls. Those few hardy souls still on the lonely streets hasten homeward under clear skies. Beyond an occasional crunch of footsteps on the snowy pavement or the distant clatter of a tram, there is little to disturb the quiet of the wintry night.

Mrs. Elfriede Kuesner, who is on her way to the National Club, by chance happens to notice a man darting out of the shadows of Portal Two, the south entrance, but later it will be firmly established that he was taking cover from the wind by standing in the doorway and jumping out to catch his bus when it arrived. It will also be determined that this fleeting incident occurred at 8:55, at the same time that Willi Otto was leaving the north entrance.

At 9:08 Hans Flöter, a student of theology and philosophy, approaches the southwest corner of the Reichstag from the adjoining Tiergarten. He is on the way home after a day spent working in the Eastern Reading Room of the State Library on Unter den Linden. He heads across the Königsplatz, parallel to the great ramp on the west side of the building. He passes the Grand Entrance on this side of the Reichstag, which is dignified by an imposing central portico upheld by six massive columns. A huge inscription across the beam at the top of the portico dedicates the building "To the German People." The Grand Entrance is flanked on either side by an exterior wall with three rows of five windows, each recessed deeply between other columns. In front of the portico a wide flight of steps leads down to the Bismarck Memorial in the Königsplatz, and halfway between the memorial and the Grand Entrance the great carriageway bisects the line of steps.

As Hans Flöter passes below the portico, he can hear his own footsteps echoing across the icy open square. Suddenly he is startled by a sound of splintering glass. His first thought is that some stupid custodian has clumsily broken a window. But just then he again hears glass shattering twice more. He spins around in time to see a dark figure crouching in a deep balcony beside the first floor where the Reichstag restaurant is located. Flöter has to look very high because he is situated far below on a level with the Bismarck Memorial, but he sees the dark shape strike a match and then bend its body through the open window into the restaurant. Flöter runs left toward the north side of the building in search of a policeman, and in doing so he almost collides with

Police Sgt. Karl Buwert beyond the great ramp. Flöter cries out, "Someone is breaking into the Reichstag!"

The policeman seems to hesitate, and the excited student gives Buwert a resounding whack on the back to get the sergeant moving. Without looking back Buwert runs up the steps and peers at the ground floor windows over the edge of the balustrade. After mobilizing Buwert, Flöter hurries to his nearby home at 4a Hindersinstrasse for dinner; the weather is too cold for him to stay outside.

Meanwhile Werner Thaler, a typesetter, has come around the corner from Simonstrasse just as Flöter finds Buwert. Thaler is on his way from Brandenburg Gate to the Lehrter Station. He, too, hears the breaking glass, and he runs up to the inclined drive to see more closely. Then he climbs on top of the curved stone balustrade and stares into the half-light. He sees two men on the balcony but no torches. He immediately runs off for a policeman whom he has seen earlier south of the building.

Thaler cannot find the policeman, so he shouts into the darkness for help and then speeds back toward the Grand Entrance. Seconds later he meets Buwert, who by this time has been joined by another young man in a black coat and top boots. The three men gawk foolishly at the bizarre sight of a flickering light moving to and fro behind a frosted window on the first floor. Then suddenly the flame races toward the southern corner of the building, and it can be seen darting from one window to the next. The men outside run after it until they reach the last window. There it momentarily pauses. Thaler, recovering first, screams, "Shoot, man, shoot!" Buwert draws his revolver and, finally convinced that the intruder is intent upon arson, fires blindly through the window. The mysterious fire disappears from sight as the window shatters. The total elapsed time from Flöter's arrival at the scene to Buwert's shot has been just slightly over two minutes.

A few moments after Sergeant Buwert's gunfire, two married couples, a salesman by the name of Karl Kuhl and his spouse, and a bookbinder, Hermann Freudenberg and his wife, happen to approach the Reichstag from the Königsplatz. While still some distance away, they notice a glimmering of fire through the windows on the ground floor of the Reichstag. Quickly running toward the carriageway ramp they shout, "Police! Fire!" By the time they reach the ramp they see one heavy drapery after another erupt into leaping, writhing flames behind the glass. Buwert, hearing them approach, requests Kuhl and Freudenberg to ring the fire alarm. They run off down the Simsonstrasse with Mrs. Freudenberg to activate the first fire-box they can find. At last they spot the German Engineering Institute, at the corner of Friedrich Ebertstrasse and Dorotheenstrasse. Ramming their way past the people coming out of the building after a course that ended at 9:00, they breathlessly hail the custodian, Otto Schaeske: "The Reichstag is burning! Call the Fire Brigade!"

Schaeske is staggered by the news, but he numbly reaches for the telephone book as he gapes in astonishment. His fingers fumble blindly through the pages until Emil Luck, who is helping him in the cloakroom, grabs the book and finds the correct number. Luck dials the number and gives the first fire alarm of the evening. The call is received at Fire Brigade headquarters at 9:13. Within one minute the alarm is issued from there to Brigade Section Six at the Linienstrasse Fire Station which responds rapidly. Less than four minutes after receiving the alarm, the first fire engines, under the direction of Chief Fire Officer Emil Puhle, screech to a halt in front of the Reichstag northwest tower by the ramp. They cannot drive up the rampway because their tires skid on the thin sheet of ice and snow covering the stone pavement. By 9:19 another unit from Section Seven arrives, commanded by Fire Officer Waldemar Klotz; it was sent in response to a separate alarm. At first there is some confusion as the firemen rush from one door to another, finding entrances locked, not knowing that only the north entrance, Portal Five, is open. Ladders are quickly thrown up against the walls, however, and already hoses lace the carriageway ramp by 9:20. At the same time two fire boats steam carefully down the River Spree in gloomy darkness to add their efforts in containing the blaze.

Meanwhile Sergeant Buwert's first instinct is to find help. He asks the young man in the black coat to spread the alarm to the Brandenburg Gate Police Station. "Tell them," he says, "the Reichstag is burning and to call the Fire Brigade." The young man does as he is told, but Buwert, who has a general distrust of civilians, repeats the order to a Reichswehr soldier who comes up a minute later. The soldier agrees, but Buwert is no sooner out of sight than the soldier catches a bus instead.

Meanwhile Sergeant Buwert's shots have also attracted the attention of two other policemen who race up from the Siegesallee. Buwert quickly orders one of them to sound the fire alarm in the Moltkestrasse. This is the second fire alarm of the evening, the one calling Waldemar Klotz and Section Seven.

A moment later Constable Helmut Poeschel appears; he was quietly patrolling near the northeast corner of the Reichstag when Buwert fired his gun. The time is 9:15. Now, startled, he hears Buwert bellow, "Fire! Tell the porter at Portal Five!" Poeschel runs off to do that, arriving a minute later at the north entrance. There his shouting brings Albert Wendt outside, but Wendt seems completely thick-witted at first. Poeschel knows that a fire alarm is located in the porter's lodge, but Wendt will not sound an alarm unless he can verify the fire for himself. After carefully locking the door behind him, Wendt rushes down the pavement without his coat or hat to see for himself. Turning the corner, he runs up the inclined ramp. To his horror he can see the entire glass dome of the Reichstag already glowing in the dark, flickering red from the flames far beneath. Already a crowd of spectators is assembling. Hearing the Fire Brigade has already been called, Wendt dashes back to his lodge at Portal Five in order to warn all of the Reichstag senior staff whom he can reach by telephone. His first attempts to reach Chief Engineer Eugen Mutzka and Chief House Inspector Alexander Scranowitz in their official apartments nearby are in vain; in his excitement he probably misdials the correct numbers. Still trying by 9:19 he finally contacts Eduard Prodöhl, the chief Reichstag messenger, and Paul Adermann, the night porter at the Speaker's residence.

Adermann in turn telephones the director of the Reichstag, Privy Councillor Galle, and the Prussian Ministry of the Interior just over three hundred yards away from the Reichstag on Unter den Linden where the call is taken by Göring's secretary, Miss Grundtmann. She in turn passes the message to Göring's adjutant, Police Captain Jacoby, who tells Göring. Göring has been upstairs talking with Ludwig Grauvert, the under secretary of the Prussian Interior. Göring is dumbfounded and cries, "What the hell is going on? Get me a car! Now! I'm going straight there!"

Meanwhile Scranowitz, hearing the ruckus from his nearby apartment where he is eating dinner, telephones Wendt at Portal Five, fearing something terrible might be happening. Wendt blurts out that the Reichstag is burning. Scranowitz, ignorant of Wendt's previously frustrated attempts to reach him, yells in rage, "And you didn't report it to me!" Dropping his receiver, Scranowitz grabs his set of Reichstag keys and sprints across to the Reichstag. His first concern is to open the doors for the firemen who already have begun to arrive. About this time, Douglas Reed, the Berlin correspondent for *The Times* of London, chances to pass near the Reichstag building and later recollected that the cupola of the Reichstag was "blazing furiously—a beacon which must have been visible for miles."

Back at the Brandenburg Gate Police Station in the Alexanderplatz, the young man whom Police Sergeant Buwert ordered to call for help arrives at 9:15. Gasping for breath, he blurts out, "Fire has broken out in the Reichstag!" The young duty officer, Lt. Emil Lateit, a small, trim figure, instantly calls out the watch and, after a moment's confusion, they pile into a police car and drive at breakneck speed toward the burning building. Such is their hurry that they forget to ask the name of the unknown man who sounded the alarm. After warming himself and waiting a short time inside the station, he leaves and is forgotten.

Part of the confusion at the Brandenburg Gate Police Station is due to the fact that they anticipated a different alarm tonight. The Social Democratic Party was scheduled to launch an election rally at the Berlin Sportpalast. The police had orders to close it down, and Lateit was detailed to handle a portion of the expected consequences of that decision. As a result the police car was already waiting in front of the station with its motor running, so by breaking a few speed records it takes only one minute to reach the fire, at 9:17.

Once at the scene of the fire Lateit quickly takes charge. He is told that the Brigade has been called, but he immediately orders Buwert to sound the "grand" or "fifteenth stage" alarm which would call in every fire engine in the city of Berlin, over sixty in all. In the mounting commotion, however, Buwert is becoming overloaded with responsibilities, and in the excitement Lateit has also ordered Buwert to stand guard on the ramp in case the arsonist should show his head. If the arsonist should come into view again, Buwert must shoot immediately. Buwert quite naturally feels his primary duty is to remain standing his watch, and he quite forgets to sound the "grand" alarm.

Meanwhile Lateit runs off to gain entrance into the building. He discovers Portal Two is still locked, as is Portal Three, but he finally reaches Portal Five at 9:20, arriving just in time to meet Scranowitz. Together with Constables Losigkeit and Graening, they enter the burning building; Losigkeit notes that the disbelieving porter still seems astonished at there even being a fire. Once inside, it becomes very dark but nobody turns on the lights. There is a strong odor of burning in the air as they race toward the restaurant. There they hope to discover some sign of the arsonist or arsonists who have so far remained at large. Upon arrival at the restaurant they see no one, so they hurry on.

At 9:22 Lateit enters the Plenary Sessions Chamber for the first time in his life. Losigkeit and Graening come to his side. Scranowitz remains in the large lobby where he is busy stamping out a small fire near the doorway to the Sessions Chamber while the others are inside the Plenary Hall. Lateit spots a broad wall of flames covering the curtains on both sides behind the Presidential dais. The flames look like "a burning organ with flames for organ pipes," he would say later on. He is able to notice little else before turning back. Losigkeit ventures further into the heat and his attention is riveted by the sight of high, bright red flames rising from the reporters' box to the left and in front of the main dais. Neither Lateit nor Losigkeit see any other flames in the Sessions Chamber, and Lateit feels certain that the structure can still be saved.

Coming out of the Parliamentary Chamber, Lateit orders his men to draw their revolvers; he is now convinced that this is a clear case of incendiarism. At this point Constable Poeschel joins them, and Lateit orders him to stay with the house inspector, Scranowitz. Lateit leaves Graening to continue on his own in the search while he returns to Portal Five with Losigkeit. On the way they pick up a suspicious cloth cap, tie, and bar of soap from the floor of the main lobby. They pass a group of firemen who already have penetrated the building as far as the west lobby. Not knowing that the Sessions Chamber is threatened by a major fire, the firemen busily extinguish minor blazes which they discover cropping up in dozens of places. Lateit sends one of the firemen to the Parliamentary Chamber with Losigkeit. At the entrance Lateit shouts, "Incendiarism! It's burning to every corner!" Outside, he runs to his police car and then drives at top speed back to the Brandenburg Gate Police Station for reinforcements. He again breaks a few speed records in the process and arrives back at the Station by 9:25, only ten minutes after his original departure. By this time the Sessions Chamber is becoming a roaring inferno. Flames can be seen actually coming out of the cupola by witnesses outside.

Meanwhile Scranowitz finally turns on the lights in the lobby and corridors, accompanied by Constable Poeschel. Everywhere Scranowitz glances he is confronted by flames. He continues dashing about trying to stamp out the smaller fires as best he can. At 9:23, only a minute or so after Lateit and the other policemen had entered the Sessions Chamber, Scranowitz looks through the door for a few seconds. He quickly takes in the whole scene and sees, as Lateit had, a mass of flames at the end of the room from the floor to the ceiling. He also notices the flames that Losigkeit saw spreading from the reporters' box. But the other things that Scranowitz observes are completely different: small fires all across the far side of the Chamber, on the first three rows of deputies' seats, each about five feet apart and about forty in number. All of these little fires are nearly identical in shape and size, and each is about eighteen inches wide. Poeschel is somewhat behind Scranowitz and cannot see beyond the doorway. Scranowitz slams the door shut and they both run down the southern corridor toward the Bismarck Hall.

Scranowitz is still slightly ahead of Poeschel when they reach the center of the hall. Just then a young, robust, half-naked man, bare to the waist, wearing only trousers and shoes, races across the room from the back of the Parliamentary Chamber. Scranowitz and Poeschel both roar, "Hands up!" The apparition is suddenly frozen, his tall body glistening with sweat from the heat. He crouches back in fear and for a moment turns as if to run, but seeing Poeschel's leveled revolver, he meekly surrenders, raising his arms high as ordered. His chest is heaving from exertion, and his long mat of tangled hair is plastered over his damp face. Constable Poeschel rapidly searches the suspect's pockets, discovering a pen knife, wallet, and Dutch passport bearing the man's likeness and his name—Marinus Van der Lubbe.

Quivering, beside himself in fury, Scranowitz screams, "Why did you do this?" With a wondering stare at Scranowitz and in a strong foreign accent, the intruder breathlessly puffs, "Protest! Protest!" Scranowitz, a big burly man with a shaved head and Kaiser moustache, is incensed. Scranowitz's fist explodes against the young man's flesh. The time is 9:27. At that moment there is a loud detonation in the Sessions Chamber as the pent-up gases explode through the glass dome. Seizing his suspect by the naked shoulder, Poeschel wrenches him toward Portal Five. There the prisoner visibly shakes in the cold and a policeman tosses a rug over the young Dutchman's back. By 9:30 Marinus Van der Lubbe is in Brandenburg Gate Police Station.

By this time the fire is a virtual sea of flames, leaping upward with incredible ferocity. At 9:31 the "tenth stage" fire alarm is

given, automatically calling out two-thirds of Berlin's entire fire-
fighting force. Eleven minutes later the decision is taken (for the
second time) to give the "grand" alarm, and the city's last remaining fire forces are committed in a desperate bid to save the
building. From all parts of the city, over sixty fire engines con-
verge on the burning Reichstag and surround the building.

Searchlights are thrown on the walls and in their reflections
tons of water pour out through the entrances and flush past the
massive crowds that have gathered for the spectacle. Hundreds
of policemen arrive by the truckload and on horseback to push
the onlookers back to a safe distance. The fireboats on the River
Spree are making their contribution felt by sending out seemingly endless streams of river water over the roof on the north
side of the Reichstag and into the Plenary Chamber beneath the
fractured glass dome. Above everything the blood red flames,
billowing smoke and steam hiss and snort out of the gargantuan
sandstone monstrosity.

About 10:00 Joseph Goebbels is informed of the fire by a call
from a guest of Hermann Göring, Ernst Hanfstaengl, who is
spending the evening bedridden with a bad cold at Göring's official state residence. Göring, the Speaker of the Reichstag as well
as Minister of the Interior in the new Nazi Government, has already left his office at Unter den Linden for the Reichstag.
Hanfstaengl can see the flames rising high above the central ro-
tunda of the Reichstag from his room in the Speaker's House,
which stands only a short distance from the east side of the
Reichstag.

Hanfstaengl's telephone call reaches Goebbels at home, where
he and his wife Magda are entertaining Hitler. They are listening
to records and making light talk after dinner when Goebbels receives Hanfstaengl's message. Goebbels' first reaction is utter
disbelief; he refuses to report this "bit of wild fantasy" to Hitler.
Goebbels is convinced that Hanfstaengl is playing one of his frequent miserable bad jokes. Later, however, Goebbels discovers
that the fire is real; he had sent his press secretary, Hänke, down
to the Reichstag to double-check Hanfstaengl's story, and Hänke
came back with confirmation of the news. Goebbels informs Hit-

ler, and they quickly drive to the Reichstag in Hitler's big Mercedes at eighty m.p.h., arriving there about 10:30.

Goebbels and Hitler meet Göring, who arrived at 9:35, nearly an hour ahead of them. They all make their way over the jumbled fire hoses and reach the main lobby through Portal Two, which Scranowitz has long since opened for the firemen. Within minutes, Franz von Papen, Prince August Wilhelm, and a few ranking civil officials arrive and join the small party of Hitler, Göring, Goebbels, and a half dozen others, who are now looking over the scene of desolation in the Plenary Chamber where the firemen are finally extinguishing the blaze. Hitler seems mesmerized as he stares fixedly at the dying flames from a balcony.

By 10:45 the fire is almost suppressed, although some mopping up will continue until the early morning hours. It has been less than two hours since the first small flame was ignited in the Reichstag. The ramparts are untouched by the fire, and damage to most of the building is slight (except for the pools of water). But the Parliamentary Sessions Chamber is completely gutted as though plucked out from the rest of the building by the voracious flames that had filled the entire room and burst through the glass dome. The iron pillars supporting the broken dome have been convulsively twisted out of shape; they simmer, and the intense red glow slowly fades dead black as if in anticipation of the new era and its colors. Debris lies everywhere, scattered like burned cobwebs. Few witnesses to the scene escape a visceral certainty that Germany has symbolically lost the heart of her parliamentary democracy by an incision worthy of a prehistoric sacrifice to chaos.

Marinus Van der Lubbe was a 24-year-old Dutch Communist. He admitted to lighting the fires, and retraced his course through the building to show the police exactly how he had done so. He said his act of sabotage was a protest against fascist capitalism in Germany, and that he hoped it would trigger a revolution. He maintained stolidly that he had acted entirely alone. He seemed a little crazy but not stupid. . . .

When Vice Chancellor von Papen arrived at the scene Adolf

Hitler met him, grasped his hand and said, "This is a God-given signal, Herr Vice Chancellor." Hitler chose to believe that the fire was the work of a Communist "conspiracy" threatening all Germany. He moved quickly and brutally to suppress it. A decree the next day amounted to martial law. Sabotage and arson were made punishable by death. Communist members were rounded up by the thousands. Torgler, the Communist deputy who happened to be in the Reichstag that night, was arrested to make the conspiracy charge sound more credible.

(Communist propaganda also had strong views on this matter of a conspiracy. The Communist version was that the Nazis encouraged Van der Lubbe to set the fire and then betrayed him —a theory which still survives despite lack of any real evidence.)

Van der Lubbe, along with Torgler, was brought to trial before the Supreme Court in Leipzig. The trial lasted from July to December of 1933, and some 250 witnesses were called. As time passed the prisoner retreated more and more into a torpor, a sullen dreamlike world of his own. He seemed resigned to his fate, although he never wavered in claiming that he had acted alone.

Van der Lubbe was condemned to death, and beheaded shortly afterward by the State Executioner. Torgler was acquitted. The case for a conspiracy remained totally unproved. But Hitler and the Nazis had taken advantage of the fire to gain a stranglehold on Germany.

It was a hold that they never relinquished until they themselves went down in smoke and flame twelve years later.

PART TWO:
WORLD WAR II

A Word About
the World War II Selections

SABOTAGE as a technique of war came into its own during the second world conflict. There were several compelling reasons why this was so. One was that, almost inevitably, it became a favorite weapon of any nation lacking in guns and tanks, planes and warships and manpower. Such were the have-not nations. One good example would be the British in North Africa at the time when General Rommel was driving for Cairo. Italy striving to be a Mediterranean power, outnumbered and somewhat over-awed by the Royal Navy, is another. Any country, like Poland or Norway or France, which in defeat and under occupation lost all ability to wage conventional war would also fall into this have-not classification. Germany, as her fortunes waned, is a good case in point.

But there were other reasons for the rise in sabotage activities. Such matters as national inclination and temperament figure. The British have always loved small, gallant operations—and the greater the odds, the more desperate the mission, the better. As far back as World War I the Italians showed that they had a

special skill and verve with small surface craft and small submersibles. The hardy Norwegians seemed almost to welcome
secret operations calling for great reserves of courage and
endurance.

The World War II exploits or near-exploits of sabotage which I
have chosen fall into four divisions:

(a) Commando-type operations behind enemy lines.

(b) Acts by underground or resistance groups in countries occupied by the enemy.

(c) Sabotage by sea, employing surface craft or small submarines.

(d) Training and technical innovations (the latter known in
the trade as "dirty tricks").

In the interests of smooth reading I have arranged the World
War II selections chronologically rather than by category.

7

Norway Goes Underground

Oluf Reed Oslen

The Nazi invasion of Norway, by sea and by stealth, was one of the best-planned operations of World War II. On the squally night of April 8, 1940, the German fleet, with no lights showing, pene- trated the fjord leading to Oslo. Although the attackers achieved almost total surprise, they met spirited opposition. The battleship Blücher *was sunk and several other troop-laden ships were dam- aged. Nevertheless the Germans were able to occupy Oslo the next day, and they quickly overran the Norwegian peninsula. But they never quite conquered the Norwegians. From the very outset of the occupation, underground groups began to form.*

Oluf Olsen's account of his first attempt at sabotage embodies this spirit of Norway in defeat but not in despair.

MOST Norwegians didn't know until after the Nazi invasion that our government and population had been sown with German agents and Norwegian traitors; or that, for weeks, merchant ships had been entering the ports of Norway, their holds crowded with German soldiers.

Like most of my countrymen, at first I was completely bewildered, and, as a lad of twenty-one with no previous military training, I did not understand the seriousness or full significance of what was taking place. Still, I was filled with a sense of outrage, with a fierce desire to fight back against the invader. And I was not alone. With a good friend of mine, Kaare Moe from Bestum, a suburb of Oslo, I tried to get a clearer idea of what we ought to do, and where we could report for duty once our course was clear.

The morning of the ninth, at the East Station, we approached a cadet officer in the army, but his reply was the same one that hundreds of patriotic Norwegians had been given: "Just go home, resistance is useless!"

Such a rebuff from a military officer had undoubtedly been influenced by enemy instructions, and the same evening we laid our plans for a long trip northward. These plans were not carried out, however, for other friends gave us an account of conditions at Hvalsmoen, where we had thought of reporting.

The whole region was being bombed by the Germans, and evidently confusion prevailed there just as it did in the far south of Norway. Moreover, we came in contact with a British captain working for the secret British intelligence system in Oslo. He urged us to abandon our plans for a journey to northern Norway through Sweden, and to report for service with him instead.

Our first assignments were small and seemingly insignificant ones, yet our greatest wish was being fulfilled—we were doing our duty as Norwegians.

We were put to work photographing, sketching, and mapping German airfields, defense works, and military positions and installations; also, finding out all we could about German troop movements: what kind of troops were concerned, to what units the troops who passed through Oslo belonged, where they came from, and where they were going.

This was work which often led to exciting minor incidents which suited our then fairly modest demands. But at that time our activities were inspired to some extent by a thirst for adventure; the whole business was a manifestation of sporting enthusiasm.

It was while fighting was going on a little way outside Oslo that we were given our first sabotage job. Small parties of Norwegian volunteers were fighting a hard battle against German motorized detachments; the enemy was far superior in both numbers and equipment.

One of these volunteer parties sent out a runner on skis through the German positions. He arrived early one morning with the following information: the Norwegian forces about Skaret (about twenty miles from Oslo) and the road along the Tyrifjord could not hold out much longer. Supplies for the German forces along the roads from Oslo, and along the Drammen Road via Lysaker and Sandvika, must be cut off at any cost so that the Norwegian troops could prepare fresh positions to the north.

Four bridges were to be blown up—one on the road from Drammen to Hönefoss via Skaret, both bridges at Sandvika, and the bridge over the Lysaker River at Lysaker. All were to be blown up at exactly four o'clock the next morning, so there was not much time. The Lysaker Bridge was our job.

Neither Kaare nor I had the least idea of how a bridge should be blown up, although we had handled dynamite before when clearing the ground where our Scout hut stood. We knew how a charge was fired with fuse, percussion cap and ordinary dynamite, but that was a far cry from blowing up a bridge. How much dynamite was needed and how should it be placed? Clearly we were not qualified for the task. But there was no time for talking; the job had to be done, whether we got others to carry out the actual blasting or did the best we could ourselves.

As it was, we knew no one else who could be enlisted for the job in so short a time. It was up to us to blow up the bridge, and our plans were laid accordingly. I had a stock of dynamite, stolen two days before from different establishments in the neighborhood, with the object of making hand grenades.

We needed a third man, however, and it was not hard to find

people who would be glad to have a hand in it. The difficulty was to find a man who could hold his tongue, who could control the desire which, especially in those days, was a common failing of practically the entire Norwegian population—the desire to make oneself popular through taking part in some exciting escapade, and telling about it.

There was another factor, too, to be considered. Among the friends we consorted with daily, nearly all were eager to join the fight in progress. Discussion and fantastic plans were first on the daily program. The greatest mistake here was that every action was planned on private initiative, which could as easily hurt our own side as the Germans; often, indeed, that was more likely. We therefore made it our guiding principle from the very beginning that no one but ourselves should know that we were working for a particular organization, regardless how many helpers we were obliged to recruit for the various tasks.

Kaare's brother Leif became our third man for this special job. The afternoon was used for a short reconnaisance of Lysaker Bridge and its surroundings. The bridge was probably being watched, but no regular sentry was to be seen. For ten minutes we stood hanging over the parapet, while motorized equipment passed over the bridge in long convoys. To our great disappointment we perceived that the middle pier, which we had thought of "moving" a bit, was enclosed in timber from below the surface of the water up to the top, where the three main beams of the bridge rested.

This was a serious setback to our plans, for obviously we could not begin to strip off a board covering in the middle of the night to reach the most effective places between the large stones of which the pier was built. It would make too much noise.

Around the pier of the bridge, however, down close to the water's edge, there was a wide projection, probably intended for reinforcement. By means of a ladder about twelve feet long, let down on a rope and leaning against the pier itself, it would be possible to get down under the bridge in a matter of seconds.

From that point, the possibility of blowing it up effectively could be investigated more closely.

The evening was spent in further preparations. The dynamite was packed in four separate parcels, sixteen pounds in each; each parcel was fitted with a double fuse twenty feet long and a powerful charge with two percussion caps on the end of each fuse. A twenty-foot fuse would give us about a quarter of an hour to get away, according to the calculations we had made with the material we had in stock—if everything went as planned.

At one o'clock that morning a rather curious silent procession made its way toward Lysaker Bridge: Leif with a light ten-foot ladder over his shoulder, Kaare with a pack containing thirty-two pounds of dynamite, and myself with a similar parcel containing dynamite, fuses and percussion caps.

There were not many people out so late, but every time we heard someone approaching we flung ourselves into the ditch for a few minutes and lay motionless until he had passed.

About a hundred yards from the bridge we stopped, took off our loads, and went on under cover of some bushes and trees. Some fifteen yards from our goal we lay still, watching the outline of the bridge. Now and then a German car passed, but otherwise the neighborhood seemed deserted.

We lay there for a good half-hour. Then the now familiar sound of iron-tipped boots rang through the silence of the night. The steps came from the Drammen Road itself, from Oslo toward the bridge. We lay as silent as mice, staring till our eyes nearly left their sockets, and listened.

The light shone on two helmets—two German sentries stood out in silhouette against the night sky as they passed over the bridge. I stole cautiously after them in rubber shoes, only to discover in the next five minutes that the Germans had a larger area to patrol than the immediate neighborhood of the bridge—they went on up through Lysaker itself.

Minutes passed while we lay waiting for the sentries to come back, so that we could roughly time their round and get an idea of how long the intervals would be in which we could work undetected.

The plan of procedure was repeated in whispers for the last time: every man knew exactly what was to happen—and exactly what a mistake would mean both for our task and for himself. The bridge must be blown up at all costs. Leif's task was to keep a lookout from a place fixed in advance, while Kaare and I did the work under the bridge. If the sentries discovered anything while we were setting the charge, it would be up to Leif to warn us. At sixteen minutes to four Leif was to leave his post and go home as quickly as he could by a roundabout route.

Time passed. The sentries crossed the bridge; five minutes past three! Forty minutes to do it in! A pressure of Leif's hand, a last checkup of the revolvers, and Kaare and I crept noiselessly toward the bridge with the dynamite on our backs and the ladder between us. At that moment the sound of a car engine broke the silence and forced us to lie flat in the ditch for a few seconds. A German truck passed with troops on board, then the road was clear again. We reached the middle of the bridge, lowered the ladder cautiously over the parapet, and made fast the rope which held it. Kaare climbed over and down onto the pier of the bridge; I followed, and the rope was jerked loose from the parapet. We stood side by side under the bridge and listened—all was still.

Kaare chose that critical moment to whisper a joke in my ear. "Shut up!" I whispered back, "or I'll set a match to the dynamite when you've got it!" Even though it was too dark to see, I knew Kaare was smiling mischievously. . . .

We continued our preparations in silence. The ladder was moved under the bridge and set up against the center of the pier. Kaare held it while I climbed up to find the best places for the charges. It soon became clear that it was impossible to use four different places. Instead of blowing the whole pier to bits, as we had originally planned, we would have to content ourselves with shattering the roadway and doing as much other damage as possible.

Our reflections were suddenly interrupted. Footsteps! It could only be the two German sentries. We remained motionless. Kaare hung onto the ladder with both hands while I clung to the top of it. Two pairs of iron-tipped boots resounded on the road above us, grew louder—and died away again.

We had only twenty minutes left when something happened which almost took our breath away. A car came from the Lysaker side, drew near, and stopped in the middle of the bridge right over our heads! Orders and loud talk reached us, standing on tenterhooks below. I felt a slight trembling of the ladder, perhaps from my own trembling legs, perhaps from Kaare's convulsive grip. The vehicle on the bridge was a German car!

We did not understand all that was said, but this much was clear: someone had been discovered trying to blow up the Sandvika bridges farther out along the Drammen Road, and now orders had been given to reinforce the guard at the Lysaker Bridge by two men! An extra close watch must be kept!

The car started again and disappeared in the direction of Oslo.

Now there were four men on the bridge. They talked together in low voices as they went over toward one parapet. For a few breathless seconds they stood discussing the possibility of the bridge's being effectively blown up; then they moved on again, and this time their steps died away toward Lysaker. From the looks of things, they did not take their task too seriously, nor the attempt to blow up the Sandvika bridges. But what were their plans?

I glanced at the illuminated face of my wrist watch: quarter to four! The sweat ran down me as I worked ferverishly; the whole charge under the central beam, the fuse down—and I after it. We had not a second to lose: the Germans might be back at any moment! An old raincoat served as a screen while I lighted the fuses.

Meanwhile Kaare had set up the ladder against the outside of the pier, and it took him a fraction of a second to clamber up, stick his head over the edge, and report that all was clear. A moment later we were both on the bridge. We left the ladder where it was and made off as quickly as we could up toward the Vekkerö Road. For the first hundred yards we went cautiously, and silently. After that the only consideration was speed.

Fourteen minutes later we stopped, panting, and listened expectantly. Not a sound! Fifteen minutes—still as quiet as the grave! Kaare turned quickly to me and said: "You don't think we've got to do it again?"

Before I could open my mouth to reply, the roar from Lysaker shattered the air. One handshake, and Kaare disappeared up toward the Baerum Road, I homeward, toward Montebello.

Next morning, we were the anonymous subjects of an excited attack in the Oslo radio news bulletin. Vidkun Quisling *— whose name has become a synonym for "traitor" but who in those days was the pillar of the law, peace, and order—made a speech of "admonition" to the Norwegian people! He said among other things that during the night there had been one regrettable case of sabotage and attempts at sabotage elsewhere. Fortunately these attempts had been foiled and the malefactors taken into custody by the German police. On the other hand, a bridge in the Oslo area had been partly destroyed, but the police were hot on the trail and expected to make an arrest in the course of the day.

At nine o'clock the telephone rang. It was Kaare. Had I heard the fearful explosion in the night and did I know that someone had tried to blow up the Lysaker Bridge?

No, I hadn't heard anything—I was such a sound sleeper.

Yes, his brother Leif had just heard about it from another friend who had gone down and had a look at the bridge, so there must be something to the report.

At ten o'clock I was up at Kaare's, and with Leif we joined the many inquisitive Sunday walkers who had collected around Lysaker. The bridge itself was closed to traffic, but unfortu-

* Quisling, a Norwegian, helped the Germans plan the invasion of Norway, and immediately became the leading collaborator when it took place.

nately, as far as we could see it had not been completely destroyed. Still, the damage was sufficient to stop the transport scheduled to leave Oslo the same morning with reinforcements for the troops engaged in the country near Skaret and Hönefoss, and to delay it for a day and a half, thus reducing the pressure on our Norwegian troops in those parts.

All through the long night of the Nazi occupation, the Norwegians continued to harass the enemy. Their exploit in blowing up the heavy water plant at Vemork in February, 1943, was perhaps the most famous of many, for it slowed down the Germans in the race for atomic power.

Oluf Olsen went on to other feats of arms, as his book, Two Eggs on My Plate, *tells. The title refers to the fact that the resistance workers were given a slightly better breakfast on the day that they were to carry out a secret mission.*

8

A Stroke at the Brain

Combined Operations

In November, 1941, the British Eighth Army in North Africa mounted an offensive against the German Commander of the Afrika Korps—the legendary Erwin Rommel. Part of the plan was a commando-type raid on Rommel's headquarters, with specific orders to kill the general. The death of "the Desert Fox" would have been as much of a loss to the Germans as the loss of many thousands of sabotaged guns and tanks.

Sometimes the official account of such an episode is as effective as a first hand narrative. These pages from Combined Operations, *a British government publication, are a good example of this "documentary" style.*

EARLY in October six officers and fifty-three other ranks* of the Scottish Commando were placed under the operational command of the Eighth Army. It was decided to use them in a bold and daring attempt to strike at the brain of the enemy by landing far behind his lines and attacking his headquarters. . . .

The first problem was how to get the force to its destination.

---

* The British term for enlisted men.

It was not possible to use destroyers, for the risk of air attack was too great, and it was therefore decided to take them in two submarines, HMS *Torbay* and HMS *Talisman*. On reaching their immediate destination they would paddle themselves ashore in rubber boats.

On the evening of November 10, the *Torbay* and the *Talisman* slipped and sailed from Alexandria, moving westward in fair weather, without incident. The Scottish Commando was in the highest spirits. "All ranks were greatly interested," runs the official report, "in what was to us a novel method of approaching our objective, and the soldiers were high in their praise of the way in which they were fed and accommodated." The first landing was made from HMS *Torbay,* which closed the chosen beach at dusk on November 14. That the submarine reached her exact destination without undue difficulty was due not only to sound navigation, but also to the calculated daring of a British officer, Capt. (later Lt. Col.) J. E. Haselden, who, dressed as an Arab, had been moving behind the enemy's lines and had established friendly relations with some of the local inhabitants. His signals from the beach were seen, and preparations to land the Scottish Commando began. The weather was deteriorating; the wind had freshened, and the swell was now considerable. Four of the rubber boats were washed away, and much time was lost retrieving them. Eventually the landing was successfully made; but, instead of the estimated one hour, it took five to accomplish.

Meanwhile HMS *Talisman* was lying some distance off, awaiting the signal that the landings from HMS *Torbay* had been completed. The weather got worse, and Colonel Laycock, the leader of the mission, had just decided to postpone the operation until the following night, when the expected signal from the *Torbay* was received. The landing from the *Talisman* took place in a heavy sea which capsized most of the boats, throwing the men into the water. All of them, with the exception of Colonel Laycock and seven other ranks who reached the shore, swam back to the submarine.

Once ashore, Colonel Laycock and his small party, which had

now joined those who had landed from HMS *Torbay,* took cover in a convenient wadi for the remainder of the night and for the day which followed. The weather continued bad with a considerable sea still running, and it did not seem possible that the *Talisman* would be able to land troops when darkness came. On the other hand, General Auchinleck's * offensive against Rommel was about to open, and Colonel Laycock was well aware that any immediate action he could take against the enemy would be of great and immediate value to the Eighth Army now making ready to advance.

He decided not to wait, but had therefore to modify his plan and divide the party into two detachments. Lieutenant Colonel Keyes, in command of the first detachment, was to attack the German headquarters and the house of General Rommel. He had with him Captain Campbell and seventeen other ranks. The second detachment, Lieutenant Cook and six other ranks, was ordered to cut the telephone and telegraph wires at the crossroads south of Cyrene. Colonel Laycock decided to remain at the rendezvous with a sergeant and two men, to form a beachhead and keep the reserve ammunition and rations. They would also be ready to receive the remainder of the Commando, who, it was hoped, would be put ashore on the following night.

Thus did Colonel Laycock and his officers plan through that long day hidden in the wadi. The weather was at no time good, and became very bad as the hours went by. A gale of wind, accompanied at times by torrential rain, howled through their place of concealment, and soon everyone was once more wet to the skin.

The detachments moved off at seven o'clock in the evening, accompanied by Arab guides who, however, abandoned them after a few miles. They therefore lay up in a suitable wadi and slept for four hours. The next day they hid in another, and in the evening, meeting with a party of Arabs who were friendly, were guided to a spot some ten miles from Beda Littoria, where they

* General Sir Claude Auchinleck, British Eighth Army Commander.

dumped their surplus clothing and rations. On both those nights Colonel Laycock visited the beach, but there was still a heavy surf and conditions for landing were impossible.

At seven in the evening of November 17, the detachments made ready to move to their objectives. Torrential rain had fallen all day; they were cold and soaked to the skin, but their spirit was high. No. 1 detachment under Lieutenant Colonel Keyes was guided to within a few hundred yards of General Rommel's headquarters by friendly Arabs. Here they lay up awaiting zero hour, which was one minute to midnight, and while there they were apprehended by a party of Arabs in uniform. Captain Campbell, however, allayed suspicion by explaining in German that the force belonged to a German unit.

The plan was for Lieutenant Colonel Keyes, with Captain Campbell and Sergeant Terry, to enter the house of the German Commander-in-Chief and search it. Outside, three men were to destroy the electric-light plant, five to keep an eye on the garden and the car park, two to stand outside a nearby hotel and prevent anyone from leaving it, and two more to watch the road on each side of the house. The two remaining men were to guard whichever way Lieutenant Colonel Keyes chose for entering the house.

Everyone was in position a little before midnight. The house was reconnoitered, but no way in could be found either through the back or through any of the windows. Lieutenant Colonel Keyes and his companions therefore went up to the front door and beat upon it, Captain Campbell loudly demanding in German that it should be opened. Inside was a sentry. Hearing a peremptory order shouted at him from outside, he pulled open the door and was at once set upon. He showed fight and was overpowered, but not silently; Captain Campbell was compelled to shoot him, and the shot roused the house. Two men began to run downstairs from the first floor, but a burst of tommy-gun fire from Sergeant Terry sent them scampering back again. The lights in the rooms of the ground floor were extinguished, but no one attempted to move.

Lieutenant Colonel Keyes and Captain Campbell began a search of the ground floor. There was no one in the first room, but in the second the Germans were awaiting them, and on throwing upon the door Lieutenant Colonel Keyes was met by a burst of fire and fell back into the passage, mortally wounded. Sergeant Terry emptied three magazines of his tommy gun into the darkened room; Captain Campbell threw a grenade into it and then slammed the door. He and Sergeant Terry picked up Lieutenant Colonel Keyes and carried him outside, where he died. He received the posthumous award of the Victoria Cross. While bending over him, Captain Campbell had his leg broken by a stray bullet.

The enemy had been taken by surprise, but most unfortunately General Rommel himself was absent. He was apparently attending a party in Rome. Three German lieutenant colonels on his staff were killed and a number of soldiers killed and wounded. Captain Campbell ordered Sergeant Terry to collect the detachment and throw all their remaining grenades through the windows. This was done, and Captain Campbell then ordered the party to withdraw and to leave him behind, since in his wounded condition they could not hope to carry him over eighteen miles of difficult country to the beach. He was taken prisoner. The party moved off, being joined by the three men detailed to destroy the electric-lighting plant. In this they had been partially successful, though some of the charges, soaked by the torrential rain, had not exploded. A grenade placed in the armature had, however, done considerable damage. Sergeant Terry led his party back and eventually reached Colonel Laycock at the rendezvous on the evening of November 18.

The ensuing British offensive shook but did not destroy Rommel's German-Italian forces. Early in 1942 he attacked again and swept to the Egyptian border. The British beat him in the battle of El Alamein (October, 1942) and Rommel was on the run at last.

9

De La Penne and the Dreadnought

Collier's *Magazine*

The raid on Alexandria in December, 1941, is the most celebrated single triumph of the Italian small-craft operators. They were members of the Tenth MAS Flotilla, which carried out both surface and underwater attacks. This unit had been formed in World War I for antisubmarine work by small surface craft. Its original name, Motoscafi anti Sommergibili (*motorboats against submarines*), remained during World War II, even though the MAS operations were now directed against capital ships and merchantmen.*

Prince Junio Valerio Borghese, who commanded the mother submarine Scire *in the Alexandria raid, was the guiding spirit and, ultimately, the commanding officer of the Tenth MAS.*

This account—the first complete and accurate version of the Alexandria raid—was written by a naval correspondent for Collier's magazine, working from battle reports and the log of the Scire.

ONE mild December night back in 1941 an Italian by the name of Luigi De La Penne was sitting on a buoy in Alexandria harbor. It was a year when very few Italians were sitting on British buoys anywhere, let alone near vital British naval installations. Although the night was warm, De La Penne was shivering. He loosened the collar of his rubber diving suit, took deep gulps of the sweet night air. He was very tired. Earlier that evening he had spent considerable time underwater—slithering his torpedo into the well-protected anchorage, placing his heavy "package" beneath the keel of a British dreadnought, and finally making his way to the mooring buoy to which his victim was tethered. Still trembling slightly, he wondered how his companions in the night's work had fared. He felt almost relieved when the long fingers of a searchlight caught and held him, when at last a Royal Navy launch came knifing toward him. . . .

December, 1941. That was the month of Pearl Harbor, of the siege of Singapore, of the destruction of the British ships *Prince of Wales* and *Repulse* by Japanese torpedo planes. Most of the fateful happenings of the fading days of 1941 are history, but no one ever thinks of Lieutenant De La Penne shivering on his buoy. Yet his night's work could have proved as costly to the Allied cause as Singapore, Pearl Harbor, *Prince of Wales* and *Repulse* all rolled into one. For the skill of De La Penne and his comrades gave the Axis overwhelming naval supremacy, gun for gun, in the Mediterranean, at a moment when the great inland sea was the cockpit of the world. . . .

Luigi Durand De La Penne was born in Genoa in 1914. From his childhood he loved the sea, and as a child he learned to swim like an eel in the warm waters of the old seaport city. He grew into a blond, deep-chested six footer. By the time war came he was already embarked on a promising career in the navy—a popular officer with a Genoese wife, a small son, and a friendly, even-tempered disposition.

De La Penne volunteered for the arduous training course of the Tenth MAS Flotilla just before the war. First he passed the medical examination, and the rigid tests to weed out latent claustrophobes and psychotics. Then, at the school near La Spezia, for months on end he was drilled in the intricate art of shallow diving. He mastered the technique of placing explosives and he learned to control and repair the various small craft designed to deliver the packaged charges.

At last he completed the course. Now the small boy who had swum for pleasure in the Bay of Genoa was entitled to wear the insignia of the Flotilla, a silver torpedo superimposed on the Roman numeral ten.

De La Penne got his baptism of fire in the second Italian raid on Gibraltar in October of 1940. He and Bianchi—who was to be his second man on the Alexandria expedition—were released from *Scire* in the inner reaches of Algeciras Bay. On their Maiale, or two-man submersible, they were to make a reconnaissance for a reported aircraft carrier in the harbor at Gibraltar. If they did not find her, their orders were to attack one of two battleships definitely known to be tied up there. But a mechanical failure and the jamming of his compass forced De La Penne to abandon the mission. He and Bianchi swam ashore and were spirited back to Italy by skillful staff work on the part of the Italian underground in Spain.

Valuable lessons were learned. Training and more training went on. Again and again De La Penne and Bianchi went through simulated raids on the harbor of La Spezia. A torpedo boat would release them seven miles out. With every harbor defender alerted, every net line watched, they would try to violate the sanctity of the port and place their charges on a mock target.

The Maiale was quite a craft. Electrically propelled, easily able to submerge to a hundred feet, with a twelve-mile cruising range, it was an oversize torpedo twenty-one feet long, with a maximum diameter of three feet. The drill, as perfected at La Spezia, remained comparatively unchanged throughout the war: the two operators—pilot and mechanic—rode astride. They wore diving masks and respirators and were equipped with cutters and lifting devices with which to make their way through or under harbor nets. Arriving at the target area, the pair tethered the craft on the bottom like a milk horse. Then they detached the massive, slightly buoyant six-hundred-pound explosive charge which formed its nose, and secured it magnetically to the keel of the victim. After starting the time device, they remounted their faithful steed—headless now but still operable—and drove away at "flank" speed of something over two knots.

The maneuverability of these odd little sea horses—they could "porpoise" like dolphins— and their near-invisibility even when running awash were still their chief assets.

Because the Maiale was also known as the human torpedo, it is still widely believed that it was a suicide craft. The term was in fact one the Surface Division men of the Tenth MAS used jokingly. "There go the human torpedoes," the E-Boat boys would jeer, preferring their own more direct method of delivering explosives. Early in the history of the flotilla the question of some kind of suicidal device to blow up both craft and operator had actually been discussed and discarded. It was agreed that every effort had to be made to ensure the survival of the operators.

At long last De La Penne's big chance came. In December, 1941, Prince Junio Valerio Borghese, in command of the Underwater Division of the Tenth Flotilla, picked him to lead the projected raid on Alexandria.

The expedition against Alexandria had been planned down to the last diving helmet and oxygen bottle. The submarine *Scire,* Borghese commanding, was to act as mother ship. Word came from Rome that the great Egyptian port was crammed with shipping. The 32,000-ton *Queen Elizabeth* was tied up there, so was the *Valiant,* another floating fortress bristling with batteries of fifteen-inch guns. There were also fleet tankers, cruisers, merchantmen, even an unidentified aircraft carrier.

Ever since the Battle of Cape Matapan in March of 1941 the Italian fleet had confined itself to support of convoys, leaving the raids on Allied convoy lanes to the submarines. Now, at one crack, there was a chance to balance the naval books, to revenge the three cruisers sunk off Matapan, and to pave the way for an Italian fleet sortie on overwhelmingly favorable terms.

To the Axis planners, the stakes seemed tremendous ones. With control of the Mare Mussolini asserted by a naval victory, beleaguered Malta would surely fall. Erwin Rommel's squadrons in North Africa would be sure of a flow of supplies and the small British army there would wither for lack of the same. There would be no telling where Rommel's next end-run might lead him.

The *Scire* sails for Egypt. On deck are three metal cylinders containing the Maiali. Along with Borghese and the regular crew go the six special operators, with nothing special to do except wait and wonder until the signal is given. Also aboard as one of the reserve crew is Surgeon Sublieutenant Giorgio Spaccarelli, skilled in both medicine and underwater operations and so doubly useful.

De La Penne is happy that his chance has come at last. Bianchi is worried about his wife's confinement, which is nearing its final stage. The others are restless—drowsy—phlegmatic—sanguine, according to their temperaments. But they all share one emotion. They are much too well aware of the hazards that lie ahead not to be frightened. A probing searchlight, a well-placed depth charge, a machine-gun burst and it would be all over.

A final air reconnaissance on the afternoon of December 18 reveals that the harbor is still a "hot" target. The report is communicated to the *Scire* with the instructions to proceed with the operation as planned.

The wireless crackles again. *Petty Officer Bianchi's wife has had a daughter and both are doing well.* The word is passed. In the tension every one agrees it is a fine omen.

They reach a point a mile off the entrances to Alexandria harbor. It is now 8:30 P.M. on the evening of the eighteenth. Borghese, in the nearness of action, is everywhere. His confidence and skill are reassuring to the six who are preparing to sortie from the friendly bulk of *Scire* into the unknown.

One by one, the three Maiali are slipped out of their metal

containers and mounted by their crews. Then, with De La Penne and Bianchi in the lead, they surface for a bearing. There is no wind, the sea is calm, the night black velvet. The three little craft are alone now, for the submarine—still submerged—has withdrawn to a position farther offshore where she can safely surface and observe the results of the operation.

It is too dark to make out any landmarks, so De La Penne sets a compass course for the harbor entrance. After an hour of steady, almost-silent progress they are able to make out the bulk of the royal palace and the tall Ras-el-Tin lighthouse. As they watch, the beacon in the lighthouse tower begins to glow, which helps.

Another hour and they are abreast the light.

Now De La Penne, crouched in the saddle of the leading torpedo, is alarmed by an unforeseen hazard: a motorboat is dropping depth charges at regular intervals to seaward of the harbor boom. The detonations grow steadily more jarring as the Maiali creep closer to the steel obstruction athwart the narrow entrance.

De La Penne knows only too well that a sneak-craft operator, fully exposed in his thin rubber diving-suit, is terribly vulnerable to depth-charge attack. There is only one thing to do and he does it: he gives the prearranged signal for the attackers to scatter. From here on, each crew is on its own. With great good luck one of them may get through.

Then something happens which would seem improbable even in the wildest adventure film. First of all, the red and green lights at the harbor entrance are switched on. De La Penne, still playing tag with the launch that is dropping the depth charges, is so close to the breakwater now that he can see people moving about, hear voices. With infinite care he raises his head a few inches above water to confirm what he hardly dares to hope: *The gate in the boom is opening. A ship is coming through.*

This is the chance of chances—to ride into the inner harbor in the wake of the entering ship. The launch drops one final depth charge as if in protest, shatteringly close, blindingly close, and roars away. The entering vessel comes up fast. By her long, lean lines De La Penne knows she is a destroyer. He can hear the clank of chain on her deck and see the men forward readying the anchor gear. A second destroyer looms up not far behind. De La Penne and his mechanic ride through the gate abreast of her, running awash. Just two small dots in the turbulence. Then a third destroyer emerges from the dark, and her wake nearly throws De La Penne's cocklecraft against the gate. But he manages to steer clear of it, and like the destroyers—but for somewhat different motives—he gains the sanctuary of the harbor.

There is rich hunting now, no doubt about it. They pass two cruisers at anchor, and then the bulk of the French battleship *Lorraine*. But the lieutenant is well drilled in his task. He knows to a nicety where the *Valiant* is berthed—nor will he be diverted from her. For this is the hour of truth for De La Penne, this is the homecoming. It is between him and the battleship now. . . .

Some hundred and fifty feet to seaward of the loom of the battleship, De La Penne, running awash, comes to a close-protection net. He submerges, tries to raise it, but finds it too heavy. He decides to flip his craft over the top and does so, feeling terribly conspicuous. He is cold now, too—his hands are stiffening —and a little water is leaking in. There is no real light—only gradations of darkness. It is nearly five hours since he left the submarine, and it seems even longer. High time to finish the job and away!

De La Penne moors his craft on the soft, muddy harbor floor. At this point in the often-rehearsed operation his mechanic is supposed to come forward and help detach the warhead. *But he discovers to his horror that Bianchi is not there.* Has he fainted? Has his body been discovered? De La Penne flippers his way to the surface for a quick look-see. But all is quiet aboard the ship nearby and only a few fingering searchlights disturb the dark. Surprise is still on his side. He decides to carry out the operation alone. But this is easier to decide than to do. Detaching the charge and dragging it along the bottom use up a lot of precious energy. Thank heaven it has some buoyancy of its own! The leak in his suit makes him heavy, he is drenched with sweat, and worst of all his goggles have fogged up. He tries to clean them —and his mask floods. It is like being in his own goldfish bowl inside a larger one. He fights back a wave of sheer panic. There is only one way to clear his mask of water and that is to drink it. The brackish water, strangled down, adds thirst to his torments. . . .

Forty minutes have now passed since he started to drag the heavy charge. Only the nearness of the target gives him the strength to continue. His head bumps into the side of the battleship a few feet above the harbor floor. Taking heart, he makes a quick reconnaissance and ascertains where the approximate center of the long keel lies. He is too tired to secure the bilge clamps, so he places the charge on the harbor bottom in close proximity. It is only a matter of a few seconds to set the detonator. Then, for the last time, he drifts upward, hands close to the sides, feet flippering with the slow, deliberate movements of the skilled diver. He has won! But he is too tired to try to regain his craft and escape.

He tears off his mask as he breaks water, throws his breathing device away and starts swimming. He has only covered a few hundred feet when a searchlight catches and holds him and a machine gun starts chattering. He takes refuge under the bow of the *Valiant* where he finds a buoy and climbs aboard. But he is not alone. Petty Officer Bianchi is lying on the buoy.

"What happened to you?" De La Penne's whisper sounds loud.

"I passed out, sir. When I came to I was floating. So I found this buoy. I—I'm sorry I failed you, sir."

"Nonsense, man, it was just bad luck. The charge is in position and the timer set. We've won . . ." It is good not to have to move any more, just to lie here, not even talking.

But the breathing spell is a short one. Another searchlight impales them. A motor launch comes up with a rush. Two men with machine guns cover the pair. It is all up now. No working their way ashore, no use for the pound notes sewn into their clothing, no rendezvous with a submarine off Rosetta five nights later as planned. But the job is done, the charge is placed.

De La Penne and Bianchi are hustled aboard the battleship. Below, under guard, they strip off their diving suits. An officer asks them who they are and they hand over their identification papers. The officer tells them they have failed. Let him believe so. The minutes are passing. The time device is ticking away. *Be calm, say little, and all will yet be well.*

De La Penne and Bianchi are bundled aboard the launch once more and taken to a naval barracks at Ras-el-Tin for questioning. Bianchi goes first. A few minutes later he is back, signaling that he has told nothing. A sleepy British officer armed with a pistol questions De La Penne in Italian. He looks rumpled and cross at being disturbed at such an hour. It is 4:00 A.M. The charge is set for 6:15 A.M.

The sleepy officer asks where he has put the charge. No answer. Then he tells De La Penne that his mechanic has told all. This De La Penne doubts. The officer says he knows how to make him talk. *Back to the motorboat again, back to the battleship.* Two hours more to go.

At this point enters the third principal character in the nocturnal drama: Captain (later Vice-Admiral Sir Charles) Morgan, skipper of the *Valiant*. He is a thick-set man, pale of face and white of hair. He speaks softly but there is the unmistakable note of command in his voice. He is on deck when the launch returns. Not unreasonably, he is worried about his ship. He wants to know where De La Penne has placed his explosive charge. De La Penne doesn't want to tell him.

"Very well," says Captain Morgan, who has been in direct communication with Admiral Cunningham, Commander-in-Chief of the Mediterranean Fleet, and is acting under Cunningham's explicit instructions. "Take him below." This time De La Penne is locked in a storeroom. The location of the storeroom is carefully explained to De La Penne. He knows that he is imprisoned directly above the spot where he laid the six hundred pounds of high explosives. But if he confesses that the charge is not secured to the ship but resting on the harbor floor, the captain will simply cast off, and all his work will have been in vain.

The British give him some rum to drink and leave him to his thoughts. He hears considerable activity in the ship, much running to and fro and curt commands.

It is not too pleasant in the storeroom. They have left him his watch and he studies it with fascination. The minutes tick relentlessly along. 5:01 . . . 5:02 . . . 5:03 . . . 5:04 . . . so an hour passes.

At 6:05, ten minutes before explosion time, De La Penne beats on the door of the storeroom and asks to speak to the captain. He is taken to him. De La Penne explains that in a very few minutes the charge will go off and there is nothing he can do but save the crew. Morgan asks him again where the package is placed. Silence.

"Very well," says Morgan in his gentle, tired voice, "Take the prisoner back to the storeroom, men."

And De La Penne is alone again, with time running out . . . 6:09 . . . 6:10 . . . 6:11. . . . He tries to squeeze through the one porthole but it is much too small. He hears the measured sound of feet. The crew is abandoning ship. *What a way to die, like a snared animal* . . . 6:12 . . . 6:13 . . . 6:14 . . . maybe the fuse is faulty. . . .

CRASH! A shattering explosion rocks the ship. The deck comes up to crush him, the deck above spins, the lights go out, smoke is everywhere. There is a sharp list to port.

But the luck of Luigi Durand De La Penne still holds. Except for a bruised knee he is unharmed. The door in the bulkhead of his cell has been blown wide open by the blast, so he walks free. The ship is still listing four or five degrees to port but has settled in the mud. Calmly, without panic, the members of the crew are carrying out the captain's orders to correct the list by counter-flooding. Others of the crew have already gone ashore or are gathered in groups on deck. No one pays any attention to De La Penne.

He goes to the rail. Scanning the harbor, he spots the *Queen Elizabeth* berthed some five-hundred yards away. He watches her steadily. Suddenly, without warning, she too gives a convulsive heave and seems to leap from the water. From her stack and topsides oil and dirt and iron scraps spray down on the *Valiant*. Then the *Queen Elizabeth,* too, settles back in the water with a heavy list. But this time her shattered bulk is resting, like her sister ship's, on the harbor bottom. Bravo, Lieutenant Marceglia and Petty Officer Schergat, you have not failed in your part of the night's work. But De La Penne is very tired.

A large fleet tanker is also put out of action. Failing to find the carrier which was their target, the team of Martellotta and Marino selected the most valuable ship they could find. They have placed their charge too near the bow of the tanker and skillful counterflooding minimizes the damage done.

Still, the toll of the night's work is impressive. Two battleships put out of combat . . . one tanker temporarily knocked out. The cost to Italy: exactly six prisoners of war.

The Italians never did take advantage of the night's work of the six operators at Alexandria. Despite temporary superiority, their fleet, kept on short rations of fuel oil by the Germans, was in no position to challenge the Royal Navy.

It took many months to repair the two battleships—so long that neither saw action again in World War II. How seriously the British reacted to the Alexandria raid was made clear by Prime Minister Churchill's report to a secret session of Parliament in April, 1942. He referred to it as a "sinister stroke" and paid tribute to the "extraordinary courage and ingenuity" with which the mines had been delivered.

10

The Secret Army

Tadeusz Bor-Komorowski

General Bor-Komorowski was a colonel in the regular Polish army when the German blitzkrieg *struck into Poland in 1939. When Poland went down to inevitable defeat, he became one of the chief organizers of the Polish resistance. By 1943 he had risen to commander of the Polish Home Army. The army was short of everything except courage, but it managed to make life miserable for the Nazi conquerors.*

Since guns and ammunition were in short supply, Bor-Komorowski and his men used their wits in many ingenious ways. This selection from his book, The Secret Army, *describes some of them:*

THE quantity of weapons at our disposal was always a small amount in comparison with the number of men to be armed, so we had to supplement armed action by attacks on the enemy's morale which would not require dynamite or guns.

One of them was what we called "Special Action N." German factories and workshops received orders from the respective German authorities that May 1, 1942, was to be observed as Nazi Labor Day. All workers were to have twenty-four hours' leave on full pay. They were also to be informed of the significance of the day in the National Socialist order. After the outbreak of war with Russia, the Germans had reduced the number of holidays to the absolute minimum in order to step up their war effort. But this order was sent out on paper bearing the authentic letterhead of the German Labor Bureau and was couched in impeccable Nazi style. Every detail had been carefully worked out. The German works managers were completely taken in and had not the least doubt that the order was authentic.

We purposely sent the order out at the last moment, and consequently the German Labor Bureau discovered the trick too late to stop it through the normal channels. Public loudspeakers and telephones were hastily used to announce that the order had been "forged by criminal elements" and to instruct all workers to return to their factories at once. It was too late, however. Most industries throughout Poland remained idle for a whole day. Among others, the Ursus Tank Works and the enormous railway repair depots at Pruszkow, of vital importance to the German eastern front, were closed for the day. The German losses in production were comparable with those of a minor RAF raid. The whole operation did not cost us a single man or a single round of ammunition.

On another occasion, all German residents in Warsaw received a communication on Nazi Party notepaper instructing each of them to deposit a food parcel for wounded German soldiers in the Warsaw hospitals. True to the German love of detail and precision, the items to be included in each parcel were minutely listed, even down to the number of eggs (and this at a time when eggs were well-nigh unobtainable, even by Germans). The German civilians all turned up on the appointed day at the office of the German Mayor in Warsaw.

Their astonishment was intense when they learned that the authorities had no knowledge of the order. Officials stated that there, too, no one knew anything of the order. But the Gestapo at once ordered all the Germans who had turned up with parcels to be held and cross-examined. The investigation took a whole day, and the German housewives, exhausted and furious, finally returned home roundly cursing the chaos of their own authorities' offices. Our object had been to hamper the work of the authorities and, in fact, we succeeded in hamstringing it for a full twenty-four hours.

Hardly a week passed in which we did not send out forged communications of some sort: orders to register, announcements, invitations to nonexistent party meetings and demonstrations and so on. The result was inevitable. German confidence in the orders of their own authorities was gravely shaken, and very often the German telephone system was so jammed by inquirers checking up on the order that urgent business could not get through. Fischer, the governor of Warsaw, was finally forced to send out a confidential circular to all his subordinates warning them against orders forged by Poles. This was what we had been waiting for. From then on, when a German official received an inconvenient order he would disregard it, on the plea that he considered it a forged one issued by our underground. Frequent confusion resulted, and all without loss of life to us. Another effort on the part of "Special Action" had an even more acute effect on the German population. Our Intelligence discovered that the German stocks of gas masks were insufficient for their civilians in Poland. We decided to take advantage of this discovery. Accordingly, all German civilians received a confidential letter, signed by Boehme, who was chief of the German Security Police at the time, which alleged that the Russians would very probably use poison gas in the near future and ordered every German civilian to procure a gas mask within the space of two weeks.

Masks were, of course, unprocurable in any shop in Warsaw, and the German administrative offices were therefore swamped with inquiries, both by telephone and in person, from the terror-stricken German civilians. The authorities were infuriated by the numerous and distracted requests. Boehme was forced to have a special proclamation posted up throughout the capital in order to cope with the panic. In it, he admitted that the original order had been forged by Poles and assured his countrymen that there was definitely no immediate danger of gas attacks. But the Germans did not react as he hoped.

"They've only just discovered that there aren't enough gas masks to go round," they complained to one another. "That's why they're trying to back out by throwing the blame on the Poles."

Bor-Komorowski's irregular forces did make good use of every weapon or explosive device that friends abroad were able to parachute in—or that they themselves stole from the Germans. The following short account and summary of "Sabotage and Diversion Action" from January, 1941, to June, 1944, is an eloquent testimony to the men and women who kept the spirit of Poland alive in those dark years:

. . . In the scope of our anti-terrorist and revenge action, much effort was sacrificed in fighting the Gestapo and the German police, from whom the civilian population had so much to dread. Sentences were executed on the most obnoxious members of the Gestapo, usually in broad daylight, in streets or public places. In the course of the first six months of 1944 we "liquidated" 769 prominent agents of the Gestapo.

These activities went a long way toward lowering the morale of the Germans in Poland, and indirectly protected the civilians. They formed, in some respects, a method of self-defense. The diversion detachments also protected radio transmitters and convoyed transports of arms and equipment.

The transport of arms from the parachute drops to the hidden distribution depots was in most cases done by means of captured motor vehicles, the arms being disguised under various forms (oxygen bottles, etc.). Obviously, the best method was to have our men dressed up in either Wehrmacht or SS uniforms, and more often than not transport took place under strong armed escort. Skirmishes with the German police and armed units often took place on these occasions, both in towns and out in the open; our troops, who always employed bold shock tactics, usually emerged victorious. . . .

There is hardly space to describe all the sabotage and diversionary activities. The following list gives some idea of the results achieved:

Railway locomotives damaged	6,930
Locomotives further delayed during repairs	803
Rail transports derailed	732
Rail transports set on fire	443
Railway carriages damaged	19,058
Railway bridges blown up	38
Motor transport vehicles destroyed	4,326
Aircraft destroyed	28
Fuel tanks (cisterns) destroyed	1,167
Tons of fuel destroyed	4,674
Petrol wells spiked	3
Rail-cars of wood destroyed (burned)	150
Military store depots set on fire	122
Breaches in electrical power in the Warsaw network alone	638
Major army depots set on fire (destroyed)	8
Complete stoppage of factories	7
Faulty assemblies of aircraft engines	4,710
Faulty casts of cannon barrels	203
Faulty manufacture of artillery missiles	92,000
Faulty manufacture of aircraft radio transmitters	107
Machines of major importance in war-production plants destroyed	2,872
Various acts of sabotage executed	25,145
Lethal bodily assaults on Germans	5,733

11

Long Island Landfall

George J. Dasch

The Germans made one major attempt at sabotage against the continental United States. The Abwehr (German Intelligence) called it Operation Pastorius. Eight saboteur-spies were involved, to be put ashore from two submarines. One landfall was off the Florida coast and one off Long Island. The spies' main objective was the crippling of aluminum plants in the Tennessee Valley. They hoped to accomplish this by blowing up some of the towers carrying the high-tension lines which powered the plants.

George Dasch commanded the Long Island team. He had spent seventeen years in the United States, returning to Germany in 1939. By his own account he became a violent anti-Nazi, heartsick at everything he saw in Hitler's Germany. His one ambition was to get back to America somehow, and to help the Allied cause if he could.

After training in a special school for saboteurs, Dasch and his three companions boarded U-boat 202 at L'Orient in occupied France. The date: May 26, 1942.

The trip took seventeen days, under a "very Nazi type" sub-

marine commander, "with the Iron Cross dangling at his neck."
The anxious, vulnerable moment of landfall and landing is told
in Dasch's book, Eight Spies Against America:

AROUND eight o'clock on the evening of June 12, U-boat 202
reached the coastal waters of the United States just off Long Island. We submerged, hit bottom in about 100 feet of water and
lay there for the next five hours, waiting for the right time to
land. For two days the fog had prevented us from shooting the
sun to determine our exact position and we had come down
from Newfoundland by dead reckoning. As near as the captain
could figure, we were just about two miles out from Southamp-
ton, but as the two of us pored over the charts together, he could
not pinpoint our location for me. It turned out later that we
were lying off Amagansett, just a few miles farther east than the
captain had figured. Not knowing exactly where we would land
added to the strain of those last few hours of waiting to go
ashore. We could hear stones and gravel washing against the bottom and sides of the U-boat as it rested there on the ocean floor.

About midnight the sub surfaced and headed at slow speed for
shore, propelled only by its nearly silent electric motors. Everything was ready for the landing. The other three men had their
final instructions. I had handed out the money belts and divided
the $1,000 in smaller bills. Two crewmen had been selected to
take us ashore in the rubber boat. Our boxes and explosives, a
couple of shovels, a duffel bag full of clothes, and my Gladstone
bag with the money sewed in its lining were on hand, ready to be
loaded on the rubber raft. Should we encounter anyone upon
reaching the beach, we were under strict instructions to overpower him or them and take the body or bodies to the boat. The
two sailors were given light submachine guns or carbines to be
used if the four of us were not able to subdue whoever might be
on the beach. It was unlikely that we would meet anyone, but
the captain wanted to be prepared in case stray fishermen, midnight bathers or a couple of lovers should happen to be on the
beach at that unlikely hour. He told the two sailors, who were

going ashore with us, "You bring the bodies back and we'll feed them to the fish when we get out to sea again."

The submarine nudged the bottom again. The already slow speed was reduced by half and we pushed in a little closer. Soon we hit solid bottom again and the captain ordered the motors cut. Without delay the rubber boat was launched. Our things were loaded and we climbed aboard. There was barely room for all six of us and we had trouble holding on as the overweighted boat bobbed up and down on the waves. The paddlers got to work and we slowly moved away from the sub. In a minute or two we were completely swallowed in fog. Even the sub could no longer be seen. For a time we couldn't even tell whether we were headed toward the beach, along the beach, or out to sea. The muffled sound of the surf seemed to be coming from all directions. Suddenly through the fog I sighted a stretch of white sand ahead. "We made it, boys," I called and jumped overboard. In the excitement and poor visibility I had misjudged the distance to shore. The water was over my head. Half climbing, half being pulled, I got back into the boat. A few more strokes by the paddlers and I jumped again. This time the water came to below my waist.

While the others unloaded the boat I ran up the beach to look around. Except for the surf, there wasn't a sound. The fog and darkness obscured everything but sand dunes and a few scraggly bushes and beach plants.

Returning to the boat, I ordered the men to carry the boxes of explosives back from the water line to higher ground. Burger * took the money bag which I had assigned to him while we were still aboard the sub. The two sailors were trying to tip up the rubber boat to empty the water that had splashed into it as we landed. I was giving them a hand with the job when I happened to glance over my shoulder. My heart nearly stopped beating. A light was moving slowly down the beach! It was only a short distance away. Burger and the other two men had gone in the other

* Ernest Peter Burger, one of the three men under Dasch's command.

direction to higher ground, and thus couldn't see it through the thick fog. Hardly taking time to think I left the two sailors and ran in the direction of the rays. The order to destroy anyone seen while landing burned in my mind and the last thing I wanted, now that I was safely in America, was to have some innocent American get killed. "Damn," I thought. "Put that out. You don't know what danger you're walking into!"

Coming up to the light, I found myself confronted by a young man in an American sailor's uniform, holding a flashlight. "Are you guys fishermen?" he asked. "Are you having trouble? Did you get lost in the fog?"

Catching my breath I begged him to put out his light, which he did. "No, we're not fishermen," I said, "and I can't tell you what this is all about."

He looked down the beach and then at me. Saying something like, "Hey, what is this anyway," he started toward the two German sailors who were now faintly visible through the fog.

I grabbed his arm and pulled him back. "Look here boy, I can't tell you what's going on just now. This is only a matter for Washington." He didn't seem to understand and made a move to continue down the beach. I pleaded again: "You have a mother, don't you, boy? Well if you ever want to see her again, please do exactly what I tell you."

In my urgency I wasn't making too much sense and he seemed uncertain about what to do.

"What is your name, boy?" I asked. He answered something that sounded like John Cullen or Collins.

With that I pulled my hat back and said, "My name is George John Dasch. I want you to shine your light in my face so that you'll recognize me when I have you called in Washington."

Just then Burger came up. I couldn't be sure whether he had heard what I said or not. Stopping a few yards away he called in a startled voice using first German and then English, "Is there anything wrong, George? Do you need any help?"

I turned to Burger and, using harsh tones that must have shown my irritation, snapped, "Go back to the others. I'll handle this myself."

The sailor, who I later learned was a Coast Guardsman, was obviously alarmed by now. Turning back to him I said, "You have undoubtedly given your oath to do your duty, and you are performing your duty by doing exactly what I tell you."

The young man was still confused and showed no sign of realizing in what danger his life stood. In my desperation to find some way to get rid of him, I reached into my pocket and pulled out some bills. "Here, please take this. This is not a bribe. Please go now and you'll hear from me in Washington."

The young man said, "Thank you, sir," and somewhat hesitatingly backed off into the fog.

Running back to the German sailors waiting at the rubber boat, I told them to take off. They asked about the light and I assured them everything was fine and instructed them to report back to the captain that our landing had been accomplished as planned.

After burying their uniforms and explosives in the sand, the four managed to catch an early-morning train to New York. But Cullen raised the alarm, and the hunt was on. Once in New York, the spies scattered. Then Dasch did what he had planned to do all along: he reported to the FBI in Washington.

Using the information which he supplied, the FBI was able to round up all the other invaders, including the Florida four.

The eight operators were promptly tried by a special Presidential commission of general officers. Six of them were condemned to death and executed soon after. Dasch's action saved his life. He served over five years in various Federal prisons and was then deported.

Coast Guardsman Cullen received the Legion of Merit for his coolness on the beach and the speed with which he raised the alarm.

12

Department of Dirty Tricks

Corey Ford

President Roosevelt created the Office of Strategic Services (OSS) in June, 1942, "to collect and analyze strategic information, and to plan and operate special services."

Under the direction of the Joint Chiefs of Staff this famous agency was run by Maj. Gen. William J. (Wild Bill) Donovan. Beneath the bland official language of "special services" there took place many unusual behind-the-lines operations. Such operations were made possible in good degree by the OSS's department of "dirty tricks," spurred on by Donovan himself.

Corey Ford's biography of the director, Donovan of OSS, tells of some of the more outlandish devices:

JUST as Donovan's energy gave OSS its vitality, so the agency was buoyed by his fertile imagination. From the beginning, he had encouraged boldness and inventiveness in devising ingenious ways to harass the enemy; and any suggestion, however bizarre, was welcomed in the front office. "Go ahead and try it." He would nod. "We learn by our mistakes." No project was so implausible, no weapon so outlandish as to be discarded out of hand.

Someone might come up with the idea of making a land mine in the shape of camel dung, which members of a resistance group could plant on a desert trail. Donovan would order his researchers to explore the possibilities. Someone else might hit on the scheme of camouflaging a powerful explosive as a lump of coal, to be tossed into a passing coal truck and eventually shoveled into the fire box of a Nazi locomotive. Donovan would beam in approval: "Why not give it a whirl?" After all, he felt, it was no more fantastic than the other lethal inventions emanating from Dr. Lovell's Research and Development unit. . . .

Dr. Stanley Lovell, in charge of the agency's calculated mischief, was a sunny little nihilist, his spectacles twinkling and his chubby face creasing with merriment as he displayed his latest diabolic devices. This simple candle could be placed by a female agent in the bedroom of an amorous German officer, Lovell chuckled, and would burn perfectly until the flame touched the high explosive contained in the lower half of the candle. This innocent-looking plastic cylinder called the Firefly, dropped furtively into the gas tank of a car by a Maquis filling-station attendant, would explode after the gasoline had swelled a rubber retaining ring. . . . This limpet, fastened by a powerful magnet to the side of a ship below waterline, would detonate when the magnesium alloy was eroded by salt water, long after the saboteur had left the area. It was used effectively by the Norwegian underground to sink Nazi troop-ships in the narrow fjords of Oslo and Narvik and sent thousands of German soldiers to a watery grave.

One of Dr. Lovell's favorite products was "Aunt Jemima," a powdered form of TNT resembling ordinary wheat flour, activated by a time-delay detonator. If the Gestapo were suspicious, the flour could be kneaded into dough and baked into biscuits or bread which the agent could eat safely, though it was not advisable to smoke a cigarette immediately afterward.

Some R & D devices were so old that they were new again. A

special shoe was prepared with a space in the sole to secrete messages, over which an upper sole was stitched and smoothed and
stained at the edges—the same method employed by Nathan
Hale to smuggle his maps of British fortifications out of New
York. Another popular saboteur weapon was a four-cornered
steel spike which would land on a highway or airplane runway
with three prongs down and the fourth upraised, its sharpened
point guaranteed to puncture the stoutest tire. Back in the American Revolution, these identical spikes, called "crow's feet," were
scattered in the streets of Boston behind Howe's retreating army
to discourage American pursuers. . . .

It was Mrs. Eleanor Roosevelt, Lovell always insisted, who
dreamed up the Bat Project, perhaps the strangest of all R & D
ventures. According to her plan, a number of bats would be
transported to Japan, armed with incendiary bombs, and released from an airplane or submarine. The bats would make for
the eaves of the Japanese paper and bamboo houses and cling
there until the delayed fuses fired, causing a conflagration which
would wipe out the enemy city. The initial task was to acquire
the bats. One of the project officers told me later that they first
erected nets on top of a Manhattan hotel, but it turned out that
New York bats were not the desired type. The operation was
transferred to the Carlsbad Caverns, where a number of bats
were captured, chilled until they were comatose, and shipped in
refrigerator trucks to an abandoned Western mining town which
had been selected for the test. In the OSS equipment shed, tiny
fire-bombs were attached to the bodies of the frosted bats, they
were revived and stowed in the bomb bay of an Air Force plane,
and turned loose over the ghost town. Instinctively they homed
in on the OSS shed and settled under the dry eaves, and the re-
sultant blaze destroyed all the experimental equipment and leveled
most of the town. Mrs. Roosevelt was eventually persuaded to
give up her idea.

An influential United States senator was responsible for a parallel venture, called the Cat Project. A constituent had pointed
out to him that a cat hates water, and always makes for dry

land. His suggestion was to sling a cat in a harness below an aerial bomb, with the mechanism set so delicately that the cat's least movement would direct the vanes of the bomb, and release the feline-guided missile over an enemy battleship. The startled cat would see the water below it, and struggle and claw to reach the one dry spot in sight. "We had to drop a cat in a harness," Lovell wrote, "to prove that the animal became unconscious and ineffective in the first fifty feet of fall." The senator yielded, and Project Cat was duly scrubbed.

General Donovan, who had won the Medal of Honor for World War I heroism, was a great believer in being where the action was. Such appearances were sometimes over and above the duties of a top-ranking Intelligence officer, stuffed with top secrets and therefore a rich prize if captured by the enemy. A K-capsule, or suicide pill, to be carried on his front-line forays, was one precaution.

Here, also from Corey Ford's Donovan of OSS, *is a glimpse of Donovan, in person and in character, on the most famous D day of them all:*

On June 6, 1944, General Donovan was aboard the *Tuscaloosa* at the Normandy invasion, wearing a woolen cap and nonchalantly munching an apple while the cruiser's big guns blasted the shore defenses. As he rode in on a landing craft with Colonel David Bruce, chief of OSS/Europe, Bruce groaned aloud at a belated realization. "I forgot to bring my K-capsule," he confessed.

"That's all right," the general shrugged, "I'll lend you one." He groped through the pockets of his uniform blouse, and his expression grew embarrassed. "I guess I forgot mine, too," he admitted, "but there's no need to worry." He patted Bruce's shoulder reassuringly. "If anything happens, I'll shoot you first."

13

For the Glory of France

Maria Wilhelm

*After the fall of France in June, 1940, an underground move-
ment was soon started in the areas occupied by the Germans. By
1943 this movement had been organized into an active resistance. In both, the youth of France did good service. They
helped put out the various underground and resistance newspapers which in themselves were a form of sabotage (in that they
helped keep alive the spirit of revolt and the dream of freedom).*

*French boys and girls reported on troop movements, strewed
glass and nails in front of German convoys, helped in the slowdown of vital industry. When they could, they escaped to England
by small boat and even canoe. Some were not lucky enough to
escape or survive, as this episode from Maria Wilhelm's book,* For
the Glory of France, *shows:*

ONE of the most moving stories is that of the five martyrs of the
Buffon High School, in the vicinity of Paris. Their real names
were Jean Arthus, Jacques Baudry, Pierre Benoit, Pierre Grelot
and Lucien Legros—but they were known to the police only by

their pseudonyms, Marchand, André, Francis, Paul and Janet. Whenever there was a demonstration, "the Five" were there distributing leaflets, encouraging their comrades. They also practiced active sabotage, and after a successful grenade attack in June, 1942, the Nazis decided to arrest them. Only Benoit managed to escape. He immediately went to work to set up a network of students trained to sabotage. Once he succeeded in destroying by fire ten Nazi planes at a local airport, but he was wounded in the raid and had to hide in a sewer for eight days. On August 22 he too was arrested, and on October 15 "the Five" were sentenced to death. All of them were under eighteen and were later honored by the *Ordre de la Nation,* usually reserved for soldiers.

All of them wrote letters to their families just before they were executed. Here is the one sent by Pierre Benoit:

Dear Parents & Friends,

This is the end. They are coming to take us to be shot. Too bad. To die when one is victorious is rather annoying, but it doesn't matter. One's life is built on dreams.

Nano, don't forget your brother. Up to the end he was correct and courageous, and I do not tremble at the thought of death. Good-by, father, I thank you for everything you have done for me. Keep good memories of your son.

Toto, good-by, I love you as I do my parents.

Nano, be a good son. You are the only son left to them, don't do anything foolish.

Good-by all you whom I love, and who love me, those in Nantes and everywhere.

Life will be beautiful again. We leave you singing. Have courage. This won't be so bad after six months in prison. I embrace you all.

14

A Passage to Persia

Fitzroy MacLean

When World War II broke out, Fitzroy MacLean was working in the British Foreign Office. His job there like many others was promptly frozen, meaning that he was not allowed to leave it for military duty. Wishing a more active role, he hit on an ingenious scheme. He ran for Parliament, got himself elected and then promptly resigned to go to war—a procedure both legal and politically feasible. Not unimpressed, Prime Minister Churchill—later a great backer of MacLean—growled a famous comment, calling him "the only young man who ever used the Mother of Parliaments as a public convenience."

By temperament Scottish Fitzroy MacLean was drawn to commando work. After a tour of North African duty in the Special Air Service (basically a sabotage outfit), he was ordered to General Headquarters Persia and Iraq at Baghdad (Gen. Maitland Wilson commanding). The time: late 1942, when the German pincers were threatening the whole Middle East. General Rommel would soon launch that new offensive of his which carried him to within a hundred miles of Cairo. The second arm of

the pincer was another German force reaching down through the
Caucasus to Persia (now Iran).

MacLean was ordered to recruit and train a volunteer unit for
commando-type work. But first of all he received an assignment
that proved a fair test of ingenuity and nerve. His account of it
appeared in his celebrated book, Escape to Adventure.

JUST as I was thinking of pitching my camp and starting to train
the nucleus of my force, I received a signal instructing me to report at once to General Wilson's Chief of Staff, General Baillon,
who, the signal informed me, had just arrived in Teheran from
Baghdad.

I found General Baillon at the British Legation in conference
with the minister, Sir Reader Bullard. They told me that they
had a job for me. For some time past, they said, there had been
signs that some kind of trouble was brewing in south Persia. The
tribes, the Qashgai and the Bakhtiari, had German agents living
among them and seemed likely to rise at any moment, just as
they had risen in 1916, when their rebellion had caused us a dis-
proportionate amount of trouble. Were this to happen, our supply
route to the Persian Gulf might be cut. There was also discontent in Isfahan and other towns, largely caused by the hoarding
of grain by speculators, which we were unable to prevent. This
discontent might at any moment flare up into open rebellion.
Worse still, if there were trouble, the Persian troops in south Persia were likely to take the side of the rioters.

A sinister part was being played in all this by a certain General Zahidi, who was in command of the Persian forces in the Isfahan area. Zahidi was known to be one of the worst grain
hoarders in the country. But there was also good reason to believe that he was acting in cooperation with the tribal leaders
and, finally, that he was in touch with the German agents who
were living in the hills and, through them, with the German high
command in the Caucasus. . . .

The situation was a delicate one. The Allied forces of occupation in northern Persia had been reduced to a minimum, in order

to meet demands from the fighting fronts; there were practically no Allied troops in south Persia at all. The nearest British troops to the seat of the trouble were at Qum, two hundred miles north of Isfahan. There was very real danger that any sudden movement of British troops in a southward direction might provoke a general rising which we should have serious difficulty in containing with the small forces at our disposal. On the other hand, if we allowed events to take their course, the results would be equally disastrous.

In short it was essential to nip the trouble in the bud, while avoiding a full-scale showdown. General Baillon and Sir Reader Bullard had decided that this could best be achieved by the removal of General Zahidi, and it was this task that they had decided to entrust to me. How it was to be done they left me to work out for myself. Only two conditions were made: I was to take him alive and I was to do so without creating a disturbance.

My first step was to go to Isfahan and see for myself how the land lay. That city's mosques and palaces, unrivaled in the whole of Asia, provided an excellent pretext for visiting it. I let it be known in Teheran that I was going to spend a few days' leave sight-seeing in the south, and set out.

I reached Isfahan the same night after driving all day across a bleak plateau fringed with distant snow-capped mountains. The flickering lights of a *chai-khana* shone out of the darkness, showing two or three dim figures squatting in the doorway, drinking their tea and smoking their long pipes; then a group of houses; then some shops; and then we were in the main street in a seething stream of carts, donkeys and camels, whose owners turned around to stare at the first jeep and the first British uniforms to make their appearance in Isfahan.

I drove to the British Consulate, where I was welcomed by the consul, John Gault. Soon Guardsman Duncan and I, in the time-honored phrase of the British soldier, had "our knees under the table" and were making good progress with a brace of the local brand of partridge, washed down by delicious wine from the town of Shiraz, which, according to some, disputes with Xeres the honor of being the birthplace of sherry.

Over dinner I disclosed to my host, a robust young man who gave the impression of being equally alert both mentally and physically, the true purpose of my visit. He was delighted. General Zahidi, he said, though pleasant to meet, was a really bad lot: a bitter enemy of the Allies, a man of unpleasant personal habits, and, by virtue of his grain-hoarding activities, a source of popular discontent and an obstacle to the efficient administration of south Persia. He, too, had heard that he was plotting with the Germans and with the tribal leaders. Indeed, according to information which had reached him, one of the opening moves in General Zahidi's plot was to be the liquidation of the British Consul in Isfahan, a piece of news which completely outweighed all the general's personal charm, as far as he was concerned.

I asked Gault where Zahidi lived. He said he would show me, and after dinner we strolled out of the consulate, across a narrow many-arched bridge, and along a broad avenue of plane trees, until we came to a massive pair of gates, set in a high stone wall and flanked by a sentry box and guardroom. Outside, a Persian infantryman was marching up and down while others, all well armed, slouched at the door of the guardroom. We took a turn around the back premises, where the surrounding wall was pierced by another gate, guarded by another sentry. This was the general's residence. Then we continued our stroll along the avenue under the trees. A few hundred yards farther along we came to a large modern barracks, which according to Gault contained the greater part of the garrison of Isfahan, ready to rush to the assistance of their commander in case of trouble. It did not look as though a frontal attack by a small raiding party would have much chance of succeeding.

If Zahidi could not conveniently be winkled out of his place of residence, the obvious alternative was to ambush him when he was away from home, traveling from one point to another. I ascertained from Gault that at the same time every morning he crossed the bridge on his way to his headquarters. Would it not be possible to take advantage of the narrow bottleneck formed by this ancient monument to hold up his car, drag him out of it, and make off with him?

I gave this plan careful consideration, but there were two serious objections to it. In the first place Zahidi was reputed to go nowhere without a heavily armed bodyguard, whom it would be necessary to overcome by force. Secondly, even assuming that we managed to avoid a pitched battle with the bodyguard, we were unlikely to succeed in kidnapping a general in broad daylight in the middle of so populous a town as Isfahan without attracting a good deal of attention. The two of us driving peaceably along in the jeep had been a sufficiently novel spectacle to hold up the traffic in the main street of Isfahan; the same party with the addition of a struggling general and his bereaved bodyguard could scarcely fail to introduce into the proceedings that very element of uproar which my superiors were so anxious to avoid. I went to sleep that night with the feeling that the problem before me was not as simple as it had at first sight appeared.

Next day, after further thought and another talk with Gault, I came to the conclusion that, unless I was prepared to risk a serious incident which might have unforseeable repercussions, I should have to rely primarily on some kind of a ruse in order to get my man. In short, what was needed was a Trojan horse.

Once I had started thinking on these lines, it was not long before there began to shape in my mind a plan which seemed to offer a better chance of neatly and successfully eliminating the source of the trouble without setting light to the powder magazine of south Persia. That afternoon I sent off a cipher telegram to Teheran, giving my proposals for Operation Pongo, which was the code name I had chosen for the abduction of the general.

The first thing was to find a pretext for introducing myself into Zahidi's house. I suggested that I should be given authority to assume for the occasion a brigadier's badges of rank; that I should then ring up the house and announce myself as a senior staff officer from Baghdad who wished to pay his respects to the general. If the latter agreed, I would drive up in a staff car, accompanied by Duncan and one or two other resourceful characters, hold him up at the point of a pistol, hustle him into the car, and drive away with him out of Isfahan before the alarm could be given. I also asked for a platoon of infantry to lend a hand in case anything went wrong. I undertook to work out some means of introducing these into Isfahan in such a way as to attract as little attention as possible.

Having sent off my telegram, I spent two agreeable days making a detailed reconnaissance of the city, with special attention to the best line of withdrawal in case of an emergency, and at the same time enjoying its peerless beauty.

The arrival of an urgent message from General Headquarters in reply to my telegram, submitting my proposals and requesting instructions, brought me back to the realities of World War II. My plan was approved in principle and I was instructed to go ahead with my preparations. Only one item of my highly unorthodox program stuck in the throats of the well-trained staff officers at the other end. It was not (repeat: not) possible, they said, to authorize an officer of my age and seniority (I was a captain) to masquerade, even for a day, as a brigadier. Rather than allow this, they would place at my disposal, for a limited period of time, a genuine brigadier, for use as bait or for any other purpose within reason. Moreover this officer, for the purposes of the operation, would receive his instructions from me. For administrative purposes I was directed to report to General Anderson, the corps commander at Qum, some two hundred miles from Isfahan, who had been asked to furnish the brigadier and also such troops, equipment and transport as I might require.

I lost no time in reporting to Corps Headquarters, where I was provided with a platoon of Seaforth Highlanders, who were told that they had been specially selected for training in commando tactics. As surprise was clearly essential to the success of our enterprise, secrecy was of the utmost importance, and at this stage practically no one except the corps commander and I was aware of our real objective. The Seaforths were equipped with tommy guns and hand grenades and we repaired to a secluded part of the desert near Qum to rehearse our act.

I had decided that the Seaforths should only be used in case of an emergency. My plan was that on the appointed day they should arrive in Isfahan in two covered trucks, disguised as far as possible to look like civilian vehicles, shortly before I set out for the general's house. One would draw up under the plane trees on the far side of the avenue, opposite the main entrance to the house, and stay there. The other would take up a position covering the back entrance. The men, clutching their tommy guns and hand grenades, would remain in the back of the trucks, out of sight. Only if they heard firing or a prearranged signal of three blasts on the whistle would they emerge from their hiding place, overpower the guard and force an entrance, after which their task would be to cover the withdrawal of the party in the staff car, which it was hoped would include Zahidi whatever happened. If, on the other hand, all went well, the two trucks would simply wait until the staff car drove out with Zahidi in it, and then fall in behind and escort us out of Isfahan to a point in the desert where an aircraft would be waiting, ready to fly our prisoner out of the country.

For our rehearsals I chose a ruined fort in the desert. Again and again the two trucks took up their positions outside; the staff car drove in; the whistle sounded; the Seaforths poured out of the trucks and into the fort; an imaginary victim was bundled unceremoniously into the car, and all three vehicles drove off in triumph, the occupants tossing dummy hand grenades out of the back at imaginary pursuers, as they went. The Seaforths gave a splendidly realistic performance. Indeed their enthusiasm was such that my only anxiety was lest on the day itself they would emerge from their place of concealment, whether things went well or badly, and massacre a number of harmless Persians out of sheer ebullience.

It now only remained to fix the day. This was done after a further exchange of signals with General Headquarters Baghdad

and with the Foreign Office via Teheran. I also extracted from
the authorities, not without difficulty, permission to shoot General Zahidi, should he be armed and resist capture.

Our D day was fixed, and on D minus one we set out from
Qum. I had decided that the Seaforths should spend the night
well out of sight in the desert about ten miles from Isfahan. Next
day, while the main party entered the town in the two trucks,
smaller parties were detailed to cut the telegraph wires connecting Isfahan with the neighboring Persian garrisons. Meanwhile I
collected the brigadier, a distinguished officer whose well-developed sense of humor caused him to enter completely into the
spirit of the somewhat equivocal role that had been allotted to
him, and set out for the British Consulate.

On our arrival a telephone call was put through to the general's house and an appointment made for the same afternoon.
After a copious lunch we took our places in the staff car, which
was flying a large Union Jack. A reliable NCO, armed to the
teeth, occupied the seat next to the driver, while Guardsman
Duncan and a Seaforth Highlander, both carrying tommy guns,
crouched in the luggage compartment at the back, under a tarpaulin. Gault followed in his own car. As we approached Zahidi's house, I was relieved to see our two trucks, their tarpaulin
covers concealing the battle-hungry Seaforths, drawn up in their
appointed places. At the gate the Persian sentry was deep in conversation with Laurence Lockhart, a Persian linguist from RAF
Intelligence, whose services I had enlisted for the occasion. So
far everything had gone according to plan.

On our appearance, the sentry at the gate reluctantly put out
the cigarette which Lockhart had given him, broke off his conversation, and presented arms. We drove on up the drive and
drew up in front of the house immediately outside a large pair of
open French windows. A servant ushered us in and went off to
fetch the general.

When, a couple of minutes later, General Zahidi, a dapper
figure in a tight-fitting gray uniform and highly polished boots,
entered the room, he found himself looking down the barrel of

my Colt automatic. There was no advantage in prolonging a scene which might easily become embarrassing. Without further ado, I invited the general to put his hands up and informed him that I had instructions to arrest him and that, if he made any noise or attempt at resistance, he would be shot. Then I took away his pistol and hustled him through the window into the car which was waiting outside with the engine running. To my relief there was no sign of the much-advertised bodyguard. As we passed the guardroom, the sentry once again interrupted his conversation to present arms, and the general, sitting bolt upright, with my pistol pressed against his ribs and Duncan breathing menacingly down his neck, duly returned the salute. The two "plain vans," with their occupants now bitterly disappointed, fell in behind; and the whole convoy swept at a brisk pace over the bridge and into the main avenue leading out of Isfahan.

Some miles outside the town we passed a large barracks, full of General Zahidi's troops, but the telephone wire from the town had duly been cut by the wire-cutting party, and there was no sign that the alarm had been given. Meanwhile Zahidi continued to sit bolt upright and to assure me that there was a very good explanation of any aspects of his conduct which might at first sight have seemed at all suspicious. Soon we reached the point in the desert where we had spent the night, and here I handed over my captive to an officer and six men who were standing by to take him by car to the nearest landing ground where an airplane was waiting to fly him to Palestine. . . .

Having said good-by to the brigadier, whose duties were now at an end, and sent a signal to General Wilson announcing the completion of Operation Pongo, I went back into the town to clear up any outstanding points, taking a few Seaforths with me. My first objective was Zahidi's headquarters, which I entered at the head of six Seaforths carrying tommy guns. Gault had told me that Zahidi's Chief of Staff was also very hostile to the Allies, and, in addition to this, extremely truculent in manner. The exaggerated amiability with which this dignitary now greeted me accordingly left me in no doubt that news of what had occurred had already got out. Taking him with me, I returned to Zahidi's house, which I proceeded to search methodically. In the general's bedroom I found a collection of automatic weapons of German manufacture, a good deal of silk underwear, some opium, and a large number of letters and papers which I took back with me to the consulate.

That night the Seaforths camped in the consulate garden in case there was trouble, and Gault and I sat down to examine Zahidi's correspondence. One of the first letters that caught our eye was a recent communication from a gentleman styling himself "German Consul General for south Persia," and apparently resident in the hills somewhere to the south. He spoke of Zahidi's activities in terms of general approval and, like all agents living in the hills, asked for more supplies. His letter left no doubt that the general's arrest had not come a moment too soon.

MacLean went on to serve in Yugoslavia with Tito and his partisans. After the war he became (more permanently) a Member of Parliament as well as a writer whose vigorous style is much admired.

15

Cockles and Muscles: Operation Frankton

Burke Wilkinson

The Italians were the most brilliant small-submersible operators in World War II. Using the same type of two-man human torpedo which carried out the spectacular Alexandria raid, they also sank ten merchantmen in the Gibraltar roadstead in a series of bold attacks. Ultimately their base of operations was a tanker called Olterra, *which was tied up across the bay in neutral Algeciras. By cutting a trap door in her hull and then flooding a forward compartment, she was converted into an innocent-looking mother ship for these strange little craft.*

The British—prime victims of these Italian raids—finally managed to capture and copy one of the Italian two-man craft. They called their own creation the Chariot. Also ridden astride, she did good work in the last two years of the war.

Meanwhile, with their love of long odds and dangerous missions, the Royal Navy used small surface-running craft to carry out several model operations that come under the heading of sea-borne sabotage. Perhaps the most remarkable was Operation Frankton. I learned about it as a naval officer in World War II, when it was still classified Most Secret. Finally, after the story came into the public domain, I was able to publish it in a collection of Navy true stories called By Sea and By Stealth *(1956):*

IN the summer of 1943 I was ordered to report to the U.S. Naval Attaché in London for liaison work with the Admiralty. One of my first assignments was to cover the Most Secret trials of a one-man submersible mechanized canoe (SMC) designed by an ingenious army officer, Major H.Q.A. Reeves. The trials were held off Portsmouth and the man who spelled Reeves at the controls of the SMC was a thickset, sandy-haired Royal Marine officer by the name of Hasler. He wore a flaring mustache of the type usually associated with the RAF and seemed quite immune to fatigue—despite the fact that the operator of the SMC spent many hours immersed in the chill waters of the English Channel. Hasler was fun to be with at the Portsmouth pubs after the long days at sea. Yet, for all his good fellowship, it was obvious that he was held in some awe by his brother officers. In the course of time I learned the story of the exploit that had already made him a legendary figure—an exploit that had also dramatically demonstrated the need for small submersibles in certain types of surprise attack. This is it.

Back in early 1942, British Combined Operations was confronted with a grave problem. The problem was this: German blockade runners carrying valuable war cargoes were eluding Allied submarine and air attack by hugging the French, Belgian and Dutch coasts. Could Combined Ops think of a way of ferreting them out?

Various measures were suggested. Major H.G. Hasler, OBE, a Royal Marine Commando with a record of expert sabotage work in the Norwegian campaign, came up with the boldest idea. *If the blockade runners were hard to catch on the run, why not go in and get them in their key hideaway at Bordeaux?*

Hasler proposed that twelve Marines in six light, limpet-carrying canoes do the job. Since the canoes could not submerge,* the raiders would run by night, and hide by day. Surprise and smallness would be their chief assets.

Rear Admiral Lord Louis Mountbatten, Chief of Combined Operations, said *splendid*. The project was christened Frankton, with Lord Louis as godparent, and plans were soon under way.

Training was long, Scottish and arduous. Of the thirty Marines originally selected, twelve were hand-picked by Hasler for the final team. If each had received a degree at the end of the course, it would have read: *Frogman of the first order, master of the delicate science of small explosives, long-range silent canoeist.*

Hasler was leader in the old, exemplary sense of the word. He could do everything better than anyone else; he never asked anything of his men that he could not do himself. As for the craft, they were beautiful cockles, fifteen feet long, with flat, plywood bottoms and canvas sides. But *could* twelve resolute men negotiate ninety miles of busy estuary and river, both closely patrolled, attach their limpets and make good their escape? Just possibly, night tests in the Thames and off Portsmouth showed. But escape would have to be overland by ones and twos. To expect to slip down river after so brazen an attack was a little too unlikely even for Hasler and his Royal Marines.

By December of 1942 he was ready. On the world scene things were brightening a little. Rommel was backpedaling toward Tripoli. United States Marines were mopping up a blood-soaked bit of jungle known as Guadalcanal, and Adolf Hitler still had a mirage named Stalingrad on his mind.

With somewhat more immediate objectives in mind, Hasler and his team board HM Submarine *Tuna,* Lieutenant R.P. Raikes, DSO, commanding. They have with them their six cockles: *Catfish, Crayfish, Coalfish, Conger, Cuttlefish* and *Cachelot.* Flag-

* The prototype X-Craft, first of the British small submersibles, was not delivered to the Fleet until January, 1943.

ship of this oddest of all small flotillas is *Catfish,* for she is Hasler's craft, with a husky Marine by the name of W.E. Sparks as stern paddle.

Corporal Lavers and Marine Mills are the crew of *Crayfish.* *Coalfish* is manned by Sergeant Wallace and Marine Hewitt. Corporal Sheard and Marine Moffat have *Conger.* Hasler's second-in-command, Lieutenant McKinnon, along with Marine Conway, will bring up the rear in *Cuttlefish.* As for *Cachelot,* she and her crew will not figure largely in this narrative, as we shall presently see.

Lieutenant Raikes points *Tuna* for the Bay of Biscay. Six hours out of port, Hasler calls his men together and tells them their destination at last. He breaks out a large-scale map, allots specific targets and rehearses the escape drill.

"I want you all to know" says Hasler, in his friendly, serious way, "that if any man thinks this thing is too much for him, he can speak up now." No one speaks, but they all grin back. It is far too good a show to miss.

Hasler takes inventory.

"Every man have his compass?"

"Aye, aye, sir," they answer in chorus.

"Limpets? Chemical fuses? Aerial photos? Escape maps? Sten guns? Automatics? Knives? Grenades? Canoe capes? Bird whistles? Camouflage cream? Badges of rank and regimental insignia?"

Each man answers in the affirmative after checking his gear. The last item is especially important: badges and insignia have been sewn inside the hooded canoeing jackets. They may just possibly save the wearer from the firing squad if caught. But all of them know that behind-the-lines operators can expect short shrift at best.

Fifteen miles southwest of the Gironde estuary, *Tuna* breaks surface. It is eight o'clock on the moonless night of December 7, and it is very cold.

Cachelot is the first casualty. In launching her from the submarine, she takes an eighteen-inch slash below the waterline.

There is only one thing to do. Hasler orders her crew back aboard the submarine and scuttles the craft with a longer slash.

So where there were six craft now there are five. In line ahead *Catfish, Crayfish, Coalfish, Conger* and *Cuttlefish* vanish like shadows into the murky night.

Soon they spot the yellow light of the lighthouse on the Pointe de Grave, on the southern side of the estuary. Tilting their double blades, the men dig to port, dig to starboard, with a will. *Dip —swing, dip—swing, dip—swing* goes the rhythm of the paddles.

Two things happen at once. The raiding party raises the bank of the estuary, gray against black. And they hear a distant roaring sound that seems to grow louder. Hasler identifies the sound. It is a tide race. Before any uncertainty can communicate itself to his men, he makes his decision. His hand signals *forward.* The boats will meet for muster on the other side of the race. The five craft plunge into the white inferno. Ten minutes of flailing paddles and spinning cockles and the lead boat is through. Then, one by one, *Crayfish, Conger,* and *Cuttlefish* appear. Of Wallace and Hewitt in *Coalfish* there is no trace. Hasler and Sparks plunge back into the white water, their bird whistles mewing like gulls in the agreed signal. Now they are battling the six-knot tide as well as the boiling water. No welcome gull cry answers theirs. *Coalfish* has vanished.

And so there are four.

They dare not linger. It is nearly midnight and soon the flood tide will slack. Hasler gives the signal to press on, keeping close to the west bank. Within minutes, a second tide race capsizes *Conger*. Again Hasler and Sparks turn back to help. The craft cannot be righted, so Sparks, on orders, holes her with his knife and she slips under. But what to do with Sheard and Moffat, helpless now, one clinging to the bow of *Catfish,* one to the bow of *Cuttlefish?* Hasler steers for land, making heavy weather of it. *Cuttlefish* follows, equally weighed down. A hundred yards offshore Hasler does what must be done. He explains to Sheard and Moffat that they are on their own now. They take it well, shake hands all around and strike out for shore.

And so there are three.

Time is of the essence, for dawn is near. By now the favoring tide is less strong, and the major obstacle of the patrol craft still lies ahead. *Catfish* and *Cuttlefish* rejoin *Crayfish* and the three race upriver at a flailing, back-breaking pace. Half-an-hour later they make out the blue light in the bows of the patrol craft. But two other gray shapes loom behind her, and the gap between them and the landing jetty at Le Verdon is only seventy yards. They had hoped to slip by one craft undetected. Three is an unforeseen hazard. Hasler must choose either to run the gauntlet between ships and jetty or make a wide detour to the east bank. Failing tide and flushing dawn sky decide for him. *Catfish* will shoot the narrow gap. If no alarm is raised, *Crayfish* and *Cuttlefish* will follow, well spaced.

Low in their cockpits, each using one blade only now for their burst of speed, Hasler and Sparks spring for the gap. They drive past the first ship and are abreast the second when a signal lamp aboard her starts chattering to shore. Figuring they have been spotted, Hasler and Sparks brace themselves for the probing searchlight and the lash of machine-gun bullets. But nothing more happens. Incredibly they are past the third patrol craft at last. Even the signal light has stopped blinking by now.

Fifty yards farther on they stop and gulp the night air. While they are still gulping, Lavers and Mills come surging out of the graying blackness. Of *Cuttlefish*, last in line, they see nothing. Now all thoughts and prayers are with the missing pair. Still *Cuttlefish* does not join them. That signal light starts blinking again. They hear a challenging shout. A single shot rips the night. Silence shuts down abruptly, oppressive now and full of waning hope. Whether McKinnon and Conway have been sunk or have turned gallantly away—after being spotted—to mislead the patrol craft, the alarm has surely been raised by now. The weapon of secrecy is gone.

And so there are two, where once there were six.

Bone-weary and sick at heart, the four survivors—Hasler and Sparks, Lavers and Mills—press on upstream. The situation looks bad-to-hopeless. The alarm is raised. Two thirds of their force is gone already. Bordeaux is still nearly seventy miles away. And their enemy the December dawn is coldly flooding the eastern sky. But Hasler, the exemplary one, is not the man to indulge in despair. He gives the familiar signal and sets a brisk pace.

As the day brightens and the river turns to blue, they come to an island. Not an ideal island, for there is little cover, but they cannot be too particular about where to picnic for the day. They drag their cockles across the mud and into the reeds. There they shake out their camouflage nets and crawl under them.

But sleep is not yet to be. Hasler, the lookout, curses a good round Anglo-Saxon curse, which rouses the others. They look where he is pointing and see a fleet of fishing boats bearing directly down on the island. The four scatter for better cover. From the shore side they hear voices and laughter. The island, it seems, is no island, but connects by causeway with the mainland. Across the causeway, laughing and skylarking, comes a crowd of women and children to join the fishermen, now beaching.

So it is to be the end after all. There is no chance of not being seen. Still, Hasler chooses the bold course.

"Bon jour," he says in his guttural, slightly Germanic French. *"Permettez que je vous présente mes amis. Nous sommes tous des soldats Anglais."*

One of the fishermen shrugs. "How can one be sure?" he asks, skeptical as only a Gascon can be.

"Please believe. Please don't mention seeing us."

"How can one be sure?"

"We are on a special mission. You must believe us."

"How can one be sure?"

The other fishermen are inclined to be friendly; their women are fearful and suspicious. Cigarettes and chocolates help. Finally, after a half-hour in which Hasler's eloquence is taxed to the full, the whole group moves off, promising not to give the raiding party away to the enemy.

Hasler resumes his interrupted watch. Lavers, Mills and Sparks slide into sleep. They would probably have slept less well, even in their exhausted state, had they known what the survivors learned many months later: the two extra patrol craft were part of a full-dress rehearsal of the Gironde defenses. German radar had even picked up *Tuna* when she surfaced in the Bay. The whole area is now fully alerted.

Yet the day passes quietly enough. River traffic seems normal. A plane or two drones overhead, too high to be searching. At dusk the little camp comes alive. Craft and arms are checked. Hasler briefs his men on the night's objective. To make up for the slow start, they must put at least twenty-two miles behind them. Hot tea is served, and hope again runs high. Twilight comes and with it the running of the tide across the mud flats. Squelching and slogging along, they drag their cockles for nearly a quarter of a mile to where the river is. At last they launch. Sweating, they climb into the cockpits. With powerful strokes Hasler and Sparks send *Catfish* shooting diagonally across stream; *Crayfish* is not far behind.

The plan is to hug the east bank, which their air maps tell them is higher and so gives better cover. The night is freezing cold and very dark. In seven hours the two cockles cover the twenty-two miles, zigzagging across river when necessary for better protection. The flashing lights which mark the shipping channel help to guide them. Once a convoy of seven ships goes by, heading upstream with a wash and a rush, rocking the cockles with its passing.

"More targets for us, boys," Hasler observes. Reassured, the men laugh and press on. By the time their objective is reached —the marshy area opposite the Médoc vineyards—the sea water is freezing on the cockpit covers, the men are drowsy and almost numb with cold. But Frankton is on schedule again. After a meal of tinned meat, biscuits, chocolate and compressed fruit, they dig in for the day.

Toward noon a fighter plane zooms them so low that they can see the swastikas on the wings and the pilot's face peering down at them. Other planes follow, beating both shores for stray Britishers. They know for certain now that the dragnet has been thrown.

But the day passes without further incident and again, with

dusk, they are waterborne. That night is memorable for one near-miss. A gray motorboat, showing no lights, goes hurtling by them, so close there was no time to hide. Surging along at twenty knots on some mysterious mission, the motorboat acts as a powerful depressant. As the frail canoes rock like corks in her wake, the four men wonder once again how they could have failed to be spotted.

Dawn comes suddenly, catching them short of the Bec d'Ambes, which is the low tongue of land at the place where the Gironde estuary divides into the rivers Garonne and Dordogne. They are forced to beach where they are, a small, flat, sandy island with almost no cover. Hasler makes a quick reconnaissance, comes back at speed with some unsettling news: the small island is a German ack-ack position. Jerries by the dozen are swarming around the gun site.

Again they shove off, and find somewhat better cover in the tall grass at the south end of the island. There, with double sentries posted, they sweat out their worst day, within sight and sound and smell of the enemy. Sitting in their boats, with the camouflage nets over them, they wait for the miracle of darkness to come. But time it seems has died. The day that started like a rocket has no end. They watch a German work party digging a ditch, and envy the men their freedom of movement. They smell cigarette smoke, and the urge to smoke is almost unbearable. Hasler doles out some rum and water. Occasionally they nibble on a biscuit. Toward noon a small, cold rain begins to fall, adding to their discomfort. Sometime in the afternoon they find themselves surrounded by a herd of cows. The cows study them patiently, incuriously. Finally they wander away.

At last it is dusk. By now the days and nights are beginning to form a pattern all their own. Time as such has become meaningless, something to be measured in freezing limbs, close escapes, cubes of chocolate and cups of boiling tea, rather than in hours and minutes. That night they enter the Garonne. The indelible moment is when they first see the pale glow of the city itself against the night sky. Bordeaux is within reach at last! There are other signs of civilization, too—a railway along the east bank, the sounds of motor traffic faintly from the west.

Four hours of paddling brings them to a jetty, blazing with light, where two fat merchantmen are loading. The sight is heartening. They know from their maps that they are at Bassens, some three miles below Bordeaux proper. They also know that, across from the jetty, there is a field of tall grass where they can hole up if necessary and make ready for the final phase.

It is in fact high time to go to cover. They dare not paddle past the jetty in the blaze of the loading lights. Looking for a likely spot, they nose along the opposite bank. Now, at long last, comes a real windfall. The field of grass turns out to be a reedy marsh. And into the marsh runs a three-foot-wide creek, into which they waste no time in turning. They are almost exactly opposite the jetty, yet perfectly screened by the tall reeds. And the noise from the jetty is such that for once they can even talk in natural voices.

The rest of the night passes in fitful sleep and high excitement. But by daybreak they have grown used to the nearness of the targets. By turns they sleep, more soundly now. They smoke and talk. They eat. They listen to the grunt of the cranes, loading the ships they have come so far to see. To their dismay one of them sails as they watch. Hasler promises other, riper targets. They speculate what the weather will be for their night of nights.

Gray and drizzling all day, the weather is another windfall, for the night, when it comes at last, is cloudy, with fitful rain and a slight, southerly breeze. The water is flat calm, another asset when it comes to the securing of limpet mines.

At seven they eat their last meal together. Then Hasler says to break out the limpets, of which each canoe has nine. The next hour is spent pleasantly inserting the fuses in their sockets. Hands tremble slightly over the delicate work, but from anticipation not fear. At last both acid bulbs and precautionary percussion caps are secured. The time setting is nine hours.

One final time Hasler briefs his men. The east bank belongs to Lavers and Mills. If necessary they will take their hungry *Cray-*

fish right into Bordeaux itself for likely targets. If none are found even there, whatever is tied up at the Bassens jetty is theirs for the sinking. They will scuttle *Crayfish* not later than five o'clock, and then escape by land. As for *Catfish,* the west bank is her hunting ground.

The major cocks his wrist. "It is now eleven o'clock. Time to get cracking."

At the entrance to the little creek they part, with mutual *good lucks* and *cheerios* and promises to meet soon at a favorite Portsmouth pub. Hasler and Sparks turn *Catfish* briskly to starboard and head for the growing halo of light where the seaport city lies. In exactly one hour they come to the dock area. They are suddenly in the midst of more ships than they had ever dreamed of, ships by the dozen tied up almost bow to stern.

The first one is a tanker. Fussy now, like someone choosing a meal at a good restaurant, Hasler shakes his head. Tankers have too many compartments for limpets to do a thorough job. In deep shadow, in the lee of the jetty lights, they work *Catfish* along the dark, outboard side of the line of ships. Clear to the end of the narrowing basin they go. The major, it seems, wants to read the whole menu before he decides what he is going to have. Finally, on the way back, he makes up his mind. The main course is a gray merchantman of some 15,000 tons. Using a magnetic holder, Sparks keeps the canoe firm under her stern. Hasler clicks on three limpets, under water. He uses a six-foot placing rod they have brought along for just such an eventuality.

Now they come to a big German Naval auxiliary (a *sperrbrecher*). They click a limpet on her hull. Suddenly from the deck above comes the clanging of hobnail boots. There is a shout. A dark figure leans over the rail. A beam of light plays on the canvas deck of *Catfish,* touches the remaining limpets in the cockpit. Hasler and Sparks freeze, bent almost double, and listen to small, metallic sounds on deck, as if the sentry were cocking his rifle. As they crouch, suspended in time, the tide begins to ebb. Gently, it carries them the length of the ship. The sentry follows them, clanging along the deck above, uncertain now, perhaps not overbright. Out of the flashlight's beam at last, *Catfish* goes to cover under the bow-flares of the *sperrbrecher*.

It is too good a chance to miss. In that anxious moment, while the puzzled sentry is still flashing his beam aimlessly out over the dark water, they click on two more limpets. Then, still feeling a little naked between the shoulder blades, they sprint for the next target.

They have three limpets left. The final victim is a cargo vessel which they had ignored on the way in. The reason for ignoring her was the fact that a small tanker was tied up outboard of her, making access to the hull difficult. Now, having reached the dessert course, with time and limpets running out, Hasler is less particular. He takes *Catfish* boldly between the two ships, securing a limpet on the stern of the larger one in passing. There is a bad moment when the ships swing closer at the whim of the tide. *Catfish*'s plywood bottom groans under the pressure. In a hopeful, hopeless gesture, Hasler pushes against the steel walls that are about to crush them, and Sparks follows suit. But luck rides with them still. The tide drifts the ships apart again. *Catfish* is able to back out of the trap. Once more, with no wasted time, they run between the two ships, placing one limpet to port on the tanker, one to starboard on the bigger ship as they pass.

Then, on the ebbing tide, they shoot downstream as if the devil were after them, as well he may be. Forty minutes later they hear the familiar, wickering cry of a gull. *Crayfish* materializes out of the murk. In some excitement Lavers explains how their side of the harbor had contained less than prime targets. So, as instructed, they have mined two ships tied up at the Bassens jetty.

Hasler makes a quiet, rather formal little speech. He thanks all three of his men for the job they have done and the trust they have placed in him. Everyone shakes hands. Then *Crayfish* turns eastward to carry out final orders. Mills waves his paddle in salute as he and Lavers vanish in the darkness.

Hasler and Sparks scuttle *Catfish* off the west bank and head inland.

Nine hours later the eighteen limpets, well and truly placed, detonate. Results: six ships sunk or so gravely damaged as to be useless for the rest of the war. Frankton is finished, mission accomplished.

The rest is silence and sadness. Lavers and Mills were captured and executed by the Germans. So were five of the other six who had been forced out of the operation in transit. One was drowned. Only Hasler and Sparks came home to tell the tale, working their way through to Gibraltar in five nerve-wracking months.

Yet the final lesson of Operation Frankton is one of comradeship and of surpassing valor. It contains the very essence of the offensive spirit, proving that nothing is impossible to those who greatly dare.

For their parts in Operation Frankton, Hasler was made a member of the Distinguished Service Order and Sparks was awarded the Distinguished Service Medal. The excellent 1956 motion picture, "Cockleshell Heroes", with José Ferrer and Trevor Howard, was based on Operation Frankton. Ferrer played a fictional counterpart to Hasler, and Hasler himself acted as a technical advisor to the production.

16

The Foxes Go to War

Ladislas Farago

In January, 1972, one of the great, secret stories of World War II broke at last: the story of how the British converted scores of German spies and saboteurs in England into double agents. In the words of reporter Alfred Friendly, "The British did more than blind the German wartime intelligence system in their country. They ran it."

The Twenty Committee, a special division of British Intelligence (MI.5), actually directed the show. Twenty is of course XX in Roman numerals, and so stands for Double-X or Double-Cross. Mostly men from academic life, the committee did a brilliant job—using a blend of fear and flattery—with the agents who fell into their hands.

A very high percentage of the one-hundred-odd captured German spies chose to work for the committee. A few stubborn or romantic ones with a high sense of duty refused, and were either executed or imprisoned. This merely made those who survived and remained "at large" seem more convincing than ever to home base.

By converting the German agents and still allowing them to ply their trade in freedom, the British could (a) feed false intelligence to the enemy, and (b) discover from the German requests to their agents exactly what they were most interested in finding out.

The British doled out bits of useless but convincing-sounding information to the double agents, or outright lies, such as where the D-day landings would supposedly take place. Proud of their spies' splendid work, more and more anxious to believe in the apparatus they themselves had created, the chiefs of German Intelligence swallowed the feedback data hook, line and sinker.

In 1944 a German agent who had defected to the British received two decorations in the same month: the German Iron Cross and the British MBE (Member of the Order of the British Empire)!

A most astonishing British achievement was the use of false sabotage to convince the Germans that one of their key men in England was really earning his pay. Here is the story, as told in Ladislas Farago's recent book, The Game of the Foxes. *Its publication played a considerable part in the British decision to release the official account of the Twenty Committee—as the afterword to this selection explains.*

THE double agent called "Zigzag" in Double-X was actually Eddie Chapman, the notorious British criminal whose specialty was safecracking. Wanted several times over by Scotland Yard in the 1930s, he had hoped to escape by moving to the Channel Islands, where he was arrested nevertheless. When the Germans occupied Jersey in the summer of 1940, they found Chapman languishing in jail, whence he promptly volunteered his services for espionage. He was accepted by the Abwehr,* which was satisfied that Eddie, who had ample reasons to loathe his native land, would make a reliable spy.

Actually Chapman never intended to become a traitor. He

* German Intelligence

reached Double-X in due course, traveling his own route. As soon as he arrived in England in December, 1942, he checked in with the police. The people at XX welcomed Eddie into the fold. Coming as he did for a specific assignment—to blow up the de Havilland aircraft plant at Hatfield—it became mandatory to carry it out, if Chapman was to return to the Germans as originally planned, where he could function as a British agent.

Eddie was left to his own devices to arrange the outrage. This was done in accordance with one of the cardinal principles of the organization that "a double agent should, as far as possible, actually live the life and go through all the motions of a genuine agent."

Chapman, or Zigzag, was allowed to visit the plant in Hatfield and steal explosives at Sevenoaks. He was physically on the spot in the dusk of a foggy winter evening at 6:00 on January 27, 1943, when the powerhouse of the de Havilland factory was to be blown to bits.

It took him so long to "accomplish the mission successfully," as he reported afterward to his case officer in Paris, because MI.5 needed time to make the wanton act appear as realistic as possible. It was taken for granted that the Germans would seek confirmation for Eddie's claim by reconnoitering from the air the damaged plant. An elaborate scheme was devised to show the Germans exactly what they expected to see.

The British had serving in the Camouflage Experimental Station of the Royal Engineers a major named Jasper Maskelyne, the scion of a famous dynasty of magicians and himself an accomplished make-believe artist. His job was to adapt on a huge scale the conjurer's tricks to the fields of battle. He invented dummy guns, dummy shell barrages, dummy tanks and even dummy men; hid naval harbors; launched a fleet of dummy submarines each 258 feet long; built a dummy battleship. Once, with the help of mirrors, he conjured up thirty-six tanks in the desert where in fact there was only one; and concealed the Suez Canal for part of its length.

Major Maskelyne and his "Magic Gang" also invented all

sorts of paraphernalia for secret agents. He was now called in by
MI.5 to devise the damage Eddie would be doing at the doomed
plant so as to look real on the photographs of the German reconnaissance planes.

Maskelyne used a big relief canvas to cover the entire roof of
the powerhouse. Painted on it in technicolor was the damage
that supposedly had been wrought below. In one of his magic
factories (of which he had three), he built papier-mâché dum-
mies that resembled the broken pieces of the generator. He strew
them, as well as chipped bricks, battered blocks of concrete,
smashed furniture and other such props all around the place,
until it looked thoroughly wrecked to observers from the air.

*The Luftwaffe sent a couple of JU-11 planes to verify Eddie's
report. What they brought back satisfied the worst skeptics in the
Abwehr. The damage seemed extensive.*

It was Maskelyne's masterpiece rather than Eddie's handiwork
which the German reconnaissance planes photographed. Chapman was allowed to go back in triumph, and was received like a
conquering hero in Paris. The Germans were so impressed with
his feat that they sent him to England again in June, 1944, this
time on a straight intelligence mission. At MI.5 he participated
in the massive deception campaign that upset German disposi-
tions at the time of the Normandy landings. This time, too, he
was permitted to return to his German friends, but by then the
Abwehr had been smashed and the Nazis who were now running
the intelligence establishment put him on ice. In November, 1944,
he was abruptly dropped by Double-X on grounds of what was
cryptically noted as "lack of security on the part of the agent."

*When, if ever, to tell what you did is one of the most controver-
sial aspects of the cloak-and-dagger world of Intelligence. The
British rule of thumb is never if there is any good reason not to.
For you may well want to use the same device or subterfuge
again. We tend to be a little more outgiving.*

In this connection, Farago's The Game of the Foxes *has an interesting history. As Farago, an old hand at spy-writing, tells us in his introduction to the book, he made a major discovery back in 1967. In the dark attic of the National Archives in Washington, Farago found a metal footlocker. It was sealed and had obviously not been opened in many years. Inside were a thousand roles of microfilm, a million pages of documentation. They turned out to be the records of the Abwehr office in Bremen, from which the German wartime activities in England had been directed. Captured by the United States Navy, they had been shipped to Washington, sifted and then left to gather dust for twenty years.*

Stitched together, there emerged a full account of what the Abwehr fervently believed was first-class espionage, and spectacular sabotage, in England. Not only were the code names of the German agents given—"Tricycle," "Giraffe," "Celery," "Dragonfly," "Zigzag,"—but the real names of the agents themselves.

When the British learned of Farago's find, they asked him and his publishers please not to make this material public. The request was politely brushed aside and the book appeared, to excellent reviews, in January, 1972.

Realizing that there was now nothing to be gained by further secrecy, the British released the official report by Sir John Masterson, mastermind of the Twenty Committee.

Originally written as a secret operational report back in 1945, the book is called The Double Cross System. *It appeared in February, 1972. In its cryptic, understated way, it is every bit as fascinating as Farago's gaudier prose. But in one area it is less revealing: there are no actual names of the agents. "Tricycle," "Giraffe," "Celery," "Dragonfly," "Zigzag" and the rest remain anonymous throughout.*

17

The Labyrinth

Walter Schellenberg

The Germans had their own successes in the field of double agentry, as well as in the closely allied department of dirty tricks. Not without pride, Walter Schellenberg, head of the Abwehr (German Intelligence) in the last year of the war, described some of them in his book, The Labyrinth. *Cheerfully ambitious, not brutal and neurotic like his many masters, Schellenberg is one of the less-unsavory figures of the Third Reich.*

The time he is writing about in these selections is 1940–1941, the early years of the war, when the Nazi star was still in its ascendancy.

ALTHOUGH in the occupied territories our security measures against the British Secret Service were not without considerable success, the gradually increasing resistance among the civil population in Holland, Belgium, France, and Norway made for a struggle that grew ever more bitter between our Counter-Intelligence and the British Secret Service. The British made full use of the resistance in order to gain footholds for their organization, even in the heart of Germany, by infiltrating the swollen ranks of forcibly recruited foreign labor. However, these underground resistance movements in the occupied countries were not only often traced by us, but were infiltrated by our own underground agents. There were even cases where resistance groups were jointly "directed" by the British and ourselves, and we were sometimes able to "order" from England radio equipment required by us, as well as currency and explosives (these, incidentally, were superior to our own) to be dropped by parachute. Sometimes it took no more than ten days for our "order" to be given and the necessary material to be parachuted into occupied territory. The British Secret Service thus became my never-failing currency reserve. The sums collected by me in this way ran into millions, though whenever the British discovered such treachery by their agents in foreign resistance movements they did not hesitate to liquidate them.

The situation in regard to the foreign currency and gold reserves of the Reich was always very strained, and the Secret Service had begun relatively early to forge the pound notes, banknotes, and gold rubles required for its own needs. It took two years to imitate the so-called grease-proof paper needed for English pound notes, and two paper mills, one in the Rhineland and the other in the Sudeten territory, were devoted solely to this task. The highly complicated process of engraving could only be started after the 160 main identifying marks had been determined; then the most skilled engravers in Germany were drafted, sworn to secrecy, and set to work in three shifts. Professors of mathematics worked out, with the help of complicated formulas, the system of British banknote registration numbers, so that our output was always one hundred to two hundred notes ahead of the Bank of England. These forgeries were so accurate that even the most cautious cashier in a bank would not have suspected anything.

A plan had been worked out to send bombers over Britain which, instead of dropping bombs, were to drop forged pound notes by the ton. The country was to be flooded with them. One can imagine what the result would have been. The government would probably have been forced to withdraw all treasury notes from circulation which, apart from the expense involved, would have placed a great burden on the administrative machinery. The population would have been entirely confused, and would have lost confidence in the Bank of England. However, this plan was dropped because the air above Britain was too well defended, and the fuel situation was critical.

We were assured of the technical perfection which our bank-note production had achieved when at the end of 1941 one of our men changed a large quantity of five- and ten-pound notes in Switzerland. Boldly he requested to have their validity checked, saying that he had acquired them on the black market. The Bank of England withdrew about ten per cent of the notes as forgeries; but the rest they confirmed as bona fide Bank of England notes. This was the sign for me to change over to mass production. . . .

I used the notes myself for the financing of enterprises abroad where I knew that I had to deal with cold-blooded and mercenary businessmen. The forged money was also used in the extensive trade of smuggled arms in which the Secret Service was employed. Wherever there was a resistance movement—in Italy, Greece, and also in France—the trade in such arms flourished, and we were able to acquire British and American weapons with our forged pound notes. Most of them were automatic hand weapons which we used in combating the partisan groups. It seemed ironical that the partisans should have sold us the very weapons which we used against them.

As the war drew on, life in the labyrinth of the German High Command became more and more nightmarish. Sabotage by assassination, at the highest level, was just one of the measures dreamed up by Hitler. His plan was relayed to Schellenberg via the Nazi Foreign Minister, Joachim von Ribbentrop, at the close of a routine conference in the Ministry.

"One moment, Schellenberg. I have a matter of considerable gravity to discuss with you. The utmost secrecy is essential—no one knows of this except the Führer, Bormann, and Himmler." Fixing me with a penetrating stare, Ribbentrop went on, "Stalin must be removed." I nodded, not knowing quite what I was supposed to say. He explained that the whole strength of the Russian regime lay in the ability and statesmanship of one man— Stalin*. Then he turned away and strode to the window. "I have intimated to the Führer my readiness to sacrifice myself for the sake of Germany. A conference will be arranged with Stalin, and it will be my mission to shoot down the Russian leader."

"Alone?" I queried. Suddenly he turned to me. "That is what the Führer said—one man alone cannot do it. The Führer asked me to name a possible accomplice"—here he stared at me intently—"and I named you." Hitler, he said, had directed him to discuss the matter with me alone and was sure that I would see the practical aspects of the plan in a realistic light. "And you see," Ribbentrop concluded, "that is the real reason for my sending for you."

I don't know what kind of face I made, but it can hardly have been an intelligent one. I felt utterly at a loss and more than a little confused.

Ribbentrop had thought everything out very carefully and now began explaining the details to me. Undoubtedly there would be an extremely close security check, and it would scarcely be possible to smuggle a hand grenade or a revolver into the conference room. But he had heard that my technical department had developed a revolver disguised as a fountain pen, from which one could shoot a heavy-caliber bullet with reasonable accuracy at a range of between eighteen and twenty-five feet. He had been told that it was so cleverly made that a superficial inspection would not reveal its real purpose. We should certainly be able to take it, or something like it, into the conference room —then all that would be needed would be a steady hand. . . .

At last he stopped talking. I had been watching him very closely. He had talked himself into such a state of enthusiasm that he seemed like a boy who had just enjoyed his first thriller.

* Up to June, 1941, when Hitler's armies drove east in a surprise onslaught, Germany and Russia were shaky allies.

But it was quite clear that I was confronted by a determined fanatic, and all he wanted was to hear me express my agreement with the plan and my immediate readiness to join him in it.

I considered the whole thing as the product, to put it mildly, of a neurotic and overstrained mind. But the situation was not a very comfortable one. I had to assume that every word I said would be reported at once to Hitler. At last, I thought I saw a way to wriggle out of the dilemma. I said that, though I considered the plan technically feasible, the whole project was based on whether we could succeed in bringing Stalin to the conference table. This, I thought, would be extremely difficult. . . . Therefore, I refused to have anything to do with any attempt at making contact with the Russians. . . . I suggested that he himself should try to establish the necessary basis for his plan and get Stalin to agree to come to a conference. Once he had accomplished this, I would be ready to stand by him both in word and deed.

"I will consider the matter further," Ribbentrop said, "and discuss it again with Hitler. Then I will call on you."

He never mentioned the matter to me again. But Himmler did, and was obviously very pleased about the reply I had given to Ribbentrop. However, after further discussion with Hitler, Himmler himself suggested that something on the same lines as Ribbentrop's plan should be attempted. Accordingly our experts constructed a special device for Stalin's assassination. It consisted of an adhesive charge of explosives which was about the size of a fist and looked like a lump of mud. The idea was for it to be attached to Stalin's car. The charge contained a fuse which was controlled by short wave and was so powerful that very little remained of the car on which we tried it out. The transmitter, which would automatically set off the explosives, was the size of a cigarette box and could send out an ultra-short wave for a distance of about seven miles.

Two members of the Red Army who had previously been exiled for a long time to Siberia, and one of whom was acquainted with a mechanic in Stalin's garage, accepted the assassination assignment. They were flown in a large transport aircraft at night and dropped near the place where our agents had informed us by short wave that Stalin had his headquarters. The two men jumped and, as far as we could ascertain, landed at the correct place; but that was the last we ever heard of them, although they both carried short-wave transmitters. I doubt very much whether they attempted to blow up Stalin. I feel it is more likely that they were either picked up soon after they landed, or that they reported their mission to the Soviet Secret Service (NKVD).

18

The Monastery

William J. Morgan

Before World War II, William Morgan, a young American doctor of psychology, was doing pioneer work in his field. Early in 1943 he was sent to England by the Office of Strategic Services. His specific job was to help the British select and train spies and saboteurs for undercover work in German-occupied countries.

After some months in England he began to grow restless for more active duty. His first step was to persuade his British masters to let him attend an advance course in sabotage. The "school" was in an ancient monastery, and his classmates were French patriots who had escaped their homeland. These classmates were in due course to be parachuted into the Maquis—the scrubby back country of France from which resistance groups were beginning to operate and from which they took their name.

With his professional skill he was already well ahead of the Frenchmen in the necessary arts, as this chapter from his book The OSS and I *amusingly tells:*

THE Maquis School was housed in a 14th-century priory, or monastery, in Sussex. It was built by the monks themselves of solid stone, but some later owner had added an incongrous wing of red brick. The chief instructor in this ancient building was, appropriately, a Shakespearean actor. His name was Vincent and he was a crack shot and a first-class beer-drinker. At the end of the course our class bought him a silver mug with a penny under glass at the bottom.

At the monastery we learned how to read maps, blow bridges, cut railroad ties, frisk suspects, and arrange recognition signals. We were also instructed in briefing and de-briefing and in the use of the Sten, Bren, Marlin, tommy gun, carbine, .45, .32 and bazooka. The course included a number of situation problems . . . some of which were carried out at night.

Our first night problem was to enter the heavily guarded monastery and remove a document—supposedly a Gestapo plan for crushing local opposition—from a desk in the drawing room. Once the plan was in our hands the problem was over. We did not have to fight our way out again. Even so, we ran some risk, for we were forbidden to beat up or otherwise mistreat the unsuspecting guards, while they were quite likely to shoot any intruder or clobber him over the head. To make things harder for us, the instructors drove us out in a lorry ten miles from the monastery and let us off half an hour before sunset on a lonely farm road. Too late it occurred to us, as we watched them drive off, that we could have seized the lorry and driven back, leaving the instructors to hike the ten miles.

As usual, we had been instructed to keep out of sight of passers-by, so we left the road and walked along the hedgerows through the fields. As darkness fell we stepped into bogs of mud, bumped into trees, trod on fallen branches whose crackle alarmed the standing cattle and scattered them mooing in all directions. Two of the students who were rather nervous tried to persuade the rest to crawl all the way on their bellies. At that rate we should have taken a week to reach the monastery and arrived plastered with cowdung.

As we plodded along we discussed how we could enter the building. The French students were set on entering by a window.

I was against it, because the monastery windows were shut every night and, like all windows in blacked-out England, so heavily curtained that, even when the light was on inside, it was impossible to see from outside whether anyone was in the room. But the students had an *idée fixe* about the window and refused to consider any alternative.

The drawing room was on the first floor so they decided to force an entry through one of the windows in the dormitory above, on the chance that the instructors would not be guarding the second floor. One man remembered seeing an extension ladder in the repair barn. I pointed out the difficulty of carrying it unseen and unheard to the main building, and also the likelihood that the instructors would guess our reasoning and be waiting for us on the second floor. I asked leave to go ahead and scout the area, but the leader of the group had a better idea. I was to constitute myself a one-man mission to capture the document, while the rest followed their ladder-and-window plan. In this way the group's chances of success were doubled.

I set off at a brisk walk along the road toward the monastery, which was still eight miles distant. There was no moon but my eyes had grown used to the darkness and I walked almost as fast as in daylight, in spite of occasional painful jars when I stepped into potholes in the road. Half a mile from my destination I began to keep close to trees and bushes, and to watch for sentries and listen for footsteps.

The grounds were enclosed by a red brick wall, a foot thick and covered with vines. The gate was guarded day and night, and sentries constantly patrolled the wall. To reach the building I had to pass within this cordon of guards. Grasping the vines, I slowly worked my way to the top of the wall and peered over. A dense hedge screened me from behind, and for ten minutes I stayed on the wall and scanned the grounds, but I could see nothing that looked like a sentry. So I eased myself down on the inside. There was no invisible sentry waiting to blow my head off, and I made my way very cautiously and noiselessly toward the main building. Sometimes I walked crouching over like a chimpanzee, sometimes I wriggled forward on my belly. I contrived always to keep some bush or tree between me and the building until I reached the monastery graveyard, where I could hide behind the tombstones. The British had certainly not wasted any granite or marble in that graveyard. The stones were no bigger than headmarkers in a military cemetery. A brick pathway led through the graveyard and across the lawn to the front door of the monastery. Suddenly I heard the unmistakable *clop-clop* of hobnailed boots smacking on the bricks. A sentry. Was he after me? I froze behind a laurel bush as he marched by, and then resumed my creeping progress. Fifteen minutes later he clopped past again. This must be his beat.

Instead of going straight toward the monastery, I began to move in a circular direction which would bring me around to the front of the building. All the while I was turning over in my mind possible ways of entering it, but none seemed promising. Outside the front door was another brick walk leading to a circular driveway, and in the middle of the circle was a clump of shrubs. I inched my way to this clump and concealed myself there. Now I could watch the front door and the sentries walking their beats and stopping to exchange a few words as they passed each other.

So far so good, but what was I to do next? For half an hour I lay in the shrubbery and tried to devise a way of entering the monastery unseen. The stretch between me and the front door was in full view of the guards and without a patch of cover.

As I lay fishing around in the depths of my mind for an answer I brought to the surface a piece of advice that Colonel Vincent had given us:

"Always try the obvious way first. Look for the key under the doormat. Don't be furtive. Don't climb in at a window when the door is open, however illegal your entry may be."

Just then a whistle blew. Had I been spotted by the sentries? Or had they seen the rest of my group? I did not think so. I had left the group three hours ago, and at their laborious pace they could scarcely have caught up with me yet. *Clop-clop, clop-clop,*

clop-clop, went six pairs of heavy British boots as six sentries assembled in front of the door, presented arms, lined up in twos and marched into the house. It was the changing of the guard. As far as I could see not a single sentry remained outside.

The plan flashed into my mind. I knew exactly what I was going to do. It was as simple as Vincent's advice. I stole quickly up to the house and flattened myself behind a brick projection in the wall alongside the front door. Next moment six guards walked smartly out of the door and down the pathway. As the last two guards went past me I stepped out, caught the door before it slammed shut, and slipped inside.

To my right along the corridor lay the open door of the guardroom. I walked past it. No one challenged me. Quickening my pace, I turned left into another corridor and flung open the drawing room door. All the instructors were sitting there with drinks in their hands. I waved my pistol at them.

"Don't move! Don't make a sound!"

Still keeping my pistol pointed at them, I walked over to the desk and picked up the "Gestapo Plan," which was neatly spread out there.

"Okay, Morgan, your side wins. But where are the others?"

I explained that I was a one-man advance unit of the team, and was about to set off to tell the others that the problem was over, but the instructors deterred me.

"Don't spoil it for them; it isn't fair. Let them have a chance too. They may have a good plan."

So we all sat up and waited, and waited. At half-past three we heard whispering and scuffling on the lawn outside. A few moments later there was a crash of splintering glass upstairs followed by an agonized scream. *"Non! Non! NON!"* and then a heavy thud on the lawn. We all rushed out through the French window. The team had stuck to their misguided plan of forcing an entry through the dormitory window on the second floor. The sleepers there were awakened by the crash of glass and one of them, a British sergeant, ran to the window and shoved the ladder, man and all, away from the window and sent it toppling down onto the grass. Mercifully the Frenchman fell clear of the ladder and was only bruised and shaken.

Why have I described in such detail a long-ago wartime training problem? Am I trying to glorify myself, and show how much cleverer I was than those naïve Frenchmen? Far from it. The point I am trying to make is this. Wars come and wars go, but the mechanisms of the human intellect do not change. When faced with a practical problem our minds work in much the same way whether we are organizing a resistance movement or any other enterprise. My training as a psychologist had taught me the basic principles of learning and also the importance of firsthand observation.

First, the ground is thoroughly explored. Then there is a period of casting about in the mind for possible answers. It is important to keep flexible—not to freeze on to the first solution that offers itself. The French team thought first of the window plan and fell so much in love with it that they were blind to its defects. The mind must grope around, feeling this way and that, testing solutions and discarding them until the right one is found. It is no use trying to hurry. Before attempting to enter the monastery, I made a very careful reconnaissance and then spent some time thinking over the problem. I managed to solve it, not by any flash of genius but by patience and good luck.

The same advice came in handy on another problem, in which messages had to be passed from one man to another at a meeting place, a hut on the local golf course. Some students would creep and crawl all over the fairway, and even crouch for hiding in bunkers at the risk of being hit by a golf ball. There was a policeman patrolling the road which ran across the course, and the students seemed drawn toward his beat like moths to a candle. Our team, on the contrary, made no effort to slink about unobserved. We dressed up in sports clothes, hired or borrowed bags of clubs, and strolled openly over the course without arousing the least suspicion. It was another instance of walking in through the front door.

The French students were very kind to me. Since I was older

and more experienced they gave me *carte blanche* to act as a one-man team in the group's interest whenever I felt like it. In this way I was able to try out my own ideas even if they did not appeal to the group, while they learned from their own successes and mistakes without any short-circuiting from me. Vincent was not told of this informal agreement, which he probably would not have approved. At any rate, he began to grow more and more irritable toward me. Late one afternoon he briefed us on the evening's problem—to blow up a motor pool. The demolitions, he said, were already in our possession, carefully cached underneath a wooden trap door which opened from the orchard on to a stairway leading down to the monastery cellars. The motor pool itself was only half a mile away, but we were to be driven in a lorry to the nearest town, eight miles off, receive detailed instructions there, walk back to the monastery, pick up the demolitions and go on to the motor pool. The pool was closely guarded, and we were to use great caution there, but until we reached it, Vincent assured us, we should expect no difficulty.

Somehow this briefing had a fishy smell. I wondered if Vincent were hinting that we ought always to expect the unexpected. And I was not especially anxious to tramp eight miles in the dark through wheat and barley fields if I could help it. So immediately after dinner I slipped away through the shadows of dusk to the orchard. For a while I hid behind an apple tree and peered this way and that in search of a guard. Seeing none, I crept on all fours, as fast as I could without making any noise, through the long grass until I reached the trap door. Very slowly I eased my hand under the edge of the trap door and felt around for the demolitions. They were there, all right, and by fingering them gently I discovered that they were in a bag tied by wire to a beam underneath the trap door. It looked as though the instructors had tricked us by wiring the bag. If so, the mechanism would be either push or pull, more likely the latter, since a man grabbing the bag would naturally pull it toward him. I had no wire-clippers so I tried to break the wire by twisting it back and forth, not knowing whether the booby-trap would be an electric shock, a horrendous noise, a fragmentation grenade or a gun shooting me. The Maquis School played rough. I broke one wire and had to hold up the bag—a good twenty pounds—with my right hand while I twisted the remaining wire with my left. I must have jerked it, for suddenly there was a loud explosion about thirty feet behind me, startling me out of my skin and showering me with dirt and stones. In the brief bright light of the explosion I saw a soldier running toward me. I gave one final tug at the demolitions bag, but it stayed firm, so I let go of it and began to run, bent double, from one tree trunk to another until I reached a side entrance to the monastery and ducked inside. Meanwhile students and instructors were galloping out of the back door and into the orchard. Most of them thought that enemy planes had dropped a small bomb. I found the dormitory empty except for one Frenchman lying on his bed. He looked me over and asked cooly, "Was it you, Morgan?" I told him it was, but that he, of course, understood that I had been in the dormitory all the time. *"Entendu,"* he replied. In a few minutes the students streamed back, and with them Colonel Vincent and the soldier whom I had glimpsed in the orchard. "Was it him?" cried Vincent, pointing dramatically at me. "I couldn't say, Colonel. It was dark and he was running. I didn't spot him while he was working on it." Vincent was furious. "Morgan, you're the only one who would pull a dirty dodge like this. I know it, because I've worked with you bloody Americans and this is the kind of thing that only a Yank would do. You did it!" He appealed to the Frenchman, who at first seemed unable to grasp what all the fuss was about, but finally grunted, "Why are you yelling? He's been up here ever since dinner."

I was herded into the lorry with the others, Vincent abusing me all the while and calling me a yellow-bellied rat and a number of other names. Just as we were ready to start, I lost my temper and shouted back, "You Boy Scout! You claim to be teaching us to use our wits, and when we do, you squawk, 'It's not cricket!' Of course I did it. Why didn't you guard the place? Why don't you go yell at your guard for being asleep on duty?" We were still shouting at each other when the lorry drove away.

An instructor traveled with us to the town of Midhurst and

gave us some further briefing about the motor pool before he dropped us off. As we trudged back across the fields I reflected that Vincent would be determined to catch me as soon as I appeared on the scene, so I worked out a plan with the others whereby I would be the decoy. When we reached the monastery grounds I took off my socks, put them on over my shoes, and crept stealthily across the orchard. Two of the Frenchmen followed about fifteen feet behind me, with even greater stealth. As I reached the trap door, Vincent and another instructor sprang out at me with drawn guns. I stood up straight, flung up my hands and cried, "Don't shoot, don't shoot! You've got me. I surrender!"

Big grins overspread the faces of Vincent and his companion. They called a third instructor to come over and look at Morgan, the smart operator who had been caught red-handed. I was ordered to walk to the house.

"But I can't see very well," I complained. "Can't one of you lead the way?"

They merely laughed at my obvious ruse and flashed their flashlights on the path ahead of me. I slowed down in the hope that one of them would overtake me so I could try to snatch his weapon, but a voice behind me said, "Hurry up, Morgan. We know all the tricks. Don't try to get funny with us." They walked me up to the door of an old repair shop. I knew this place. It was cluttered with old paint cans, boards and saws. There was only one small window, no light, and five steps leading down from the door. I refused to go in, protesting that I would break my neck in the dark. The other two instructors walked off, apparently bored with the argument, and left me arguing with Vincent. He commanded me to enter, so I pushed the door inward, while I grumbled that it would be the worse for him if I broke my neck. Vincent was close behind me. I pretended to stumble over the threshold and cursed Vincent loudly as I slipped behind the door. He took a step in after me and I slammed the door in his face with all my might, knocking the flashlight out of his hand. I heard it break on the ground. I bolted the door on the inside, ran across to the window, which to my astonishment was unbolted, climbed out, ran across the grounds, and joined my group at the motor pool. Everything had gone smoothly for them. The two Frenchmen who followed me had removed the demolitions bag without trouble. They had wire-cutters ready, but the bag had not been wired.

The French students had gained experience and confidence since the early problems. They had devised an ingenious plan for dealing with the sentries at the motor pool. Two men fired revolvers on one side of the pool and a few moments later two more men fired on the other side. The sentries were distracted by this double diversion and it was easy for the rest of us to enter the pool and "blow it up," i.e., blow the tread off a derelict tank.

When we returned to the monastery Vincent greeted us with jovial friendliness and congratulated us on a good performance. You would never have guessed there had been ill-feeling between us. And yet I am ready to swear that, actor as he was, his fury with me and his glee at my capture were not feigned. Did he decide he had been unfair to me, and deliberately let me escape from the shed? Or did the other instructors put pressure on him? I shall never be sure.

Dr. Morgan parachuted into Occupied France, as he had so very much wanted to do. He organized a band of over five hundred guerrillas with marked success. By the war's end—still under forty—he had risen to the rank of lieutenant colonel.

19

Sabotage by Assassination

Fabian von Schlabrendorff

A great deal has been written about the historic attempt to kill Adolf Hitler on July 20, 1944. On that date a bomb placed in his East Prussian headquarters by Col. Claus von Stauffenberg exploded violently, killing four people. But Hitler himself was only bruised, and driven to furious revenge.

Here is an account of a less-known plot which took place over a year before. Its prime mover, Fabian von Schlabrendorff, was an aristocratic East Prussian who had hated Hitler from the start of his rise to power. Von Schlabrendorff and a close friend, Maj. Gen. Henning von Tresckow, were both stationed at Smolensk, the headquarters of Army Group Center on the eastern front in Russia.

Their brave attempt rates inclusion here, although not an act against a military *enemy. When assassination or kidnapping is designed to interfere with a specific war effort or a political program it is an act of sabotage.*

AROUND noon on March 13, 1943, Hitler arrived at Smolensk. . . .

Tresckow and I had conceived a plan to eliminate him by smuggling a time bomb aboard his plane. In this way, the stigma of an assassination would be avoided, and Hitler's death could be attributed—officially, at least—to an accidental plane crash.

Although Tresckow was especially ill-fitted for the odious and repugnant role of a sneak assassin, he accepted the responsibility of doing the "dirty job" of getting Hitler out of the way. No one except his most intimate friends knew what this decision had cost him. Once he had made up his mind, however, he hesitated no longer, but began to look around for the necessary materials. Several months before Hitler's visit to the Army Group Center's headquarters, Tresckow had managed to get explosives through Col. Baron von Gersdorff, a staff officer of the Army Group, who could obtain such material without arousing suspicion. Gersdorff, although solidly anti-Nazi, was not yet involved in the plot to kill Hitler. Here, however, was a person of such complete integrity that we did not hesitate to approach him.

Trying to find the right kind of explosive was quite a problem. We soon realized that the types used by the German army were not at all suited to our purpose, for the fuse that ignited them made a slight hissing noise which might have been noticed by some alert bystander.

We finally decided on British explosives of the plastic type and British fuses. British planes had been dropping large amounts of such material over Germany and German-held territory, in an effort to equip Allied agents for acts of sabotage. Naturally, a good deal of this material fell into the hands of our own military. . . .

Before doing anything else, Tresckow and I had to make enough tests with these bombs so that we would be familiar with every detail—familiar enough so that we could almost handle them in our sleep. Most of our tests were successful, and proved the explosive to be amazingly powerful. Our main difficulty, for we possessed no technical knowledge in this field, was to find out exactly what had gone wrong in the few tests that had not worked out as expected. In all these cases, the moment of explosion had been much—and to us unaccountably—delayed, thus throwing off our timing. Noticing that this had happened only with the bombs we had tested outdoors, we engaged in conversation with members of the Pioneer squad, casually bringing up the question of British explosives. We soon found out that the Russian winter had been responsible for the unsatisfactory results of some of our outdoor tests, because extreme cold tended to slow down the action of the chemical designed to eat through the wire holding down the firing pin, which, on being released, would strike the detonator and set off the explosion.

After we had concluded our experiments we went ahead with preparations for the assassination. Tresckow thought of a way to camouflage the bomb. Taking two packets of explosive—just to make doubly sure—we fashioned them into a parcel which looked like two bottles of Cointreau—the only brandy that comes in square bottles. The wrapping was arranged in such a way that the fuse could be triggered from the outside without disturbing the package. On the morning of March 13, I took the bomb to my quarters and locked it away. Kluge * and Tresckow drove to the airport to meet Hitler, who, as usual, arrived with an incredibly large entourage including both his personal cook and his private physician.

The official conference with Hitler took place in Kluge's quarters, with Tresckow and the other commanders of the Army Group Center present. It would have been easy to smuggle the bomb into that room, but had we done so, we would have killed not only Hitler, but all the other army leaders, including Kluge, whom we needed for the success of the coup.

After the official meeting, lunch was served in the officers' mess. Once again the fact that the bomb would have killed everybody in the room forbade an attempt at that time.

Hitler was served a special meal, every part of which had been prepared by his personal cook. It was tasted before his eyes by

* Field Marshal Guenther von Kluge, the Army Group Commander.

his physician, Professor Morell. The entire procedure was reminiscent of an Oriental despot of a bygone age. Watching Hitler eat was a most revolting spectacle. His left hand was placed firmly on his thigh; with his right hand he shoveled his food, which consisted of various vegetables, into his mouth. He did this without lifting his right arm, which he kept flat on the table throughout the entire meal; instead, he brought his mouth down to the food. He also drank a number of non-alcoholic beverages, which had been lined up beside his plate. On his orders, no smoking was allowed after the meal.

During the luncheon, Tresckow approached Col. Heinz Brandt, a member of Hitler's entourage, and asked him casually whether he would be good enough to take along a small parcel containing two bottles of brandy for Gen. Helmuth Stieff of the High Command at headquarters. Brandt readily agreed.

Now everything was arranged. Earlier that morning, I had telephoned Captain Gehre, our liaison officer in Berlin, and had given him the code word which meant that Operation Flash—Hitler's assassination—was about to be set off. We had agreed on this way of communicating, and I knew that Gehre would immediately inform Dohnanyi, who in turn was to advise General Oster of the developments. These two were then to get everything ready for the second, vital step of seizing the capital.

After lunch Hitler started back to the airport, accompanied by both Kluge and Tresckow, while I fetched the bomb from my quarters and drove to the airport. Upon my arrival there, I waited until Hitler had dismissed the officers of the Army Group Center and was about to board his plane. Looking at Tresckow, I read in his eyes the order to go ahead. With the help of a key, I pressed down hard on the fuse, thus breaking the small bottle of corrosive chemical and triggering the bomb, and handed the parcel to Colonel Brandt who boarded the plane shortly after Hitler. A few minutes later both Hitler's plane and that carrying the other members of his party, escorted by a number of fighter planes, started back to East Prussia. Fate now had to take its course.

Tresckow and I returned to our quarters, from where I again called Gehre in Berlin and gave him the second code word, indication that Operation Flash was actually under way.

We knew that Hitler's plane was equipped with special devices designed to increase its safety. Not only was it divided into several separate cabins, but Hitler's own cabin was heavily armor plated, and his seat was outfitted with a parachute. In spite of all this, Tresckow and I, judging from our experiments, were convinced that the amount of explosive in the bomb would be sufficient to tear the entire plane apart, or at the very least to make a fatal crash inevitable.

With mounting tension we waited for news of the "accident," which we expected shortly before the plane was to pass over Minsk. We assumed that one of the escort fighters would report the crash by radio. But nothing happened.

After waiting more than two hours, we received the shattering news that Hitler's plane had landed without incident at the airstrip at Rastenburg in East Prussia, and that Hitler himself had safely reached headquarters.

We could not imagine what had gone wrong. I called Gehre in Berlin immediately, and gave him the code word for failure of the assassination. Afterward, Tresckow and I, stunned and shaken by the blow, conferred on what our next move should be. We were in a state of indescribable agitation; the failure of our attempt was bad enough, but the thought of what discovery of the bomb would mean to us and our fellow conspirators, friends, and families, was infinitely worse.

Finally, after considerable deliberation, Tresckow decided to telephone Brandt, and asked casually in the course of the conversation whether the Cointreau had been given to General Stieff. When Brandt replied that he had not yet had the chance to do so, Tresckow told him that the wrong parcel had been sent by mistake, and asked him to hold it until the following day, when it could be exchanged for the one Stieff was supposed to get. Brandt's pleasant answer made it clear that at least the bomb had not been discovered. We realized that it had to be retrieved at all costs, but as Stieff at that time was not yet a member of the conspiracy, we had to keep him out of it, and could only pray that the bomb would not go off belatedly and before we could get hold of it.

On some military pretext, I flew to headquarters the following day in one of the regular courier planes and immediately went to see Brandt. As I exchanged parcels with him—the one I had brought along actually *did* contain two bottles of brandy—I felt my blood running cold, for Hitler's aide, serenely unaware of what he was holding, handed me the bomb with a grin, juggling it back and forth in a way which made me fear a belated explosion. Forcing myself to display an outward calm which I most certainly did not feel, I took the bomb and immediately made my way to the nearby railroad junction at Korschen, where a special train of the High Command was scheduled to leave for Berlin that night.

As soon as I arrived in Korschen I boarded the train and went to the sleeping compartment that had been reserved for me. Locking the door behind me, I began gingerly to open the deadly package with a razor blade. After gently removing the wrapping, I could see that the condition of the explosive was unchanged. Carefully dismantling the bomb, I took out the fuse and examined it. The reason for the failure immediately became clear. Everything but one small part had worked as expected. The bottle with the corrosive fluid had been broken, the chemical had eaten through the wire, the firing pin had been released and had struck forward—but the detonator had not ignited! One of the few duds that had slipped past a British inspection was responsible for the fact that Hitler did not die on March 13, 1943.

Mingled disappointment and relief flooded through me as I looked down at the dismantled bomb. Disappointment, because our long and carefully laid plans had ended in failure through no fault of ours; and relief, because we had at least been able to prevent discovery of the plot, with all the terrible consequences such a discovery would have brought in its train.

Von Schlabrendorff was imprisoned for his part in the July 20 bomb plot the following year, but survived. Tresckow, much more deeply involved, committed suicide immediately after its failure.

20

Pin-stripe Saboteur

Charles Wighton

His code name was "Robin." He was a Swiss, a forty-seven-year old businessman when World War II began. He is a fine example of the amateur type of underground worker, in the sense that his cover was so perfect that none of the professionalism showed on the surface. In actual fact he commanded a regiment of resistance workers in France. Using his organizing skills, he ran the regiment like the president of a company. And it throve. The number and variety of deeds he planned and carried out were unmatched by any single agent on the Allied side. With the help of a beautiful Russian girl called Tania, later captured and executed by the Germans, he was able to put the flow of arms and explosives dropped from England to spectacular use. (SOE, the outfit mentioned in the text, is short for Special Operations Executive, the branch created by Prime Minister Churchill to direct all undercover action against the Axis powers.)

Although he earned some twenty decorations, "Robin" remains a shadowy figure by his own wish. Charles Wighton, an excellent English writer, finally persuaded him to tell some of his

adventures. Here are selections from two chapters of Pin-stripe
Saboteur, *which was published in England in 1959.*

PREPARATIONS for the Second Front formed only one side of
"Robin's" activities during the earlier months of 1943. At the
same time he was planning, directing and sometimes personally
participating in a series of sabotage operations stretching across
northeastern France from the border of the Saar to the Channel
coast.

And in everything he did he never forgot the advice given him
two years before by an officer of British Intelligence to use
"economy of force."

Such a principle was completely in accord with his basic instincts. For in his years of highly successful commercial activity
he had always worked on the principle that there should never
be any greater outlay than was strictly justified by the anticipated result. In addition, he had been something of an expert in
obtaining high profits for a small outlay, and he felt that what
had been sound for francs was even more important with human
lives. And he strongly deprecated any operation, however spectacular, which involved big risks to the participants without cor-
responding damage to the German war effort.

In all this he found Tania an apt and able pupil. Ballet dancer
though she was, he found that she was that rare combination—
lovely and intelligent and still more, daring. In addition she had
a precise and logical mind which made her a perfect staff officer
—able to translate into tangible terms the aggressive and sometimes overimaginative ideas which flowed from "Robin" almost
nonstop.

Tania not only helped to plan sabotage. In the face of constant protests and sometimes threats from Robin and the others,
the nineteen-year-old Russian Jewess persisted in carrying out
some of the most daring operations on her own.

It was about this time that Robin, from his groups which were
still purveying a steady flow of intelligence information, discovered that there was a bottleneck in a vital article of German in-

dustrial equipment—belting. The great factories of the Ruhr and Silesia, working night and day under the driving force of Reichsminister Speer, were literally swallowing industrial belting. The factories of the Reich could not produce enough. Speer, therefore, had ordered one of the main French plants specializing in such equipment to produce the extra belting which German industry required.

Robin, as coldly calculating as ever, quite simply decided that this French factory must be put out of production. And he was undeterred when he discovered that the owner of the plant was a French industrialist who, although obeying the German order to produce the belting, was certainly no *collaborateur* and was in fact believed occasionally actually to have helped the Underground.

Robin, therefore, using his own peacetime identity, asked for an appointment with the industrialist. And after the usual exchange of compliments he announced quite bluntly, "Monsieur, I have come to tell you that your plant is to be sabotaged." The industrialist went white.

"What do you mean, Monsieur?" he stuttered, for no man likes to think of his factory in ruins. "And who is going to do it?" he continued nervously.

"I am sorry, Monsieur," said Robin, "but I am. But as I know you are a good Frenchman I have taken considerable risks to come here and tell you what the Resistance is going to do. And I want to know if you will help."

"Help you, Monsieur, to sabotage my own factory?" asked the by now quite speechless industrialist.

"Yes, Monsieur," said Robin, "for here is the problem. We of the Resistance can easily enough sabotage your factory—by blowing it all sky-high. But that is wasteful and moreover we know you are a loyal Frenchman. So I have come to ask you for expert advice, Monsieur. How can we sabotage your factory so that it goes out of production for months, but doesn't do too much damage to the plant itself. You are the best man to tell us that and so I have come to ask your help."

The industrialist shook his head and wrung his hands.

"You ask a great deal, Monsieur," he said to Robin, "but I must admit you are a brave and honest man to come and tell me. And so although I feel I am tearing out my own heart—*I will help you to sabotage my own plant.*"

Robin seized the man's hand and shook it. "We shall not forget you, Monsieur, in better days. France can be proud of you."

And then in the privacy of the industrialist's office the two men sat down and planned the sabotage. The industrialist, after showing Robin plans and diagrams explained that there was one machine in the main manufacturing department which if wrecked would put the whole plant out of operation for several months. If an abrasive was introduced into this machine it would be hopelessly destroyed. The industrialist already had had difficulty about spare parts for this section of the plant, and he assured Robin that none could be obtained in France. And he added one other vital fact—this department was staffed largely by girls.

Robin promised him that within a few days he would send a girl to him who was looking for a job, and that the industrialist need know nothing more.

On his return to Rue Cambon, Robin told Tania of his bargain with the industrialist, and before he could say more she announced, "O.K. I'll take the job." Robin put up every possible objection but by this time he had discovered that Tania's will power was the equal of his own. And reluctantly he gave her permission.

Next day, Tania, dressed like a typical French factory girl, left for the factory, after agreeing with Robin that the necessary sabotage abrasive should be delivered to her in a week.

As arranged, the industrialist instructed his works manager to give the girl a job, and Tania was sent to the shop where the vital machine was. As she had predicted to Robin, Tania soon had the French workers—and particularly the male foreman— at her beck and call. And when the specially prepared abrasive reached her a few days later, she began to collect it in her locker in the factory.

Within another week Tania reckoned she had enough abrasive in the factory and one day after she had been working at the plant for about a fortnight, she told her friends that she felt very tired. At the midday break she told her workmates that she would just stay in the shop where she was working. Everyone by this time knew the small dark girl with the flashing black eyes, and no one paid the slightest attention as she sat down alongside the vital machine to eat her meager wartime sandwiches.

As soon as all her workmates had disappeared, Tania, who had the abrasive in a large shopping bag, set to work. In the ninety minutes at her disposal she liberally smeared as much of the inside of the machine as possible with the British-manufactured abrasive. She had just finished when her workmates returned. Tania in the meantime had liberally powdered her face with a near-white powder and she announced she felt sick. She told the foreman that she was so unwell that she must go home —and disappeared.

She was in a train on her way back to Paris when the whole vital machine ground to a standstill. Inquiries showed that the machine had been sabotaged with abrasive but the girl who had spent the lunch hour in the machine shop had disappeared.

The industrialist wrung his hands and told the Germans what he thought of the *terroristes*. But he felt a considerable degree of inner satisfaction when, as he had predicted to Robin, he discovered that no spare parts for the machine were available in France. The Germans were informed and specialists were sent from Dortmund to find out what was required.

With German bureaucratic delays and journeys between Paris and the Ruhr it took the Germans nearly three months to manufacture the necessary parts and it was several more weeks before they were installed and the plant was once again in production. In the interval, the shortage of belting in Germany had reached a critical point and armament production was affected.

Emboldened by the success of this singlehanded operation Tania clamored for more "out-of-town jobs," and when Robin decided to attack the great railway engineering sheds at Lagny, where more of the main-line locomotives on the eastern section of the French railways were serviced, Tania insisted on doing the job.

Dressed in a beret and belted raincoat and with far too much make-up, the pretty Jewess began to frequent the cafés near the Lagny locomotive depot. She soon became friendly with the drivers and engine cleaners and, playing the coquette with great skill, she was soon invited—against all regulations—into the depot itself. After a few days she became an accepted figure around the locomotive sheds as she trudged around with a large shopping bag in her hand.

The bag contained a special jelly which she dropped into the water tanks of the locomotives as she toured the sheds. In due course the water system became clogged, resulting in loss of power, and finally blocked. In some of the more successful cases the boiler blew up for want of water. And the German Security Officers who were summoned never found a satisfactory explanation for the curious series of locomotive breakdowns and explosions which dogged the important eastern section of the French railways for weeks thereafter.

Tania's next exploit was at an alcohol factory on the outskirts of Paris, where Robin had discovered that the Germans had concealed one of their main petrol dumps for the area. Again adopting the role of a coquette looking for work, Tania succeeded in infiltrating into the petrol dump and making a full-scale reconnaissance. She mapped the layout of the main petrol tanks and discovered the whereabouts of the main control valves, where individual parts of the installation could be isolated from the rest in case of fire.

But Robin forbade her to go any farther. It was a sabotage group with Robin in command which, a few nights later, broke into the dump and, after boring holes into the walls of main tanks, inserted British explosives connected to concealed time fuses.

Robin and his men had just returned to central Paris when the whole city was shaken by one of the greatest explosions of the war and heavy, oily smoke began to drift over the city from the direction from which they had come.

But Robin himself tends to discount his sabotage operations as "just normal routine affairs" when he discusses them today. "The same sort of thing was going on all over France at the same time and to be quite honest it all became rather boring after a time," was his postwar comment.

Robin's nonchalance toward the increasingly frequent sabotage operations carried out either under his personal leadership or under his direct orders, during the late spring of 1943, betokened no indifference to the care with which the enterprises were planned. On the contrary. For all his sabotage projects, as in the espionage enterprises in which he had gained such success previously, were planned down to the last detail in a way which would have brought joy to the heart of a regular staff officer.

Robin in fact felt there was little real difference in the preparations necessary to successfully blow up a strategic railway bridge, and the preliminary move in a business coup which might bring a profit of several million francs. Indeed he often had been impressed, when among his prewar commercial friends in London, by the way that former staff officers made exceedingly shrewd businessmen. And in reverse he saw no reason why a successful businessman should not emulate the graduates of a staff college on their own ground.

The French Section of the SOE in London kept their group leaders in the field surprisingly well supplied with detailed instructions on a variety of subjects. Robin welcomed every bit of technical advice he could get—particularly the printed and typed instructions prepared by explosives experts of the Royal Engineers. He made an intensive study of the detailed instructions and advice sent from London on the various types of explosives and fuses dropped to the resistance—and how best to use them.

Moreover, with all the instincts of a lifetime he was a willing disciple of the military doctrine of economy of force; in particular he strongly deprecated the spectacular, but often comparatively ineffective, attacks, particularly on railways, which became fashionable in the later days of the resistance.

Robin's principal rail targets were on the eastern section of the French State Railways—the vital trunk lines by which German divisions and supplies were moved to and fro between France and the Reich—and the troop-consuming wastes of the Eastern Front beyond. Accepting and developing the advice of the British sapper experts, he chose as the location of his operations cuttings where a wrecked train could be relied upon to pile up and cause a blockage lasting several days. Longer interruption was seldom possible. The Germans had highly efficient rail repair commandos who were rushed to the scene as soon as one of the main German traffic arteries was cut.

Robin also insisted on one primary requirement. All his rail wrecker groups were warned that the locomotive must pass over safely before the explosion occurred. This was a viewpoint not shared by all the British officers dropped to assist the Resistance fighters, for it almost inevitably meant that the locomotives were intact—and locomotives were the very sinews of war.

But as Robin explained in after years, "I was not prepared to sacrifice unnecessarily the French crews of the locomotives, however desirable it might be to destroy the engines themselves—and particularly in these still comparatively early days. Many of these French engine-drivers and firemen were, in fact, among the most devoted members of the resistance—some of them members of my own groups—and had for long provided the British Secret Service with regular and detailed information about German troop movements.

"In addition they were able to sabotage their locomotives in their own quiet way—for instance, by running with insufficient water—and because little has been heard of this type of sabotage it does not mean that it was not often just as successful as the more spectacular type. So I gave a definite order to all my groups, in both northern and eastern France, to make sure that the crews were safe."

Robin's second standing order to the train-wrecking groups was typical of the man's wry saturnine humor. German leave trains were moving to and fro across eastern France every night, so Robin told his men: "Play fair. I don't want you to wreck the German leave trains taking the soldiers home to Germany. Wreck the trains bringing them back to France—after they've had a good time at home."

It was on one of these train-wrecking sorties in eastern France that Robin, laden with several pounds of British plastic explosive and a number of so-called fog-signal detonators in a paper parcel on the carrier of his bicycle, was cycling through a forest with two of his local group leaders. They were on their way to a rendezvous with one of his groups which planned to blow up the main line between Paris and Strasbourg.

As they cycled round a corner the three men were suddenly faced by a road block manned by toughs of the Vichy *milice*— as dangerous as the German Security Officers and often much more offensive. There was nothing for them but to cycle right into the hands of these Vichy security guards, many of whom were the dregs of the French jails.

"Who are you—where are you going?" demanded the thug in charge of the *milice* detachment.

Robin, always prepared to bluff before shooting it out, shrugged his shoulders and grinned:

"What do you think we are?" he laughed, as he slipped off the safety catch of the pistol in his pocket. He added: "Can't you see we are *terroristes*—on our way to blow up the railway? And look, in that parcel I have all the explosives we need for the job!"

Loud guffaws greeted this sally. Robin's two companions, their fingers on the pins of the hand grenades in their pockets, closed in for the showdown.

"You are a rascal," said the *milice* NCO-in-charge and at that he took Robin round the shoulders and thumped him on the back.

"Ah, *mon vieux*," said the chief *milice* tough, "I wish all the *terroristes* were like you. But be on your way, *mes amis*—and don't try that joke too often. Some of my colleagues might believe you."

"O.K.," said Robin, "I promise you I'll be more careful in the future. But now we must be on our way—for we still have to blow up the railway."

Further guffaws from the *milice* greeted this parting shot and as Robin and his two comrades cycled off they were followed by ribald advice from the Vichy toughs.

Robin, because of the technical difficulties of the planned operation, had been in two minds whether to carry it out. Now honor clearly demanded that there *must* be a train wreck . . . but it was possible only at a section of line where the Germans had recently cut the bordering trees just to prevent such an enterprise.

A quarter-of-an-hour after leaving the *milice* he reached the rendezvous where the train-wrecking party was waiting. And, in view of the special circumstances, they made haste to the line. Their knowledge of the German timetable told them that a troop train was due in less than half-an-hour and no time was lost in burying the explosive and clamping on the fog-signal detonators. The whole preparations were completed only five minutes before the train was due and, although the site chosen for the wreck was not more than two miles from the *milice* road block, Robin was quite determined to wait and make sure that his story to the *milice* should be duly confirmed.

A few minutes later came the hiss of the troop locomotive. It was traveling comparatively fast and to have blown up the locomotive at full speed would have induced a truly spectacular wreck. But Robin, personally controlling the firing of the explosive, let the locomotive and the first car—a luggage van—pass over before he gave the signal to detonate. The second and third coaches reared into the air and straddled the track while the rest of the train piled on top.

"Honor was satisfied," said Robin, recounting the tale in after years, "but in the circumstances we could scarcely be expected to carry out a personal inspection of the damage just to make a detailed report to the people in London."

21

Parachuting into Norway

Gunnar Sonsteby

The wartime saboteur is always at his most vulnerable trying to work his way into enemy-held territory. Whether swinging down into the unknown by parachute, paddling ashore in a rubber boat released from a submarine, or slipping past a border block-house, he is in extreme danger. Nor is the danger over until he can lose himself in a city or go to cover in a secret hideaway.

Here Gunnar Sonsteby, a famous Norwegian saboteur, tells what the long process of being dropped back into his native land was like.

The time: October and November, 1943. The origin of the flights: an airfield near Cambridge, England. Sonsteby's one companion in the jump: Knut Haugland, who had already served as radio operator in the celebrated attack on the heavy water plant at Vemork.

WE had to wait until weather conditions were right. We could only jump over Norway in bright moonlight and with unobscured vision. Finally we took off from an aerodrome near our secret quarters on October 11 in a four-engined Halifax bomber. It was evening when we took off and by midnight we were passing the Norwegian coast at Flekkefjord, near the southern tip of the country. There was a magical element in this nocturnal reunion with our country, and we were impatient to make our jumps.

However, there was thick mist over the Skrim plateau and the pilot forbade the jump. He circled over Drammen and Oslo and dropped a number of leaflets. On the whole, the German AA guns were not much in evidence. A few had fired at us as we crossed the coast, and also at Oslo, but nothing troublesome.

The bomber then turned west and headed for Scotland. We landed safely toward morning and later in the forenoon the plane took us back near Cambridge, where we had started from.

On October 15 we took off again, and again we had to turn back when conditions proved hopeless. Twice, now, I had sat there ready to jump through the floor of the plane; it was even worse having to be taken back again. Some days later we went through the same experience—and again a fourth time. We were beginning to be fed up and disgruntled. Then the moon was wrong and we had to sit and wait for the next full moon— November 12.

On that day, we tried again. At first all went well, but when we were out over the North Sea, gasoline suddenly began to pour in to where we were sitting. Knut Haugland was rather ill that day, having contracted a gastric chill or something of the kind, and he was lying on the floor with a blanket over him. The stink of the gasoline trickling in was scarcely calculated to make him feel better. We wondered what on earth was up. The pilot did the only thing possible: he turned and headed for the nearest airport.

We were ten miles out from the coast at the time and it was essential to lighten the plane as much as possible to maintain height. So the pilot ordered us to jettison all our equipment. For us that was tragedy, but we had to obey. Knut had spent months getting all that magnificent equipment together, and now we had to dump it into the sea! We felt we would almost prefer to land on the water.

That, apparently, was a highly probable outcome even after the plane had been lightened, and we had to take off our parachutes and put on Mae Wests. We were told that if we landed on the water, we would, if we were lucky, have three or four minutes in which to get into the rubber dinghies. Anything can happen when you land in roughish seas, and the gasoline swishing about and forming pools on the floor might contribute its own surprises.

At last the coast appeared below and we could breathe more easily. The airfield at Snoring soon came into sight. The pilot had been in radio contact and we saw that the emergency stand-by had been ordered: ambulances and fire engines and the lot. No doubt, when a plane landed soaking with gasoline that was all very necessary, or could be. However, we had no need of it. The plane landed without mishap and for the fifth time we were carted back to where we had started.

Five days later, on November 17, we were airborne once more. This time we got across the North Sea and were soon over Telemark. I was sitting beside the opening in the floor ready to jump as we crossed Lake Norsjo at Notodden. At the command "Action Stations" we were to sit upright, legs over the edge of the hole, hands clamped to our sides and our feet close together, and at "Go" we had to shove off.

Our excitement was intense. It was a minute or two after two o'clock. I saw the lake under me. Then it was gone. Then came another lake, Myklevann, up on the plateau itself, and a few minutes later I caught sight of bog and moor beneath us and there at last the lights we were hoping to see. The captain gave the green light, the warning light came on beside me, I heard the words "Action Station," then "Go" and I jumped. The next instant, my face and body were buffetted by bitingly cold air. I plunged down at great speed gasping for breath, but before I had time to wonder whether the parachute was going to open or not, I felt a violent jerk and there I was hanging.

I realized at once that we had been put out far too high. It must have been nearer 2,000 feet than the 1,000 feet that had been planned. The force of the wind was carrying me sideways. I was struck by the magnificence of the view: in the distance I could see the river Lagen shining in the bright moonlight, and in the other direction I could see away back to Notodden and the mountains beyond.

I had been so occupied with my jump, that I hadn't looked to see how Haugland was doing. Now I saw several parachutes ahead of me and assumed that one of these must be Haugland's and the others those of the containers with our equipment. We were already a good distance from each other.

As I got nearer the ground, I caught sight of the little cottage that was our objective. I was about three hundred feet above it then, with the wind sweeping me along toward some woods. Remembering what I had been taught at the parachute school, I turned in my harness so I was facing the direction in which I was going, but I was carried on and on, and was soon sailing along above the treetops. I knew I could expect a good hard bump when I finally hit.

Once among the treetops, I held one foot out in front of me as a shock absorber. Suddenly there was a great jerk as the parachute caught in a tree and, before I knew what had happened, I was hanging in my harness just a couple of feet off the ground. In a moment I had got out the knife I carried, cut the cords, and dropped into loose snow.

I had been lucky. My next job was to get my parachute down from the tree, fold it up, and hide it. That done, I took off my thick parachute suit and put it with the parachute. Then through snow to the hut, where I was met by our "reception committee," which included two others from England who had come in just ahead of us. Haugland turned up soon afterward. He had made a good landing on snow-covered bog, a bit closer to the hut than I.

We soon found the container with skis which had been parachuted immediately after us, and in it were our rucksacks. The reception group told us we were going to have considerably more trouble gathering together the twenty or so containers with arms and equipment. They apparently were scattered over a vast area; and some might even have landed as far away as the Lagen Valley, where the mountainside ended in a sheer drop. Altogether our two planes had dropped between thirty-five and forty parachutes. In the course of the day, we brought in the weapon containers and carefully camouflaged them with snow.

When Haugland made contact with London on his transmitter (which had the code name Tricorne Red), he was told to go as soon as possible to the local Milorg chief at Kongsberg, down in the valley and a few miles to the north. Filling his rucksack with equipment, he put on his skis and went off. At the first place he came to in the valley, he got a taxi to drive him to Kongsberg. Two days later, to our surprise, he turned up again at the hut on the plateau, exhausted and very much the worse for wear. His face bore the obvious marks of blows.

What had happened was this: while Haugland was with the local Milorg man at Kongsberg, the Gestapo arrived and arrested everyone present. The Germans suspected that Haugland had come from England and naturally treated him with particularly loving attention. He was subjected to a true Gestapo interrogation, hence the marks on his face. When that was over and he and the Milorg man were being taken outside to the Germans' car, he managed to ease the straps of his rucksack almost off his shoulders and, as they reached the stairs, he let his rucksack drop and took a great leap down the stairs and out. Once in the street, he ran in the direction of the arms factory and from there into the woods. Thanks to a tiny compass which the Germans had overlooked, he made his way to the hut. We were overjoyed that he had escaped. The episode was duly reported to London.

Sonsteby became the most decorated hero of the Norwegian resistance. One of his exploits was the blowing up of the Labor Office in Oslo exactly one day before the German-run draft of a Norwegian labor force was to begin. Records and draft forms were destroyed and, much to the glee of the Norwegians, the hated draft itself had to be postponed for many weeks.

Skorzeny's Secret Missions

Otto Skorzeny

When World War II broke out, Otto Skorzeny, a big, easygoing Viennese businessman, was thirty-one years old. He was almost six and a half feet tall. Even the dueling scar which scrawled down the left side of his face from temple to chin was outsize. His first three years in the German army were routine enough, except for the rather unusual fact that he carried Col. T.E. Lawrence's The Seven Pillars of Wisdom *in his knapsack while serving on the Russian front.*

In December, 1942, he was sent home with a kidney infection. For a man with a bad kidney, the next two years were exciting. In short, he became the most celebrated of all German commandos, using tactics of speed and surprise in a way worthy of Lawrence himself.

The Nazi fortunes were ebbing. Impressed by British feats of arms, like the raid on the Rommel headquarters and Operation Frankton, Hitler thought he saw in such diversionary forays a short cut back into the winning column.

Skorzeny was appointed Chief of German Special Forces early in 1943, with the modest rank of army captain. From then on, his fame rose like a star shell. He led the glider troops in the famous rescue of Mussolini in August of that same year. The Allies held the Italian dictator prisoner on a high peak in the Apennines. They prepared for attack from below, so Skorzeny, in character, attacked from above, achieving perfect surprise. Later he flushed Admiral Horthy from his own well-defended palace, at the moment when the Hungarian regent showed signs of defecting from the Axis cause.

Here, as told in his autobiography, are two characteristic exploits from the crucial year of 1944. They catch the flavor of the man himself. Apparent are his understated humor and his very real powers of command.

As the military situation grew more precarious, the field of my activities grew wider and more intense. After several half-sugary, half-acid discussions with the staff of the Wehrmacht General Headquarters, at length I was granted my great wish. My "special units" were to be increased. The sole battalion I had had so far now became the kernel of a brigade of six battalions, recruited in great part from among the 1,800 volunteers of the Brandenburg division. The Führer also entrusted me with the direction of the 2nd Section of the Army Secret Services. Its function was sabotage and demoralization of the enemy. . . .

Toward the end of the summer of 1944, "combat swimmers" from the navy and a detachment of my men were able to carry off a feat of which they may well be proud. The British armies, under Field Marshal Lord Montgomery, had just crossed the Waal, one of the chief tributaries of the Rhine. They were forming a bridgehead around Nijmegan, which threatened our front directly. To our misfortune, they had seized the bridge which spanned the river so that their convoys reached the firing line without difficulty. As the British had set up a very powerful anti-aircraft system around the bridge, the vertical dives of our pursuer bombers remained unavailing.

Advised of these conditions, I consulted experts on the employment of combat swimmers against this accursed bridge. Even partial success would be something and reduce enemy pressure in this sector for the time being at least. I knew that naval technicians had already produced "torpedo mines" destined for similar purposes. These weapons had the form and dimensions of a semi-torpedo; equipped with air reservoirs, they could float on the surface of the water. This allowed them to be handled fairly easily once launched. According to the earliest tests, the simultaneous explosion of two of these mines, moored to a column or pillar, produced so violent a displacement of water that no construction could resist its impact.

The British bridgehead extended upstream and downstream some four or five miles on either bank. The left bank was completely occupied by the enemy. One night Captain Hellmer, who directed the operation, swam away alone to reconnoiter. Thanks to his rubber fins, he advanced at high speed and almost noiselessly. To hide the white blob of his face, he wrapped netting around it; the material was close-knit but not too much so to prevent him from seeing through it. Thus equipped, he swam cautiously toward the bridge, chose the pillar he proposed to blow up, and examined it minutely. When the operation was to be executed, each man had to know exactly what was his task. Above him the Churchill tanks rolled toward the front. The roar of the motors and caterpillars would be an important factor in the success of the enterprise; it was to be hoped that it would cover any suspicious sound rising from the waters. Nor would the sentinels on guard think of watching the surface of the river. How could any danger come from that quarter when the British army occupied the terrain several miles up and down stream? Silently Hellmer allowed the current to bear him past the enemy positions on either bank and finally returned to our lines.

A few days later the meteorological station promised us a particularly dark, and perhaps even rainy night—just the weather requisite for such an enterprise. The floating of the heavy mine-torpedoes was a tough job, the more since the British artillery gratified us with not a few well-directed shells. A few of the men engaged in floating the bombs were wounded. At last the task was done. We watched the large semicylinders bobbing up close to shore. The twelve volunteers made ready and manned the torpedoes, three men on either side; then, at a given signal, they disappeared down the current into the night. Soon the heavy silhouette of the bridge rose out of the darkness; our men could hear the never-ending rumble of trucks and tanks moving from bank to bank. Presently they were under the flooring of the bridge. In a wink, they affixed two mines against the chosen pillar, one on the right, the other on the left. Then they opened the valves of the reservoirs while two specialists removed the fuses of the time detonators.

Now, the two bombs, heretofore innocuous, were deadly. Slowly these enormous "cigars" sank into the waters along the base of the bridge, while all the men swam away at top speed. Five minutes later a terrific explosion rent the air. The mines had done their work, the pillar crumbled and, in its fall, dragged the central part of the bridge down with it.

Almost at once both banks of the river came to life. The British began by shooting at random, then with a more unhealthy accuracy, for the first glimmers of dawn revealed the heads of the swimmers. After a few minutes a spray of machine-gun bullets hit one of our men. His comrades surrounded him and held him up in the water. Repeatedly, bullets splashed into the water here and there amid our swimmers but miraculously only two more of our men were slightly wounded. At last the entire unit was able to return to our position on the right bank some six miles downstream from the bridge. Completely exhausted, the uninjured men soon clambered up the bank, bringing with them the three who had been wounded.

Our operation had succeeded perfectly. But it was certain that the enemy would henceforth be on the watch and that a repetition of this feat would be very much more difficult, if not impossible.

By the autumn of 1944, the Allies were closing in on the German homeland. But Adolf Hitler had for months been dreaming of one last big offensive action. He chose the place well, with a final upsurge of his celebrated intuition: the dark forests of the Ardennes, where his armies had scored their original break-through back in 1940. The plan was to split the Allies and drive straight on to Antwerp, which would fall on D day plus seven. The United States First Army, along with the British and Canadian armies to the north, would thus be divided from the rest of the Allied forces. In due course they would be driven into the sea.

Skorzeny's share of the action would be a vital one. In a private briefing, Hitler himself told him his mission. With some three thousand hand-picked men—as many as possible English-speaking—he was to infiltrate the enemy lines. Clad in American uniforms, these men were to mix with the retreating Americans and add to their confusion. False commands, slashed telephone wires and the blowing up of fuel and ammunition dumps would all play a part.

More specifically still they were to make sure the fleeing Americans did not *destroy the three vital bridges over the Meuse as the Germans broke through.*

Skorzeny tells of some of the problems that developed in the short six weeks that he was allowed for training:

We could now go about making the necessary preparations. My troops were to form the 150th Armored Brigade. The basis for our plan was obviously the schedule drawn up by the High Command for the whole offensive. According to this schedule, our armies were to break through the enemy front the first day. The second day they were to reach and cross the Meuse. We were therefore justified in supposing that the remnants of the line divisions must have attained all their objectives on the evening of the first day; specifically in our sector, they must have gone beyond the crest of a small mountain range called Le Haut Venne. Otherwise I would be forced to give up the mission entrusted to me. Further, I asked for aerial photographs of the three bridges my troops were meant to seize.

I won ready approval of my plans for the organization of the brigade and General Jodl promised that the general staff would back me up in all my requests for matériel. I took advantage of this to solicit the loan of three experienced battalion commanders, and, in addition to the volunteers, the transfer to my brigade of a few homogeneous Wehrmacht units. These would serve as a frame and skeleton for my hastily constituted organization.

Soon I received three very capable lieutenant colonels and, shortly after, two battalions of Luftwaffe paratroops, two Wehrmacht armored companies and one signal company. These troops would reinforce the two companies of my "special units" and my battalion of parachutists.

There remained the question of "English-speaking volunteers." . . . When the first hundred volunteers arrived at Friedenthal, I struck a new low in despondency. I wanted to consign the whole thing to the devil. "Professors" attempted to divide the volunteers into three categories according to their knowledge of the English language. And Category 1, composed of soldiers who spoke English or, better still, American slang fluently and without an accent, was practically at a standstill. Whereas we needed such men by the hundreds, we would find one or two at most who deserved to be classed in this category.

Here I must confess that my own English is pretty weak. What a pity I had always made the most of English classes to raise Cain with the poor teachers! But now I tried to catch up for lost time and occasionally to put in a well-turned phrase. One day I met a young officer, a flier, who was a candidate for Category 1. Quite naturally I asked him:

"Tell me about yourself in English, please."

The poor lad grew embarrassed, hesitated, then plunged:

"Yes, Herr Oberstleutnant, I became my last order before five months." He hesitated anew, then added hurriedly in German: "If you will allow me, I will explain all that in my native tongue . . ."

So there it was! I could only be cheerful about it. A man cannot heap insults on a volunteer who is obviously filled with enthusiasm. But with such prowess, he would certainly never dupe an American, even a deaf one.

When after a fortnight the selection of volunteers was finished, we found ourselves faced with a frightful result. The first category, in its entirety, numbered some 10 men, especially former sailors who, incidentally, formed a large part of the second; the second category, made up of men who spoke more or less fluently, numbered some 30 to 40 men; the third category, soldiers who knew how to "make themselves understood" was somewhat more numerous with 150-odd men; the fourth category, lads who had not completely forgotten what they had learned at school, totaled about 200; as for the others, they could just about say "yes" and "no."

Accordingly I was compelled to form a brigade of deaf-mutes for, after assigning 120 of the best "linguists" to the headquarters company, I had, so to speak, nobody left. We would perforce mingle among the fleeing American columns with teeth tight-clenched as though the extent of the catastrophe had deprived us of the power of speech.

In order to improve this situation somewhat, we sent the second category of men to an interpreters' school and to an American prisoners' camp. But as the "courses" lasted only a week, the results were negligible.

As for the bulk of my troops, men who did not understand one single word of English, we inculcated a few lusty G.I. oaths in them, and the meaning of "yes," "no," "O.K." Also, all day long and every day, we repeated for their benefit the principal words of command used in the American army. And that was all we could do to camouflage our brigade, linguistically speaking. . . .

As time passed—and it passed terribly quickly—we intensified the training of the men. Chiefly, we repeated several versions of the general theme, bridgehead. In a somewhat different field, we strove to make our men lose the rigid bearing which results from German military training with its exaggerated and useless discipline. Finally we even accustomed them to the use of chew-

193 SKORZENY'S SECRET MISSIONS

ing gum and the typically American way of opening a package
of cigarettes.

At all events the only almost perfectly camouflaged company
we possessed was the headquarters company. We therefore decided
to be as exclusive as possible in admitting men to it. Our instructions were to leave the greatest latitude to the spirit of initiative
of the soldiers. As advanced observers at the front, they would
render inappreciable services to the bulk of our armies. They
had also to try to add to the confusion reigning among the
enemy, by spreading false rumors, by exaggerating the initial
success of the German divisions, by giving fantastic orders, by
cutting the telephone lines and by destroying reserve munitions.

One day after I had finished inspecting my troops, an officer
in this company asked to speak confidentially to me. He declared
very solemnly:

"Colonel, I now know the purpose of the operation we are
preparing."

For a moment I was perplexed. Could Foelkersam or Har-
dieck, the only persons who shared the secret, have committed
some involuntary indiscretion? But already the officer, mani-
festly satisfied by the effect his first words had produced, whispered:

"The brigade is to march to Paris in order to capture Allied
General Headquarters."

This was almost too much for me. I had to exercise great
self-control to avoid laughing. I contented myself with an inde-
finable exclamation of, "Hm! Hm!" This sufficed to set him off
again enthusiastically:

"As I know every inch of Paris, I should like to offer my help,
Colonel. Naturally I shall keep mum about this."

I asked him for suggestions; he propounded a detailed plan. A
column of pseudo-prisoners, surrounded by soldiers speaking
perfect English, would enter Paris just like that! Even German
tanks could take part in the excursion under the guise of booty
to be presented to Allied General Headquarters.

I found it difficult to stem the flow of his verbiage. At length I dismissed him, having asked him to study his plan in greater detail, to come back to see me, and especially to be sure not to talk! Much later I learned that he had not observed this last injunction. For weeks, Allied counterespionage was on the watch, notably over the Café de Paris, which I had mentioned in the course of this conversation.

Operation Greif was launched on December 16. Such was the Battle of the Bulge. Despite complete tactical surprise, the German offensive ran into stubborn fighting as the Americans dug in. There was no headlong retreat. Behind the brief, orderly withdrawal, the Meuse bridges were blown up before Skorzeny could get to them. Despite the high-sounding promises of the top brass, he had less than half the men he was promised, two captured Sherman tanks and twelve German Panthers. The latter were camouflaged with sheet metal, changing their profile in such a way as to "fool someone a mile away." Skorzeny (a lieutenant colonel now) was forced to throw a good part of his command into conventional defense to protect the northern flank of the German attackers.

Some of his Special Forces did manage to penetrate the American lines. Here he tells us how they fared in their unusual mission:

Meanwhile I received news from the groups sent behind the enemy lines to disorganize the Allied rear. Out of nine groups which had received these orders, six, or at most eight, must have really crossed the line of fire. Even today, I am still unable to tell how many. I can well understand that more than one of these young soldiers hesitated to confess that, at the moment of infiltrating into enemy positions, his courage failed him. On the other hand I know that two of these groups were taken prisoner. Subsequently four others offered such clear and precise reports that their veracity could not possibly be suspect. As a matter of curiosity, I should like to tell briefly of some of the episodes that took place during this action.

The very first day of the offensive, one of these groups had passed through the breach opened in the Allied front and advanced as far as Huy, near the banks of the Meuse. There it had settled quietly at a crossroads to observe the movements of the enemy troops. The team leader, who spoke English fluently, had the nerve to stroll in the neighborhood of the town in order to "get an idea of the situation."

After a few hours, an American armored regiment drove up and its commandant asked our men the way. With remarkable presence of mind, the team leader gave him a wholly fantastic reply. Those swinish Germans, he told the American, had just cut off several roads. He himself and his company had had to make a vast detour. The American tanks, happy to have been warned in time, took to the roads which our team leader had indicated.

On their way back, this group cut several telephone lines and removed a number of signboards set up by the American Quartermaster Corps. Twenty-four hours later they rejoined our lines, bringing with them some interesting information on the disorder which reigned on the American front at the beginning of the offensive.

Another of these small commando groups, which had also crossed the American lines and reached the Meuse, noticed that the Americans had done virtually nothing to protect the bridges in this region. On their way back to the German lines, our men had barred three main roads leading to the front by affixing ribbons, which in the American army denote mined areas, to the trees. Later we confirmed the fact that Allied reinforcement columns, preferring to avoid these roads, had taken a wide detour.

A third commando group discovered an ammunition dump. Our men hid until nightfall, then blew up the dump. Shortly after, finding a main telephone line, they cut it in three places.

But by far the most extraordinary story was that of still another group which, as early as December 16, found itself suddenly in front of an American position. Two companies of G.I.s, settling down as though to withstand a long siege, had built barricades and stationed machine guns around them. Our men must have been pretty badly scared when an American officer asked them for the latest information from the front.

Our commando leader, who wore a fine uniform which ostensibly made him an American sergeant, tried to collect himself. Probably the Americans attributed the fear still evident on the faces of our soldiers to the results of their last encounter with those "damned Germans." For, to believe the commando leader, the Germans had already gone beyond this position both on the right and on the left, so that it was practically encircled. Much impressed, the American captain gave immediate orders for retreat.

All in all, given the circumstances, the success of these commandos went far beyond my expectations. And, a few days later, the American station at Calais spoke of the discovery of an immense enterprise of espionage and sabotage conducted under the orders of Colonel Skorzeny, Mussolini's kidnapper. The Americans announced that they had already captured more than 250 men in my brigade, a grossly exaggerated figure. Subsequently I learned that Allied counterspies, filled with a noble ardor, had arrested a certain number of authentic American soldiers or officers.

As for the comical stories I was told after the war by several American officers, they would fill a volume. Captain X, for instance, found a German officer's chest in a French town and took a pair of boots out of it. As they happened to fit him, he wore them every day. But the M.P.s, set loose on a spy hunt, deduced that Captain X was, and must incontestably be, a German spy. So the luckless officer was arrested and rather roughly handled. He assured me that he would never forget the week he spent in a most uncomfortable prison.

One day, two young lieutenants who had arrived in France in 1944 were invited to lunch by the commandant of a unit which was already accustomed to the rigorous life at the front. Polite and amiable, they thought themselves called upon to voice their appreciation of this meal, though it consisted only of canned food. This praise and also their spotless uniforms made them so eminently suspect that hastily summoned M.P.s dragged them from their chairs and threw them into prison. For the veterans, disgusted with canned foods, could not conceive how an authentic American might find praise for such sickening food.

Nor was this all. Believing me capable of the most frightful crimes and of the boldest designs, American counterespionage considered itself bound to take exceptional measures to assure the security of the high command. Accordingly, General Eisenhower was sequestered in his own general headquarters for several days; he was forced to settle in a little house, guarded by several cordons of M.P.s. Soon the general had enough of it and sought by all means to escape this surveillance. The counterespionage authorities even managed to find a double for Eisenhower. Every day the pseudo commander-in-chief, clad in general's uniform, had to get into his chief's car and drive to Paris in order to attract the attention of the "German spies."

Similarly, during the entire Ardennes offensive, Marshal Montgomery ran the risk of being stopped and questioned by the M.P.s. A pleasant jokester had spread the rumor that a member of Skorzeny's band was engaged in spying disguised as a British marshal. So the M.P.s carefully examined minutely the appearance and bearing of every British general traveling in Belgium.

After the war Skorzeny was tried at Dachau for war crimes and acquitted on all counts. But his release from prison was long in coming, so he escaped from a prison camp in Germany in July of 1948 by stowing away in a transport pool car driven by a German driver.

23

An Exploit of the Battling *Barb*

John L. Steele

The USS Barb *was one of the most successful submarines of World War II. Under her red-headed skipper, Comdr. Eugene Fluckey, she accounted for a quarter of a million tons of Japanese shipping in the last year of the war. A typical Gene Fluckey exploit was the penetration of Namkwan port at night—a bottleneck-shaped harbor on the China coast between Shanghai and Canton. Once inside, he torpedoed at least six ships, escaping to deep water again despite a furious counterattack.*

As the war neared a close Fluckey and the ninety-man crew of the Barb *grew bolder still. Here is a sabotage episode against the home islands of Japan. It was written by John L. Steele, Senior Time-Life Correspondent, and this is its first appearance in print:*

COMMANDER FLUCKEY edged *Barb* in toward the beach. It was nearly midnight and the light southerly breeze barely kicked up the water. An undercurrent of expectation ran through the submarine. Lt. William M. Walker, USNR, of Columbia, South Carolina, was about to lead his seven "hand-picked" saboteurs onto Japanese soil. The men were chosen to go ashore for their brawn, coolness and agility. They held a final briefing. One gunner's mate who had refused offers of more than two hundred dollars to swap his place in the assault force with other members of the crew, mumbled, "You can buy for a nickel." The captain quietly went over the plan again—to blow up a train at a vital point in the railway system of the industrial east coast of Japan. Through days of waiting, periscope observations had given a timetable of trains traveling the heavily loaded coastal route.

Now the men checked their equipment, red flashlights, watches, knives, D rations, lifejackets, cigarette lighters, pistols, shovels, and picks.

"Mother wouldn't like this," Walker whispered with a smile to the captain. "She always writes me to stay out of trouble."

Barb edged slowly toward the beach. Even "Kamikaze," the Japanese prisoner taken from a trawler, asked to join the landing party. He had furnished information on sentry dogs and beach patrols.

Contact was made with two "spitkits," probably Japanese sampans, coming down the coast. The crew manned battle stations and the submarine headed out to sea to avoid. The sampans turned away and *Barb* turned again toward the beach. It was hard to make out the landmarks which would fix the chosen position for a landing. "In position," the Captain at last reported. A thousand yards off lay the coast of Japan, only two fathoms of water lay between the keel of the submarine and the ocean floor—no diving room. The order came to launch the two rubber boats. The men traded the tight, familiar security of the conning tower for the unknown beach.

"As the boats shoved off," Fluckey recalled later in his patrol report, "I planned to say something apropos such as, 'Synchronize your watches, gentlemen.' However, all I could say was, 'Boys if you get stuck, head for Siberia 130 miles north—follow the mountain ranges, good luck.'"

Now the boats went in. *Barb* must be easy to spot from the

beach, the men aboard her thought. Momentarily, those in the submarine feared shots, clamor, flares—but the blackness of night engulfed all in silence.

Walker and his party reached the beach. They found themselves in somebody's back yard, fifty yards from a house, but fortunately no dogs. Dog tracks and human barefoot prints were everywhere. A short huddled conversation, boat guards were left behind and Walker led his party cautiously inland, skirting the houses, then plunged into waist-high "bullrushes" which seemed to crunch and crackle with every move, shrieking out the commandos' presence. All shapes took on human form. A highway lay two hundred yards ahead. Another huddle. All clear. Walker rose, started to scurry across the road and crashed headfirst into a four-foot ditch. He cautioned his party to "watch the ditch," then, dashing across the road, plunged into a ditch on the opposite side. At last the railroad tracks. Suddenly a strange-shaped object was spotted a short way down the railroad. John Markuson, a motor machinist, was sent to check it. Without a word the men started digging to spot and plant the demolition gear.

Someone came running up the track. The men froze. It was Markuson, who reported, "Jees, that thing is a lookout tower." Asked why he didn't give the prearranged whistle signal on approaching, he replied: "I tried to whistle, but when I saw that tower my mouth just dried up." Digging began again. The picks and shovels shattered the quiet of the night so the men put the tools aside and dug dog-fashion with bare hands. A flickering light appeared down the track. A train? Work ceased. All ears pinned to the rails in frontier fashion. Not a sound.

Around a curve an unscheduled northbound train loomed, seemingly out of nowhere. The party plunged for a bordering hedgerow. "Why can't they run their trains on time?" someone whispered. The train roared by, engineer hanging far out of his cab. Walker swore that the engineer looked him right in the eye. With the crash dive into the hedge Billy Hatfield's lifejacket inflation cartridge went off. Hatfield, one of the Hatfield versus McCoy clan, was sure he was shot, then found he merely was approaching maternity as his Mae West inflated. Paul Saunders, chief of the boat, decreased the micro-switch clearance of the demolition gear just to be sure it worked. Circuits were checked and the men broke for the boats.

Aboard *Barb*, Captain Fluckey ticked off the minutes. "Are they never coming?" Then from the bridge the dim signal lights of the saboteurs were made out. At last the boats were leaving the beach. The blinking became insistent; did they mistake *Barb* for a patrol boat? The submarine gave a long, dash signal and darkness settled in again.

Now another northbound train came up the tracks. The captain broke the silence to yell to the boats, "Paddle like the devil." Warning was unnecessary: the boats spotted the train and paddles churned like eggbeaters. The train came closer and closer. Any second now and it would cross the demolition charges. Would the gear work? What a moment. Even the boats stopped paddling to look back. Everyone was choked with the expectancy of momentary destruction.

There was silence. Then there was unbelievable noise. There was darkness. Then there was a fiercely etched light. There was foreboding lest the tricky charges were improperly set. Then there was the exultant thrill of purpose accomplished and risk paid off.

The charge made a greater explosion than expected. The engine's boiler blew with a roar. Wreckage was tossed two hundred feet in the air amid flame and the smoke of escaping steam; cars were piled up and rolled off the track in a writhing, twisting mass.

Moments later the rubber boats were hauled aboard and *Barb* backed clear, circled and headed for deep water. A small fire flickered along the roadbed. That was all. *Barb* headed into the dark night and safety.

PART THREE:
UP TO NOW

24

The Mission of the Pregnant *Perch*

Clay Blair, Jr.

Despite the fact that the United States possessed the atomic bomb, the Korean War (1950–1953) was waged in conventional ways. This submarine episode from early in the war dramatizes the continuing nature of behind-the-lines operations. Certainly the mission of the pregnant Perch *bears a startling resemblance to that of the battling* Barb *five years before.*

Clay Blair, Jr. saw combat as a submariner in World War II. Then for ten years he covered the Pentagon as a Time-Life *correspondent.*

AN ungainly looking United States submarine lay to in the Sea of Japan, the sea lapping softly along her black sides. Two United States destroyers hovered off her quarter. On the submarine's afterdeck, on a stretcher covered by the British Union Jack, rested the body of British Royal Marine Commando P. R. Jones. Around the body stood Jones's comrades, their jaws working nervously and their eyes avoiding each other. The brief burial service was read and the body was hoisted over the side into the sea. An honor guard of Royal Marines fired three rifle volleys. The destroyers' guns boomed a salute. The United Nations flag dipped to half mast.

Commando Jones was the only casualty in the first combat operation of submarines in the Korean War. . . .

The submarine *Perch,* with a great bulbous projection on her afterdeck, was the laughingstock of the fleet. They called her the "Pregnant *Perch*" and, as sailors will, conjured up many unprintable theories to explain how she got that way. Actually the bulbous projection was a hangar tank which carried a motor launch, or "skimmer," in submarine lingo.

The skimmer was aboard on the chilly night in September, 1950, when *Perch* proceeded on the surface through the choppy waters of the Sea of Japan. She was bound for the coast of North Korea. Phosphorus flickered and bubbled greenly in her wake. On her tiny bridge six men ducked behind the steel plating to escape the irritating splash of spray as *Perch*'s bow plunged in and out of the sea troughs. Overhead, in the periscope "A-frame," radar antenna whirred around and around, to pick up any Russian ships or submarines based at nearby Vladivostok.

Down below the surface of the water, in the warm bowels of the three-hundred-foot sub, *Perch*'s "Motor macs" checked the roar of the 1,600 horsepower diesel engines. Up forward in the crew's mess, the ship's traditionally temperamental chief cook rode herd on the mess cooks who were lazily scrubbing white plates and cups for next chow. In "officer's country" several lieutenants and ensigns lounged in a tiny wardroom.

Throughout the boat, wherever a little space could be found amid the machinery, dungaree-clad sailors were playing acey-deucy and cribbage or were reading ragged paperbound books from the ship's library. The public address system piped music from a phonograph in the after battery compartment. Between records sailors chatted into the mike to make what *Perch*'s men called their own "disc jockey program."

Like most submarines just setting out on a war patrol, *Perch* was a jolly, noisy boat. But beneath the deliberate display of indifference ran a strain of tension—which showed when the radar antenna atop the periscope stopped whirring and fixed on one bearing: an aircraft contact. The officer of the deck sang out, "Clear the bridge." Five other men repeated it in a hoarse chorus as they ran for the conning-tower hatch. The diving klaxon gave two blasting honks and the public address system screamed, "Dive! Dive!" as *Perch* submerged in a cloud of foam and spray.

The unidentified plane passed over; *Perch* poked her snout up through the black water again and the course was reset for the coast of North Korea. Her men relaxed a little.

In her forward and after torpedo rooms *Perch* carried sixty-seven British Royal Marines under the command of Lt. Col. Douglas B. Drysdale, veteran of a dozen or more commando raids during World War II. They were members of "41 Independent Commando" and had been flown from London to Tokyo at the outbreak of the Korean War. *Perch*'s mission was to land them on the east coast of Korea and blow the railroad line that hauled supplies down the coast from Russia to the North Korean army. Meanwhile the commandos were gorging themselves on steak and, after their austerity diet at home, sometimes eating six eggs apiece.

While the commandos waited below, six pairs of binoculars scanned the gloomy black seas from the bridge topside. Finally, far up ahead, the dim, low outline of the North Korean coast could be made out. The first greenish-yellow streaks of dawn were beginning to poke skyward.

Perch's skipper, Lt. Comdr. Robert D. Quinn, came up on the bridge. He looked about briefly, then returned to the conning tower and passed the word to the officer on the bridge: "Pull the plug." The six men on the bridge went below, the conning-tower hatch snapped shut and the sub dipped under and went deep. Throughout the day she prowled along the rocky North Korean coast, occasionally sticking her periscope up for a look-see. By dusk *Perch* had closed to within four miles of the uninviting shoreline.

Soon after dark she surfaced noiselessly and Skipper Quinn

climbed to the bridge again. He studied the shore, then softly passed the word below: "Man the boats."

Crew members brought out and inflated the ship's rubber boats. The commandos clambered up the hatch ladders, spewed out onto the deck and climbed over the slippery side into waiting rubber boats. No lights were shown. Ten marines crowded into each boat, complete with equipment. On the bridge United States Marine Major Frank W. Harrington directed the loading and casting-off procedures quickly and quietly. From the bulbous tank behind *Perch*'s conning tower the skimmer was rolled out on a dolly. Then the sub dipped her tail down into the water and the power boat was launched into the sea. It gathered the six bobbing rubber boats onto a towline for the trip to the beach. Commando Leader Drysdale gave the signal and a marine leaned over to start the skimmer's engine. It would not start.

Skipper Quinn called down for haste. Still the skimmer's engine refused to start. On the shore they could see a train chuffing down the railroad tracks and through the tunnel which was their target. In the conning tower the radar party picked up the train, tracked it and jocularly reported to Quinn, "Train making twenty-five knots, course north."

Then the radar picked up a more serious target: "Enemy patrol boat, directly inshore." Steaming in wide figure eights, the patrol boat was right in the path the commandos were supposed to take. As all eyes strained toward shore, two truck lights appeared briefly and disappeared on the beach.

Skipper Quinn remembers now how he felt the blood draining from his face. It looked like a trap.

Quinn, Harrington and Drysdale held a fast conference. Their decision: it was a trap. They had been discovered. They promptly called off the operation. While Quinn kept his eyes on the patrol boat inshore, the marines scrambled back aboard and disappeared down the hatches. The rubber boats were gathered up, deflated and stowed. The balky "skimmer" was floated aboard and stored in the hangar. The hangar doors were banged shut, and *Perch* pulled the famous old naval maneuver of "getting the hell out of there."

Later that night, standing far off the shore of North Korea, *Perch* exchanged messages with headquarters in Japan and was given permission for another try. But she was ordered to make it with the help of two nearby destroyers. The submarine was to meet them at 10:00 the following morning.

By that time Quinn and Drysdale had selected another target. It looked perfect. Two razor-back mountain ridges, about one hundred yards apart, jutted out to sea. Between them stretched a broad horseshoe-shaped beach. The railroad ran across the beach and into tunnels under the ridges at either end of the beach. Between the tunnels and under the tracks ran a concrete culvert. If a pressure charge could be planted in each tunnel and the culvert could be blown up, the rail line would be closed for very lengthy repairs.

Next morning the submarine surfaced alongside the United States destroyers *Maddox* and *Herbert J. Thomas*. Quinn and Drysdale went aboard one of the destroyers to work out a plan. All agreed that the North Koreans had been alerted to the sub's presence in the area, so deception would have to be used.

It was Quinn's suggestion that was adopted: send one destroyer to the exact spot where *Perch* had been discovered the night before, to draw attention away from *Perch* and her new target. The *Thomas* was designated for the job and ordered to simulate *Perch*'s activity of the night before, with one exception: she was to raise hell with her five-inch guns. *Maddox* would stay in the general vicinity of *Perch* as an escort.

A few hours later *Perch* was closing the shore near target No. 2. This shore had been previously photographed by the United States submarine *Pickerel,* famous for her snorkel voyage from Hong Kong to Pearl Harbor. In preparation for *Perch*'s raid, *Pickerel* had patrolled the North Korean coastline, sometimes standing only a stone's throw off the beach. *Pickerel* had photographed thirty miles of the coast in detail, so now *Perch*'s commandos had photographs and silhouettes of their new target to study.

At 7:00 P.M. Quinn went to the sub's bridge. The ocean and

sky were black. He could only hope that this was no trap like the last one. After one unsuccessful attempt this one would have to work. It would be suicide to pull out of this one and then try again on another part of the shoreline. North Koreans all up and down the coast would be waiting for them.

Again Quinn passed the word to man the boats. Again the commandos stomped up the debarkation hatch ladders and climbed over the side into the waiting rubber boats. Again the skimmer was launched. This time the engine, which had been very carefully checked, started without a squawk. A rope was tossed to the six bobbing rubber boats. Half an hour after the sub had surfaced, the marines were headed shoreward, rifles, carbines and demolition equipment ready.

In the skimmer Drysdale checked his side arm and watch. The moon would soon be rising. Over a short-range radio set, he set up guarded communications with the sub, which was rapidly fading from sight in the black void astern. Off in the distance about five miles away, he spotted the lights of two enemy patrol vessels, moving slowly and ominously back and forth. There was no sound except the purr of the skimmer's engine, and the *slap, slap* of sea water pushing against the rubber boats. Then the skimmer's engine coughed and stopped.

The towrope had fouled the screw.

Drysdale immediately ordered a marine over the side. While the boats bobbed about helplessly, the marine whacked away at the fouled rope with a jackknife. In minutes he had it loose and was hauled from the icy water. The skimmer's engine started up easily, and the boats again chugged slowly shoreward.

They were about eight hundred yards from the beach when the silence was broken by a volley of rifle fire. Drysdale stopped the skimmer's motor and listened. Had *Perch* been ambushed again? Should he turn back immediately? Drysdale made his decision quickly: hold fire, he ordered; the shots had probably come from coastal or railroad guards scared by their own shadows. He would carry out the raid as planned.

Drysdale gave the signal, the boatman started the engine again and they headed for the beach.

When the skimmer was five hundred yards offshore, the engine was again stopped and the towline was slipped off. In the darkness the six boatloads of marines gathered around the skimmer. Speaking softly through a walkie-talkie, Drysdale ordered four boats to make for the left side of the beach and the remaining two to the right side. Half an hour after leaving the submarine the first rubber boat bumped onto land on the left side of the sandy beach. The commandos quietly fanned out across the sand.

One group of marines clawed up a twenty-foot embankment to the railroad track, crossed it and took positions in the scrub hills above the mouth of the left tunnel. They were to act as a covering force in case the demolition party were disturbed by North Korean patrols. . . .

While the force on the left was digging in, another ran straight inland and took positions in the hills to cover the center area of the beach; between them and the water the demolition teams would prepare to blow the culvert under the railroad. A third force was to cover the right side of the beach, near the mouth of the right tunnel.

The marines in the center section flopped down in the gravel, inland from the railroad. There was a shot and the commandos answered with a barrage into the dark scrub. One scream, then silence. The marines held their ground while the demolition crews hurried across the beach to their three stations—the culvert and the left and right tunnels.

Out on the sub, Skipper Quinn was worried by the firing on shore. He had agreed with Drysdale that the commandos would be too busy to radio a running account of what was going on on the beach; but now Quinn fretted as he received no explanation. In utter exasperation he went below for coffee; then inspected the ship's crew standing at battle stations. In the officers' wardroom the young ship's surgeon had laid out his surgical equipment and set up an operating table.

On the beach Drysdale was waiting for word that the right covering force was dug in. The demolition men in the right tunnel were planting their pressure explosive charge under the railroad tracks when they were fired on through the tunnel. They reported to Drysdale over their walkie-talkie. The right covering force should have been in position by then, and a few tense minutes passed before they finally reported in. They had missed their initial landing point on the beach but were now in action. The enemy firing through the right tunnel stopped as abruptly as it had begun. The demo team went back to work.

It was quiet again. Drysdale walked back and forth, in plain view, from one tunnel to the other, whispering encouragement and checking progress. The work was going ahead rapidly by the time the moon climbed to the horizon.

The skimmer had run to within fifty yards of the beach, where it anchored. Drysdale gave the signal for the explosives to be brought ashore. A marine went over the side and swam to the beach with a towrope. Once on land, he pulled in a small rubber boat laden with the explosives.

The rising moon lit up the bay, and from the shore they could see *Perch* swing about, to present as small a silhouette as possible. By now the North Korean countryside had been alerted by the rifle firing. Work would have to be speeded up if they were to succeed in their mission and get out alive.

Marines hurried the explosives up the side of the railroad embankment to the waiting demolition men. Soon the cheery word came from the left tunnel: the pressure charges were laid under the tracks and set to go when the next train came along. Fifteen minutes later the right tunnel crew reported all set.

The men in the culvert were still at work, sweating through their green dungarees, when firing broke out on the left again. Another North Korean patrol.

The left covering force opened fire into the scrub. Again all was silent. Drysdale received a progress report on the culvert: another ten minutes. He ordered the left-beach force to withdraw. The men dropped back across the sand to the rubber boats. Down at water's edge they hauled the boats into the water and prepared to embark. As the grimy marines huddled together to climb aboard one of the boats, they heard a single shot from the dark brush inland. One marine groaned and fell into the water. His buddies lifted him into the boat while one radioed a report to the skimmer, which relayed the word to the submarine so the "Doc" would be expecting to handle a casualty. Then the rubber boats raced toward the skimmer.

Meanwhile Drysdale ordered the right covering force to withdraw. And now the culvert crew was finished. Retreating to a safe distance from the culvert, Drysdale gave the word: "Blow it."

The culvert erupted in a dense cloud of smoke, dirt and rock. The roar set off more enemy firing, but it was wasted fire. Drysdale and the three engineers ran for the one remaining rubber boat, and were soon paddling seaward, toward the skimmer and the other boats.

On *Perch* Skipper Quinn sighed in relief as the skimmer and its strange tow chugged alongside. With him on the bridge stood the doctor, waiting for the casualty they had reported. But it was too late. Commando P. R. Jones was dead. The dirty, exhausted marines clambered aboard and, one by one, dropped down through the hatches while *Perch* sailors gathered the rubber boats, deflated and stowed them away.

As *Perch* steamed seaward, an air of almost hysterical relief swept through the boat. The United States submariners were pretending they had acquired a cockney accent, and the Britons were retaliating with mock Brooklynese. . . . Beneath the friendly kidding was every man's realization that he had just participated in an intimate demonstration of United Nations' cooperation in a common effort.

Just before *Perch* headed across the Sea of Japan for her home berth she got a report from the destroyer *Maddox,* which had stayed near the enemy shore just long enough to hear across the bay a telltale muffled *wharroomph!* An unsuspecting engineer had taken his train into one of the tunnels and tripped the pressure detonator under the tracks. The tunnel crashed down on the train and put the railroad out of business for a long, long time. The mission of the "Pregnant *Perch"* was completed.

Sabotage in Vietnam: Glimpses Behind the Bamboo Curtain

The Pentagon Papers *and* The Washington Post

During the Korean War (1950–53) it became clear that some form of guerilla warfare behind enemy lines was needed. So the United States created the Special Forces of the Army, lineal descendants of such World War II outfits as the British Commandos. By late 1952 the Special Forces were in action in Korea, and did good service in the last months of the war.

Their original headgear was a jaunty green beret, with a silver Trojan horse as emblem on it. Later the Trojan horse was changed to a flash patch in the form of a shield. "Wear the beret proudly," President Kennedy said still later, in a message to the Special Forces. "It will be a badge of courage in the difficult days ahead."

Even before President Kennedy's inauguration, the difficult days had begun in Vietnam. In June, 1954, the United States sent a team to undertake secret operations against the Vietminh and to support the shaky government of Vietnamese President

Diem. This "Saigon Military Mission" (SMM) was led by Col. (later Maj. Gen.) Edward G. Lansdale, a leading expert in irregular warfare.

The SMM operated under difficult conditions. For the Geneva Agreements, signed on July 21, 1954, called for the withdrawal of all United States personnel north of the 17th parallel, the new dividing line between North Vietnam and South. In The Pentagon Papers—*classified material made available to* The New York Times *by Daniel Ellsberg in 1971—there is a glimpse of some frantic activity in the northern capital city of Hanoi on the part of a SMM unit.*

One particular unsigned report from the Papers defines the duties of Maj. Lucien Conein, commanding officer of the northern SMM unit: "Major Conein was given responsibility for developing a paramilitary organization in the north to be in position when the Vietminh took over. . . . The team had headquarters in Hanoi, with a branch in Haiphong. Among cover duties this team supervised the refugee flow for the Hanoi airlift organized by the French."

More specifically, Conein—a veteran of the French Maquis —was instructed to do as much damage as he could before the final withdrawal. Here, from the same unsigned SMM report, giving the highlights of the year 1954, is his main accomplishment:

HANOI was evacuated on 9 October. The northern SMM team left with the last French troops, disturbed by what they had seen of the grim efficiency of the Vietminh in their takeover, the contrast between the silent march of the victorious Vietminh troops in their tennis shoes and the clanking armor of the well-equipped French whose Western tactics and equipment had failed against the Communist military-political-economic campaign.

The northern team had spent the last days of Hanoi in contaminating the oil supply of the bus company for a gradual wreckage of engines in the buses, in taking the first actions for delayed sabotage of the railroad (which required teamwork with a CIA special technical team in Japan who performed their part brilliantly), and in writing detailed notes of potential targets for future paramilitary operations (United States adherence to the Geneva Agreement prevented SMM from carrying out the active sabotage it desired to do against the power plant, water facilities, harbor, and bridge). The team had a bad moment when contaminating the oil. They had to work quickly at night, in an enclosed storage room. Fumes from the contaminant came close to knocking them out. Dizzy and weak-kneed, they masked their faces with handkerchiefs and completed the job.

From here on a bamboo curtain of silence falls over all United States sabotage activity in the grim Vietnamese War. General Lansdale's book, In the Midst of Wars, *tells us a great deal about how he tried to bolster the Diem government and nothing at all about sabotage. He is discretion itself about Major Conein's activities, not even mentioning the exploit in Hanoi.*

One reason for this curious silence is that the big new word, especially in the Kennedy years (1960–63), was "counter-insurgency." This came by definition to mean the prevention or containment of Communist infiltration, or rebellion, in an otherwise free country. Yet the countering of such tricks as insurgents use can sometimes be almost unrecognizable from the tricks themselves!

Only in such semi-fictional accounts as Robin Moore's The Green Berets *is there any clue that the United States was capable of staging behind-the-lines exploits of its own.*

As recently as June of 1972 another small corner of the bamboo curtain was lifted. The Washington Post *published a story which ran like this:*

VIENTIANE, Laos, June 14—Use of Laotian territory and specially recruited Asian mercenaries for CIA-sponsored espionage and sabotage missions in North Vietnam has been confirmed here by American sources close to the operation.

The missions are originating from a number of small mountaintop sites in northern Laos within thirty miles of the North Vietnamese border. The guerrilla troops are transported by unmarked Air America planes.

The existence of the guerrilla missions inside North Vietnam was first reported in Saigon earlier this week. Such missions were known to have been initiated in the early 1960s, but were not regarded at the time as very effective and were apparently suspended after the 1968 bombing halt.

Highly trained mountain tribesmen from northern Laos and some Thai mercenaries with long experience in special operations are said here to make up the teams. Most of the guerrillas are said to speak Vietnamese, some fluently.

Officially, the Air America management in Vientiane is unaware that the company's pilots or planes are flying such missions. Air America is a quasi-private airline under contract with United States government agencies.

Pilots used on the espionage-sabotage mission flights are carefully selected and receive special pay for hazardous duty by a "white envelope system." This means that the money received is not accountable or traceable, even for tax purposes, sources say.

Official United States spokesmen in Vientiane decline to comment on the operation, but information pieced together from American and Lao sources here indicates that virtually inaccessible CIA-maintained bases in Laos are used to train, house, and transport the guerrillas.

Nam Yu, the CIA's most secret base in Laos, situated in northwestern Laos near the town of Ban Houei Sai, is reported to be the primary training center.

Nam Yu was formerly a base for intelligence teams being sent into South China to report on telephone and road traffic, a program discontinued in 1971 when President Nixon accepted an invitation to visit China.

From Nam Yu, the guerrillas are moved to the Long Cheng area eighty miles north of Vientiane where they continue to train, making forays into the surrounding mountains inside Laos on lower-level reconnaissance missions for seasoning and practical experience in avoiding capture and inflicting harm on Communist forces.

Many of the potential North Vietnamese infiltrators are "weeded out" during this training period, sources say.

Resident newsmen here have been unable to visit Long Cheng in recent months.

Jump-off points for the guerrillas are considerably east and northeast of Long Cheng, according to the sources, most being tiny hilltop positions hardly known to exist. A major point of departure is said to be at Bouam Long, sometimes called "the fortress in the sky," about forty miles northeast of Long Cheng, a base the Communists have never been able to wrest from its Meo defenders.

Practical training exercises are also conducted at Bouam Long. Communist radio broadcasts frequently note the presence, capture or killing of commandos from Bouam Long in the Sam Neua area of northeast Laos. Caves in nearby mountains contain the headquarters of the Communist-supported Laotian rebels.

The highest priority, however, is given to missions that cross Sam Neua Province and move into North Vietnam where they conduct sabotage, espionage and propaganda missions in that country's least inhabited and defended areas. Precise information on targets and types of guerrilla action is not available here.

It is known, however, that the CIA is distrustful of many claims made by the guerrilla infiltrators and frequently equips the units with cameras so they can photograph themselves at targets. The photographs prove the missions were carried out, and provide intelligence data for CIA analysts.

Each mission uses at least one specially equipped twin-engine Otter plane, said to carry half a million dollars worth of radio and electronic gear for pinpoint navigation and locating of ground forces. Because of the twin Otter's virtual silent operation as it passes close over the ground, its short take-off and landing capability, and the load it can carry, its basic function has been the clandestine insertion, pickup and resupply of guerrilla missions.

There are also reports of guerrillas being snatched from enemy-occupied territory by a hook dangling from rescue aircraft. The guerrilla on the ground inflates a large balloon with lighter-than-air gas, attaches it to a thin line which is then attached to a harness he fastens to himself. The rescue craft passes over the balloon, hooks on and hauls him up.

Qualified sources here say, meantime, that they believe that such espionage missions will be increased in northern Laos, and may be resumed inside China itself, to sabotage war material that—because of the mining of Haiphong—is expected to flow increasingly through China's Yunan Province and the Laotian province of Phong Saly on its way into North Vietnam.

There are undoubtedly many such stories still to be told. In the meantime it is interesting—and touching too—to recall that Special Forces men formed a guard of honor at President Kennedy's burial in Arlington Cemetery.

At the end of the ceremony itself, Sgt. Maj. Francis Ruddy took off his green beret and placed it in sorrow above the place where his commander lay.

The beret bore the shield emblem, for defense, not the Trojan horse of early Special Forces days, symbol of deception.

26

"This Is a Hijacking!"

Jörg Andreas Elten

In the foreword, I mentioned that a simple hijacking for private purposes (say for revenge or greed) does not belong in a book about sabotage, but that a hijacking for political purposes does. Here is one of the most sensational examples of the latter. The account was put together from scores of interviews by a German newsman, Jörg Andreas Elten.

THE couple held hands as they boarded the Israeli Boeing 707 in Amsterdam. A steward remembers thinking: "Honeymooners." The man was in his early twenties, spare, wiry, with reddish hair and a narrow face. The girl, graceful, slim-waisted, had long black hair and an olive complexion. She was wearing a light-blue suit.

El Al Flight 219—Tel Aviv-Amsterdam-New York—was almost fully booked, but the two managed to find adjacent seats, a few rows behind the partition separating the first-class and tourist sections. Next to them, at the window, sat Mrs. Faye Schenk, an American from New York. Glancing at the couple, she thought, "What nice-looking people!" But she noted that they did not exchange a single word.

Shortly after 1:00 P.M., the aircraft took off and, with 148 passengers aboard, began climbing to its cruising altitude of 32,000 feet.

Suddenly Mrs. Schenk heard an "animal cry" and looked up in amazement. The two young people beside her had leaped into the aisle and were running forward into the first-class compartment. Again and again they cried *"Yallah! Yallah!"*—an Arabic word meaning "Let's go!"

The man was holding a silvery revolver in his hand, so small it appeared to be a toy. The woman brandished two cylindrical containers—hand grenades.

Charging through the first-class area, the pair reached the service lounge, a special compartment for the crew. Beyond this was a door leading to the aircraft's cockpit.

It was locked.

"Open up!" the man shouted and began beating on the door handle with his revolver. Behind him, the woman held the grenades aloft and warned, "The safety pins have been pulled!"

There were three crew members in the service lounge: the chief steward, Avraham Eisenberg; a steward, Shlomo Vider; and a stewardess, Jeanette Demerjean. As Israelis, they had been briefed to act differently from crews of other airlines in case of a skyjacking; they were expected to react like soldiers under Arab attack.

Today, September 6, 1970, as usual during these months of intensifying enmity in the Middle East, the El Al plane carried two security officers, one in the tourist section and one in first class. This afternoon, however, the first-class security man had gone into the cockpit.

It is an ironclad El Al rule to keep the armored door to the cockpit closed during a skyjack attempt. Thus, the security officer had little choice of action. If he left the cockpit, it would mean opening the door for the hijackers. But if he stayed inside, perhaps the three crew members—Eisenberg, Vider and Jean-ette Demerjean—could handle the situation without his help, since they had been schooled in defending their airplane.

Confronted by the locked door to the cockpit, the hijackers momentarily seemed undecided. Noticing this, Vider began slowly rising from his seat. The male skyjacker turned, weapon in hand, and then fired. Perhaps it was meant as a warning, but the bullet hit Vider in the leg.

Seeing that the skyjackers were becoming increasingly agi-tated, Vider, even though he was wounded, knew that he had to act quickly.

"Don't get excited," he said quietly. "Let me talk to the cap-tain over the telephone. I'll tell him to open the door."

The skyjackers assented. But Vider, speaking Hebrew, fully agreed with the captain's suggestion to fly on. The door re-mained closed.

In frustration the male skyjacker now grabbed Jeanette around the neck and aimed his revolver at her temple. Then he dragged her to the cockpit door and shouted, "Open up, or I'll kill the girl!"

Wounded as he was, Vider realized he had to do something. Slowly he stood up. The skyjacker immediately pointed the re-volver at him. "Let me speak with the captain," Vider said. He advanced a few steps and then, from a distance of three feet, he lunged. With his left hand he slapped the revolver aside and with his right he grabbed the skyjacker's hair and began beating his head against the cockpit door. Both men fell, and the women—Jeanette and the female skyjacker—fled to the rear of the first-class section.

At this moment, the captain of the airplane went into a daring flight maneuver. He turned the heavy Boeing 707 on its left wing and plunged into a power dive. The female skyjacker, still hold-ing the grenades, lost her balance and staggered toward a seat occupied by New York tax consultant Harry Clark. Clark leaped up and jumped her from the rear.

"I'll blow the plane up!" she shrieked.

Disregarding her threat, Clark gripped her throat and panted: "Okay, then we'll both die!"

Clark kept his hold. "I squeezed and squeezed and thought I had killed her," he said later. The grenades dropped from her hands; they did not explode. The safety pins were still in place.

In the tourist section, where few passengers could see what was happening, the dive added to the confusion created by the sound of the gunshot. Several women began shrieking, and children cried. Yet one woman kept her head. Mrs. Esther Moyal, of Linden, N.J., began singing a Hebrew folk song, "Hava Nagilla," and the others joined in.

By now the second Israeli security officer, stationed in tourist class, was well aware that he had trouble aboard. But so far he had delayed action to see if other accomplices might be on the plane. As the aircraft dived, he stepped forward with his hand on his revolver. Seeing the fighting men at the cockpit door, he fired at them. Three shots hit the skyjacker. Vider was bleeding profusely. "Suddenly the struggle was over," Vider said later. "I thought the skyjacker was unconscious. I stood over him and poked him with my foot—he did not move."

The female skyjacker had lost her wig and much of her makeup, and the Israeli security officer now recognized her as a woman reputed to be the "heroine of the Palestinian nation," 24-year-old Leila Khaled. She had established her reputation in August, 1969, when she had skyjacked an aircraft belonging to Trans World Airlines. This was precious "cargo" indeed, and under other circumstances the plane would have flown nonstop back to Israel. But Vider needed immediate medical attention. The pilot decided to land in London.

Meanwhile, word of the attempted skyjacking had been radioed to Amsterdam—much to the consternation of the El Al ground-security officer there. It was his job to check out all passengers before they boarded. Obviously, he had slipped up, but now his attention was drawn to a more crucial matter. Had he made only one mistake? Although he had allowed Leila Khaled and her companion to get on Flight 219, he had denied seats to two men who had aroused his suspicions—and these two were now aboard a Pan American plane bound for New York.

The two men in question were blacks, Semoe Gueeye and Sanghone Diop, purportedly students from Senegal, West Africa. They had aroused El Al's suspicions by purchasing only one-way tickets from Amsterdam to Santiago, Chile, via New York City, and by offering to pay for them in cash, an unusually large amount. Nothing more concrete than this developed, but it was enough for El Al to tell them, "Sorry, Flight 219 is full." However, the two had open tickets, so they decided to take Pan Am Flight 093 instead.

At first, El Al said nothing to the American airline about its unsubstantiated suspicions. But, as Flight 093 prepared for departure, the airport police were alerted and ground control radioed the Pan Am captain, Jack Priddy. The Pan Am craft, one of the new jumbo 747s, had left the terminal, but was still on the runway awaiting takeoff clearance.

"Clipper 093. El Al has refused two passengers for their flight from Amsterdam to New York because they didn't like them. It looks as if those two are aboard your aircraft."

Priddy obtained the names of the men, then left the cockpit and descended the spiral staircase leading from the lounge on the upper deck of the giant jet to the first-class compartment. The two blacks were paged, and after a short delay they identified themselves.

"It was an awkward situation for me," Priddy later revealed, "because, according to the law, I had no right to search the two. Nonetheless, I said, 'I'm sorry, gentlemen, I have a message from ground control. I apologize, but I must search you. If you do not agree to this, I must take you back.'"

The two acted surprised, but they remained polite. "We don't understand," one of them said. "But if you want to search us, go ahead, please."

Priddy frisked both from their shoulders to their socks and examined their attaché cases. He found nothing. A stewardess searched the seats with the same result.

Priddy felt a little ridiculous. "Forgive me, gentlemen," he said. "It appears to have been a mistake." The two blacks only smiled.

At 2:21, Priddy reported tersely to ground control: "093 ready for takeoff." And soon the craft was aloft.

But he had not frisked the two thoroughly enough. In fact, the polite young Negroes were very well armed: they carried two small revolvers and two hand grenades equipped with plastic explosives. They were hidden in special containers in the genital regions of both men.

The second skyjacking began in the first-class lounge. Gueeye, holding a grenade in one hand and a revolver in the other, cleared the area of passengers. Then he ordered a purser, Augusta Schneider, up the spiral staircase. Seizing her about the neck and pressing the gun to her temple, he pushed her toward the cockpit door.

"Open!" the man barked.

"My key is downstairs," she pleaded. The skyjacker shifted the revolver to her ribs and repeated his command. She beat against the door with her fist. On the other side, a flight engineer opened it a crack, and Gueeye pushed his way in, shouting, "Hands up! This is a hijacking!" Behind him, Diop also entered.

Unobtrusively, Captain Priddy flicked on radar code 3100. As a result, on a radar screen of British Airways Control in London, Pan Am 093 showed up as flaring dots. However, code 3100 was being used only in the United States at that time, and its meaning—a skyjacking—was unknown elsewhere. British flight controllers who assign air lanes over the Atlantic realized that something was amiss. But what?

One skyjacker told the captain, "Turn back to Amsterdam!" Priddy raised his air speed and put his enormous machine into a turn.

British Airways Control immediately inquired: "093, why are you changing course? What's up?" Priddy did not answer, and the flight controller on the ground seemed to understand. "Descend immediately to 27,000 feet," he told Priddy. "Avoid a midair collision."

Priddy took the jumbo down. But Gueeye became agitated.

Evidently he believed that the pilot was preparing for an emergency landing. Feeling the revolver in the back of his neck, Priddy coolly tried to reassure him. "Calm down!" he said. "We'll fly you wherever you want. Just tell us where."

The skyjacker then said he wanted to go to the Middle East, to a "friendly" country. Priddy switched on the public-address system and gave the news to his passengers.

With that, Gueeye seemed to relax. He took a seat behind the captain and confided, "This is my third skyjack."

Priddy received the news with relief. Later, he observed: "The man was a pro, thank God. In a skyjacking, it's better to be dealing with an expert than with some amateur who might go off the deep end."

It was now shortly after 5:00 P.M. For controllers in the European flight-safety centers, a sensational situation was materializing. The abortive attempt to hijack the El Al aircraft was dramatic enough. But now, just a few hours later, not only a Pan American jumbo 747, but *two other* giant jets—a Boeing 707 and a DC-8—were hurtling toward the Middle East. Obviously this was a concerted and well-organized operation, for all three had been commandeered by men and women who reported in broken English that they were acting on behalf of the Popular Front for the Liberation of Palestine.

The Front is an organization of Palestinian guerrillas which carried out previous hijackings in 1968 and 1969 and planned other bombings aimed at the West. But many people on this September afternoon were still only dimly aware of what it stood for and what its members hoped to achieve.

The hijackers themselves were representative. All were under thirty, and nearly all of them belonged to the new generation of Palestinians whose homeland is occupied by the Israelis. Most of them had spent their youth in Palestinian refugee camps, growing up in miserable housing, with short rations and a deep, inbred hatred of Israel. . . .

Planning for the skyjacking began in August soon after President Gamal Abdel Nasser of Egypt, following a peace plan put forward by the United States, agreed to a cease-fire with Israel. The Front violently opposed any such move, and so an elaborate scheme was devised to pressure the West and publicize the Palestinian cause.

It appears that the Front had available a well-trained hijacking squad. For example, Leila Khaled and her accomplice carried with them detailed instructions on radio operation and air routes from the English Channel to Amman, Jordan. The Front had obtained flight maps for Europe and the Middle East, of the kind that professional pilots use. The hijackers knew the basics of navigation, and were familiar with the instruments in the cockpit. Their hand grenades and pistols were purposely made of nonferrous substances, to thwart the electronic surveillance equipment at airports.

Unlike the skyjackings to Cuba and other countries, these were meant to have political impact. Therefore, the planes would not be flown merely to "a friendly country," but to a lonely bit of Jordanian desert where Popular Front guerrillas would take charge of the passengers. Aptly, this hard-packed bit of wasteland near Amman had been dubbed "Revolution Airstrip."

The political nature of the skyjackings became quickly evident, and within a short time President Richard Nixon and British Prime Minister Edward Heath were notified. Everywhere in the West, leaders and their ministers were kept posted on the unfolding events.

Their concern proved warranted. The hijackings crippled international air traffic, the most important means of transportation in the modern world. They opened a new episode in the guerrilla war of the Third World against the "establishment" of the rich, industrial nations. They were to trigger a civil war in Jordan and thereby plunge the entire Arab world into a deep crisis. And finally, in all likelihood, they hastened the death of President Nasser, who managed to deal with the crisis but, in doing so, sapped his last remaining physical reserves.

Meanwhile, 30,000 feet above the European continent, the lives of 477 innocent people aboard the three planes lay in direct jeopardy. But this did not bother the Popular Front. As Leila Khaled told her captors in a London police station: "One is on the side of either the oppressed or the oppressors. There are no innocent people, and there is no neutrality!"

For all their careful arrangements, the skyjackers had made one serious miscalculation. Not until they boarded Flight 093 did Gueeye and Diop realize that the plane would be a giant 747. The craft was too big to be accommodated at Revolution Airstrip, and there was a period of confusion about where to take it. At last they decided on Beirut, Lebanon.

For the most part, Gueeye sat directly behind Priddy, holding his gun and hand grenade. While flying over Salonika, however, the captain noticed that both the skyjacker and the flight engineer were crawling around on the floor, looking for something with flashlights. "What's up?" he asked. The flight engineer answered in a tone of urgency: "He lost the safety pin from the grenade!" While Gueeye searched, he held the grenade's trigger mechanism down with his thumb. One false move would have destroyed the cockpit and sent 152 passengers and 17 crew members to their deaths. But finally the pin was found and reinserted.

Beyond the cockpit door, alone in the lounge, Augusta Schneider tended the other skyjacker. At one point, he asked for some orange juice. When Augusta handed him the glass, he said, "Drink from it first."

"He thought I had put poison or sleeping tablets into it," Augusta said later. "I had to drink half of the glass."

She also served him a plate of soup. He hesitated for a moment. How was he to eat while holding a grenade in one hand and a revolver in the other? Finally, he gave the perplexed stewardess the hand grenade and said, "Would you please hold this for a moment?"

As darkness fell, they reached Beirut. For the skyjackers, the situation now became critical: the Lebanese government was hostile to the Popular Front, and would certainly prepare an unpleasant reception for them. In addition, the Front itself did not know that the skyjackers were planning to land there; they were still awaited at Revolution Airstrip.

As the 747 came in over the Lebanese capital and began circling, Gueeye first requested that a "responsible representative of the Popular Front" be put on the radio. This alone took more than an hour, and when finally a Palestinian commando reached the airport and identified himself, Gueeye did not recognize the name. An argument developed and, as it continued, a detachment of the Lebanese army, with armored vehicles, moved onto the airfield, determined to prevent a landing. When they learned this, Gueeye and Diop were close to losing their self-control. They trusted no one, not even the commando they were talking to. And then, as the excited exchange went on, Captain Priddy broke in to announce, "We have fuel left for fifteen minutes. I merely wanted to tell you that!"

This announcement forced the Lebanese regiment to withdraw, and Priddy was allowed to land. Aboard, Gueeye and Diop masked their faces in white napkins and guardedly observed a yellow jeep in which the commando slowly approached. An identification was made, and shortly the skyjackers learned their new orders: proceed to Cairo and there—to protest Nasser's agreement to a cease-fire—destroy the aircraft. So, as the plane refueled, a new cargo was brought out. A Palestinian commando in the Beirut control tower designated it as "sandwiches." In fact, it was dynamite.

A demolition expert put the sticks aboard and quietly affixed them to the washroom walls. The crew was being kept in isolation and had no idea what was happening.

In all now, there were nine Popular Front representatives on board, and they sauntered down the aisles of the vast aircraft, engaging the passengers in political discussions. Augusta Schneider remembers, "It looked like a tea party." Unnoticed, the dynamite specialist laid his detonating cord.

With the fuel loaded, Captain Priddy started up the 747 again and took off. Now Gueeye and Diop, plus the dynamite expert, were the only guerrillas aboard. Two hours later, as the plane neared Cairo, Gueeye came out of the cockpit and said to Augusta: "You will have eight minutes to get the passengers off." The crew at once prepared for an emergency debarkation.

Just before the landing, the young demolition expert got up and boldly asked Augusta for some matches.

"The 'No Smoking' sign is on," she said. He smiled and insisted.

Augusta recalls: 'I gave them to him, and then suddenly I saw this fellow lighting fuses. We were still at least 300 feet above the ground!"

Captain Priddy braked the jumbo to a halt just short of the end of the runway, and the crew hurled open the doors. Emergency slides were automatically inflated and deployed. In less than 90 seconds all of the passengers were off the plane.

In the cockpit, Gueeye rose, looked at his watch, waited until the last moment, then said to the pilot and co-pilot: "Okay, go! Good luck!"

The men dived for the exits. Even so, Captain Priddy and Gueeye were still under the wing of the jumbo jet when the first explosion shattered the cockpit.

"I felt the pressure waves on the back of my neck," Priddy said later. "At the same time, I heard rifle fire all around. I did not know what to make of that. We jumped into an airport bus and threw ourselves on the floor. Gueeye was arrested by two Egyptian soldiers."

Augusta Schneider and another group ran in the opposite direction, away from the airport building. "Suddenly, I spotted Diop standing on a sand dune," she remembers. "He was holding his attaché case in his hand, gazing at the aircraft and observing the explosions. The flames illuminated him brightly. I noticed that he was smiling. He was happy. Later, he helped us with an Argentine woman who had broken her leg, and he gave his handkerchief to someone else who was injured on the head. He was no longer dangerous. He had accomplished his mission."

Later that day, September 7, all the passengers and crew were picked up by another Pan Am plane and flown to New York.

Roughly thirty-five miles northeast of Amman lies Gaa-Khanna, a level stretch of sand resembling a dry lake bed. When the winter rains come, its fine sand becomes as slippery as soap. The rest of the year, it is as flat as an ironing board and hard-surfaced. No roads lead there—only desert tracks. This was Revolution Airstrip.

The first hijacked aircraft to reach it was the TWA Boeing 707 which had left Frankfurt that afternoon, piloted by a 51-year-old American, Carroll Woods. Although one of the hijackers, a trim, attractive young girl who sat behind Woods with a hand grenade, had charts of the area, the strip was not readily recognizable at first. Then, abruptly, the sun sank, and on a later pass over the spot, Woods made out two parallel rows of lights—smudge pots lined up to indicate the runway.

The crew made preparations to land, going through an emergency checklist for lowering and locking the nose gear, and the jet came down. "All at once the aircraft was surrounded by armed figures," Woods reported later. "I was afraid that I would roll over them. Finally, I braked the plane at the very edge of the strip."

. . . Silent and fearful, the passengers observed a half-dozen men and women climb aboard, armed with submachine guns. They wore green fatigues and *kafiyehs,* a Bedouin headdress. Stalking along the aisle, they presented a grim picture, and several children began to cry. But the commandos didn't act like pirates lusting for blood. They behaved more like officials at an international airport, distributing entry forms and asking for passport data. Even in a revolutionary situation, Arab bureaucracy triumphed.

As the passengers completed the forms, the noise of another plane startled them from their seats. It was the second hijacked craft, a Swissair DC-8 from Zurich. This flight, too, had had difficulty in locating the desert airstrip, and at one point a radio voice had advised: "Fly heading 260." Checking his maps, pilot Fritz Schreiber, 56, discovered that this course would take him straight to Lod, the Israeli airport near Tel Aviv. Apparently the Israelis had picked up the Swiss jet on radar and wanted to lure it to their territory. Schreiber deemed the risk too great. "Thank you," he had advised the anonymous voice. "We know!"

Soon the DC-8 touched down at Gaa-Khanna and braked to an emergency stop as the co-pilot reversed the engines. The Popular Front now had 286 passengers and 22 crew members in its power.

Fully armed, the commandos strolled the aisles, advising their hostages to prepare for the night and explaining their cause. On the Swiss jet, one Palestinian said in faultless English: "We are sorry for having brought you into this situation. But we had no choice. We wanted to attract the world's attention to the fate of our people."

The passengers sat listening in the dark. With the engines off, there was no electricity. The stewardesses served a few cold leftovers from the galley, holding their trays in one hand, flashlights in the other. Many passengers declined the meal. Said the co-pilot, "Morale was at rock bottom." Soon a brooding silence descended, interrupted only by the sound of the Arab guards pacing the aisle.

The sun rose the next morning on a unique scene. The two silvery planes, symbols of the 20th century's great technological advances, shimmered in the desert, while around them were pitched the flapping tents of the Palestinians. The flag of the Popular Front, planted in the sand, waved defiantly; in the distance sat several armored vehicles of the Royal Jordanian Army. They had approached in the night, but had made no move to attack.

The crew served breakfast brought by the guerrillas: flat Arabian bread, sheep cheese, hard-boiled eggs and tea. Infants were diapered with napkins from first class. By 11:00 A.M. the thermometer stood at 104° F. in the shade. The toilets, no longer operating properly, gave out a foul odor.

Around noon a black Chevrolet carrying the chief of staff of the Jordanian army, Gen. Mashur Haditha, arrived, and under the wings of the TWA jet he spoke to the guerrilla chief, Abu Fahdi. "The king is appalled," Haditha said. "You have put to shame before the whole world the Arabs' celebrated reputation for hospitality." Then, carefully, he hinted that King Hussein might order his men to free the hostages by force.

Abu Fahdi was unimpressed. "If the army attacks," he said, "we'll blow up the planes with all the hostages in them."

Finally, the two agreed on a compromise. The commandos would release most of the women and children and let them go to Amman. In return, the Jordanian regiments would retreat to new positions two kilometers from the aircraft.

Through the morning, Popular Front soldiers had been examining the papers of the TWA passengers. This plane had come from Tel Aviv, but to the guerrillas' surprise, they found not a single Israeli passport. Meanwhile, to relieve the worsening situation in the cabin, holes were dug beneath the craft and a flight engineer opened the waste outlets to the toilets. Amid the malodorous mess, a guerrilla made an interesting discovery—several torn-up Israeli passports. So there *were* Israelis aboard!

A thorough search of hand baggage was made, and more Israeli passports turned up. In fact, among the hostages possibly a dozen had double citizenship, American and Israeli, although none resided permanently in Israel.

With this information in hand, the guerrillas picked 127 persons from the two planes and loaded them onto buses for Amman. Most of the men had to remain. And no hostages of the Jewish faith were relinquished from the TWA flight. Many families were separated, and there were heartrending good-bys as the buses pulled away. A 16-year-old American, Barbara Mensch, said later: "I was traveling with my friend Nancy. We had spent our vacation at a kibbutz. Nancy was allowed to go, but I was forced to stay behind. That's the first time I cried."

Hardly had the buses left when the chief of the Popular Front in Amman came on the radio. "I hope you did not release anyone of British nationality!" he said urgently.

"We have no Britons here at all," he was informed.

To the guerrillas this was unwelcome news, and at 2:00 P.M. the leaders of the Popular Front gathered in Amman to discuss a question of highest priority: What could they do to get Leila Khaled freed? There was only one answer. After a short consultation, the guerrillas began to prepare for their next "expedition."

The plan was to hijack yet another plane—this time one belonging to British Overseas Airways. The flight chosen was that of a four-engine VC-10 jet which left Bahrein, a small island in the Persian Gulf, the morning of September 9, bound for Beirut and London. Nearly half of the passengers were Orientals, as the flight had originated in Bombay with a stop at Dubayy. But fifty-two were British citizens—more than enough to bring pressure on the British government to release Leila Khaled.

The hijacking began without a hitch. A little over an hour into the flight, one of three Palestinian commandos on board—informally garbed in light shirts and slacks—rose from his seat and calmly and undramatically proceeded to the cockpit. Capt. Cyril Goulborn turned in his seat as he heard the door open and looked into the barrel of a small pistol. Having followed the accounts of the other skyjackings, Goulborn knew at once what was happening. He reacted with the poise of an experienced wartime pilot. "I realized immediately that I had to create a relationship of confidence with the man holding the gun," he said later.

In the passenger compartment, two other guerrillas took charge. A British major named Fawkes Potts, a contract officer with the Abu Dhabi defense force, on his way to Beirut with his wife, Jenny, and his daughters, Susan and Annette, watched the men closely.

"My daughters called one 'Goggle-eyes,' " he said, "the other, 'Fleabrain.' It was my impression that these men were under the influence of drugs. Certainly they were both very tense and on edge."

Instead of flying directly to Revolution Airstrip, the guerrillas decided to stop first at Beirut. Having handled a hijacked 747 jumbo jet only a few days earlier, the men in the control tower there took the situation routinely. But, as before, there were delays. The British ambassador in Beirut, informed of this new crisis, demanded that the Popular Front release the passengers as soon as the plane landed. There were thirty-five children aboard, twenty-one traveling without their parents. What did the skyjackers want with all of them in the Jordanian desert? But Popular Front orders were: 'Don't let a single passenger leave the BOAC plane in Beirut!"

In the air, the children had their own ideas. Stewardess Mandy Thomas was sitting with two of them, Leo and Aiden Biles. Nearby stood Fleabrain. Little Aiden took a penknife from his pocket, pressed it into Miss Thomas's hand and whispered to her, "Go ahead. Stick it in his ribs!"

As Mandy later explained, "The only thing that surprised these children was that the guerrillas had no machine guns."

Landing clearance finally came through, and Goulborn set the plane down at Beirut. As soon as refueling was completed, he lifted off again, and shortly before sunset the VC-10 joined the two other craft on the sands of the Jordanian desert.

Meanwhile, sitting in her police-station cell in London, Leila Khaled exchanged banter with one of her guards. Said the guard, "Why don't you go home? We'll show you the way to the airport. You don't even need a ticket. Just skyjack the first plane and fly away."

Leila smiled and said, "I'd better not. Who knows, some Israeli sharpshooter might knock me off. But you may rely on my comrades. They'll get me out of here. I'm confident of that!"

Negotiations aimed at freeing the hostages had begun some six hours after the first hijackings. At that time, no one in the West yet knew exactly where the planes had landed or whether the passengers were safe. This lasted until a representative of the Palestinian Red Crescent (the Muslim equivalent of the Red Cross) invited the head of the permanent International Red Cross delegation in Amman to visit the hostages. After the delegate's return from the airstrip, it was learned for the first time that the jets had landed in Jordan and that the passengers were unharmed.

Through the Red Crescent, the Popular Front made a demand: Free three Palestinians who had shot at an Israeli airliner in Zurich and were being held by Switzerland. Later, the Front requested the release of three guerrillas who had been tried and convicted in West Germany for an attack on El Al passengers in Munich.

The next day, as the world read in stunned amazement of the hijackings, diplomats conferred anxiously in several capitals. In Washington, D.C., Secretary of State William P. Rogers, interrupting the Labor Day weekend, met with representatives of Britain, Israel, Switzerland and West Germany. The following day, he received ambassadors from ten Arab countries. The Arab reaction to the high-handed tactics of the Popular Front was far from favorable. Said Talat Al-Ghoussein, ambassador from Kuwait, "The hijackings do not serve the cause of the Palestinian people."

Initially, the Germans and Swiss agreed to accept the commandos' terms. The United States, however, was in a difficult position: although most of the hostages were United States citizens, the United States itself held no Palestinians and therefore had no bargaining power. In the end, all of the concerned Western nations agreed to act together and deal with the Popular Front as a unit through the International Committee of the Red Cross.

With the skyjacking of the British airliner, the poker game for the hostages entered a new phase. Within hours, Prime Minister Heath convened his ministers at 10 Downing Street, and Leila Khaled became the focal point of the negotiations.

Meanwhile, at Revolution Airstrip, the Palestinians made two moves. On the first night, they had removed six men from the TWA plane and had imprisoned them in a small room in Irbid, a northern Jordanian city which was controlled by the guerrillas. Four days later, the Palestinians took ten more men to a refugee camp on the outskirts of Amman.

The uncertainty of the fate of these men played on the nerves of the hostages left behind. They heard newscasts on their transistor radios, and so they knew that the Popular Front had set a deadline for the fulfillment of its demands. First, it was September 10, 10:00 A.M.; then it was extended by seventy-two hours.

The nervousness of the adults in the TWA jet transferred itself to the children. They became restive and noisy. Miriam Beeber, a 19-year-old American, and her friend Sarah Malka, who had been born into a Jewish family living in the Sudan and who spoke Arabic fluently, took the children to the rear of the plane and opened a sort of kindergarten. Miriam said, "Sarah had bought herself a drum during her vacation in Israel. Now she beat it, and we sang songs with the children—things like 'Old MacDonald Had a Farm.' Later, we played riddles."

Next door, in the BOAC aircraft, 15-year-old Nigel Hatcher had a special problem: he had brought a turtle with him from Bahrein, which he placed in a tin box filled with water. "The water began to reek," he said. "I should have changed it. But we only got a cup about every five hours, and I couldn't give the turtle much. It was pretty hot in the desert, and we were often thirsty."

The guerrillas told the BOAC passengers that they could go home as soon as their Prime Minister released Leila Khaled. Time passed, and the Britons began to chafe at the delay. They could not understand why Heath was letting them stew so long in an aircraft studded with dynamite. Nigel Hatcher reported: "Everybody was cross with Mr. Heath for being so slow. In fact, my brother called my turtle 'Ted Heath,' for a joke."

Nonetheless, it was partly due to the influence of the British Prime Minister that the International Crisis Staff in Bern, set up to deal with the situation, finally made a weighty and tough decision. This occurred on Thursday night, September 10. Representatives of the United States, Switzerland, West Germany and Great Britain met that evening at the Swiss Foreign Ministry, and discussed once again the ultimatum of the Popular Front, shortly due to expire. The Popular Front was now officially in-

sisting on an additional demand: it wanted to retain an unspeci-
fied number of Jewish hostages of American citizenship until the
Israelis would agree to release some Arab resistance fighters they
had under detention. But it was unclear how many of these guerrillas were involved. Numbers given unofficially ranged between
300 and 3000.

The meeting dragged on into the night. Diplomats kept leaving the room to consult their governments in Washington, London
and Bonn. There was a terrible aspect to the decision being
framed. Giving in to the blackmail of the Popular Front, in
order to save the lives of the hostages, would almost surely en-
courage the guerrillas to skyjack other planes. That, in turn,
would escalate the blackmail and endanger the lives of hundreds
of other innocent people.

Prime Minister Heath instructed his representatives to stay
tough, and finally at three o'clock in the morning a decision was
reached. Leila Khaled and the six other Palestinian terrorists
would be liberated only if all hostages, including those of Jewish
faith, were returned safely. No Arabs held by the Israelis would
be included in the deal.

The decision was radioed to Amman via the Red Cross, and
soon the guerrillas at the airstrip knew of it. They were angry. A
guerrilla girl, whom passengers called "Bombshell Bessie" for
her rough ways, stormed into the BOAC plane and shouted,
"Because of your bad government, we shall have to blow you all
up with the plane!" The children aboard looked at her in horror.
The adults fell awkwardly silent.

That night the jittery guerrillas began digging foxholes, in the
belief that a small band of Israelis was planning a raid to free
the hostages. Even without the feared attack, the guerrillas' situation was growing hourly more precarious. When the skyjackings
had begun, the Popular Front was convinced that its demands
would be met within forty-eight hours, and the barter of the hostages arranged. Now, with the passage of almost six days, logisti-
cal support for some two-hundred prisoners had become diffi-

cult, and the hostages' predicament was angering world opinion.

Nasser himself feared that the skyjackers were giving the Israelis or the Western powers a pretext to intervene in the Middle East. In fact, President Nixon had already ordered several transport planes moved to Turkey, where they would be quickly available for a rescue attempt. Aircraft carriers of the American Sixth Fleet, stationed in the Mediterranean, were heading for the Lebanese coast.

But there was danger right at the guerrillas' doorstep. For some time there had been sporadic fighting between Palestinian irregulars and the Jordanian army. This trouble had its roots in decades of Middle Eastern history; but what it amounted to was that the Palestinian guerrillas, nominally citizens of Jordan, were in open civil war with the Hussein government. An outbreak in June had killed or wounded more than five hundred people before a cease-fire cooled things down. In the past week, at least two more cease-fires had been declared, only to be violated almost immediately. Hardly a day now passed without an exchange of fire in Amman and other cities to the north.

The Palestinian irregulars embraced far more than just the Popular Front. In all, there were twelve guerrilla groups, loosely associated, and together they claimed to have some 30,000 troops. Of these, probably fewer than five thousand had ever had any training.

In the face of all these mounting pressures, the leaders of the Popular Front in Amman issued an order: the passengers would be brought into the capital; the skyjacked aircraft would be left at the airstrip; the airstrip would be evacuated.

The plan displeased Abu Fahdi, the ranking man at the airstrip. But dutifully he began to ship off his prisoners in minibuses sent out by his superiors. Before their departure, however, he had a surprise in store for them. The buses rolled only a few hundred yards from the aircraft and then began to take up a semicircular formation.

Seconds later, an explosion shattered the cockpit of the BOAC aircraft. Next, the fuel tanks of the TWA plane exploded.

Then, the fuselage of the Swissair jet went up. For twenty minutes explosions rocked the desert stillness—and $24.5 million worth of airplanes disappeared in fire and smoke. Waving their submachine guns, the guerrillas greeted the thunderous spectacle with cheers.

Suddenly, from all sides, heavy Centurion tanks of the Jordanian army advanced on the strip. For six days they had been keeping their distance. Now they hoped to free the hostages. Nervously, the guerrillas undid the safeties of their guns and trained them on their prisoners.

Abu Fahdi jumped from his bus, along with a couple of other men, and there followed a wild emotional altercation between the guerrillas and the Jordanian officers.

"What are they saying?" Miriam Beeber asked her friend Sarah.

"If the army does not withdraw," Sarah translated, "the guerrillas want to kill us all!"

"One more step," Abu Fahdi yelled, "and you'll be returning to Amman with a column of hearses!"

The Jordanians gave up and withdrew. The buses, packed with hostages and guerrillas, careered across the desert. Passing through a village on the way, the convoy turned into a propaganda procession. "Everyone into the street!" a guerrilla commanded. "Applause!"

People streamed from houses, cafés and shops and gathered at the curbs, hailing the commandos as heroes. To the simple villagers, they were daring young men who had plucked the "imperialist" airplanes from the skies and snared the "capitalists." "The crowds gawked at us like so many animals in a zoo," Miriam said. "The noise was frightening."

Where were the buses headed? Miriam was convinced that the guerrillas were taking them to the Intercontinental Hotel in Amman. For six days she had not washed, or changed clothes, or even brushed her teeth. Her dress was sweaty, her hair full of sand. She looked forward to her first bath in the hotel and to an ice-cold Coke.

But her surmise was only partially right. Most of the hostages were delivered, as she expected, to the Intercontinental. Inside the hotel, which had been badly damaged in recent street fighting, the scene was a mixture of television lights, interviews, happy reunions, tears, children running to and fro. But above the confusion two frightening questions persisted: "Has everyone been released? Who is missing?"

Representatives of the International Red Cross, diplomats, managers of airlines and reporters tried to make sense of the situation. Obviously, some hostages were still in the hands of the guerrillas. Who were they, and where were they being held? In fact, fifty-six persons were still unaccounted for. (The tabulation eventually revealed that thirty-eight Americans, eight Britons, six Swiss, two Germans and two Dutchmen were missing.)

Some of these were the men taken from the planes in the first days of the hijacking. But most of this number had actually been on Miriam Beeber's bus with salvation almost in sight. Then, as the vehicle rumbled through the sun-baked streets of Amman, it had suddenly broken away from the rest of the convoy, mounted a steep street, and halted in front of a low concrete building.

"Get out!" the hostages were ordered. "We are going to keep you as long as your governments do not fulfill our demands. You are now prisoners of war."

"For the first time in this terrible period," Miriam confessed, "I broke down."

At this point, the negotiations between the Popular Front and the Red Cross were temporarily suspended. The International Crisis Staff in Bern ceased functioning for all practical purposes, and the fate of the hostages became entwined in a bloody civil war.

Initially, the prisoners were held in Amman in four different locations. But on the night of September 15 they were regrouped. The eight British, six Swiss and two Germans were taken to a small row house at Al Wahdat, one of the Palestinian refugee camps on the outskirts of the capital.* Thirty-two of the

* The two Dutchmen, one a passenger and one a TWA steward, were released, leaving fifty-four hostages still in guerrilla hands.

Americans, previously imprisoned at three different spots, were brought together in a three-story building on a hill above the city. This occasioned a joyous reunion and talk long into the night.

The next morning Radio Amman announced the appointment by King Hussein of a military government, a move which the guerrillas considered a declaration of war. In the Palestinian refugee camps, arms and ammunition were distributed—mostly Soviet carbines—not only to men, but to women and young boys. "Brothers," the guerrilla radio declared, "keep your fingers on the trigger until the Fascist military regime is removed!"

Swissair Captain Schreiber remembers the morning of September 17. "Machine guns rattled, and there were dull explosions everywhere. We lay close together in a small room. Light entered through a tiny barred slit. It was hot. In the front of our house, mountains of ammunition crates were stored. It's unthinkable what would have happened if we had sustained a direct hit."

A pall of dark smoke hung over the city as Hussein's tanks moved along littered boulevards, firing at guerrilla snipers on rooftops and in narrow alleys. Shops dropped their steel shutters, while in the houses people took to the cellars for protection. Electricity was out; telephones were dead; a curfew had been imposed.

The Americans, on their hilltop, had a vantage point—when they were able to get near the windows. "On the second day," Benjamin Feinstein, a steel contractor from New York, remembers, "the tanks of the Jordanian army approached within one hundred yards of our house. Shells hit very close. We threw ourselves to the floor in the middle of the building. But some stood guard at the windows, ready to throw back hand grenades before they exploded. After dark, the noise abated a little. We looked down into the valley. It was like watching a fireworks display."

For days the war raged, with Hussein apparently on top one moment, the guerrillas the next. On September 19, the Syrians intervened on the side of the Palestinian guerrillas, pushing across the northern border of Jordan with an armored brigade of

Russian tanks. The fighting grew intense, and Hussein was hard-pressed.

Two days later, President Nixon sent fourteen vessels, among them the aircraft carrier *John F. Kennedy,* to reinforce the Sixth Fleet, and the airborne units of the 8th United States Infantry Division, stationed in Germany, were put on alert. The Soviets also beefed up their Mediterranean fleet with fifteen additional ships. But, under pressure from the Russians and the Jordanian army, the Syrians withdrew their tanks on September 23, and once again the scales tipped in favor of Hussein.

Preparing for a showdown, the youthful king now ordered his elite troops, the red-bereted Jordanian paratroopers, to free the fifty-four hostages, cost what it might. On the morning of September 25, the Jordanians broke through the guerrilla defenses and stormed into Al Wahdat, the refugee camp. The British, German and Swiss hostages could hear them coming. First there was the shrieking of women and children nearby. Then crowds began running through the narrow street past the house. The roar of exploding hand grenades drew closer. To alert the troops to their presence, Ernst Vollenweider, the Swissair flight engineer, thrust his white undershirt through a barred window.

By this time, the guerrilla guards had evaporated, and Vollenweider called out: "Prisoners! Swiss! Englishmen!" Suddenly, the small interior court of the house was full of soldiers in red berets. They burst through the door. Laughing, they shook hands with the hostages. But almost immediately an officer interrupted them. "Fast!" he barked. "Come along."

Filing outside, the hostages followed their liberators through the narrow quarters. Said one man, "A tank was systematically clearing the streets. When we passed it and the gun went off, it made us jump, and that made the soldiers laugh. But they were happy anyway—so happy that they emptied entire magazines from their submachine guns into the air."

Soon the hostages were led to safety after an ordeal which had lasted almost three weeks. Now there were only thirty-eight Americans left to be found.

During these tense days, President Nasser of Egypt struggled desperately to end the fighting and to avoid the larger conflict he saw brewing. He first dispatched a highranking emissary to Amman to attempt to negotiate a cease-fire between Hussein and the leader of the guerrillas, Yasser Arafat. Rebuffed by both men, he convened an Arab summit meeting in Cairo's Hilton Hotel. But Hussein and Arafat refused to attend. Despite the absence of these principals, the conference decided to send a peace delegation to Amman, led by Premier Gaafar Mohammad al-Nimeiry of Sudan.

Twice, at grave personal risk, al-Nimeiry flew into Amman, and on September 25, the same day that the first hostages were found and freed, he finally succeeded in persuading the warring parties to accept an armistice.

Concurrently, Prime Minister Heath wrote to Nasser, asking him to intercede on behalf of the hostages. As a result, Egyptian embassy personnel in Amman made contact with the Popular Front. The guerrillas were now in a desperate situation. Water had run out, food was short, and they could no longer guarantee the safety of the people they held.

At last, on September 26, in the forenoon, a guerrilla calling himself Abu Khaled appeared at the house where the bulk of the American hostages were detained. Khaled explained that TWA Capt. Carroll Woods was to be guided to the Egyptian embassy by a guerrilla girl. There he was to transmit the "final demands" of the Front. These were as follows: They wanted the curfew lifted and an end to the military government instituted by Hussein. They wanted the right to bury their dead. They wanted the armistice to be observed.

Woods and the girl left, and now everything proceeded swiftly. American contractor Feinstein recalled later: "I was in the kitchen opening a can of peas. A guerrilla entered in the company of an Egyptian and said, 'All of you are free!' Then the Egyptian—who used a walking cane to help a limp—led us through the backyard. He was very excited. He said he was taking us to some Red Cross buses nearby. Keeping close to the walls of houses, we followed him."

"Many Palestinians were watching us," said Miriam Beeber. "They knew that we were on our way to freedom. One man came running up, holding a small child in his arms. 'America! America!' he cried. He wanted to give us the child to take with us. He thought the Jordanians were going to massacre them all, and he wanted to save his child."

The Red Cross buses were not where they were supposed to be, so the Egyptian—he was a diplomat from the embassy—tied a white handkerchief to his cane and led the hostages through the no-man's-land that Amman had become. Despite the armistice, shooting was still going on.

Finally, the Egyptian deposited the group in an industrial building in the heart of Amman and left to find the buses. Two agonizing hours passed, but at last he returned with a Red Cross delegate and the vehicles. As the hostages got in, machine-gun rounds whistled about. "Duck!" the Egyptian yelled, and the buses sped away.

Fifteen minutes later, they reached a Red Cross hospital. The front of it was shot up, and broken glass was everywhere. Wounded lay in the corridors.

"The next morning," Miriam said, "a Palestinian nurse led us through the hospital. There I saw children who had lost their arms, children with eyes torn out by artillery-shell fragments. I'll never be able to forget it."

After breakfast, the hostages were taken to the airport and put aboard planes to begin their long-awaited journey back to New York.

At noon the same day, in Cairo, Nasser crowned his role as negotiator. After six hours of talks, King Hussein and his main foe, Arafat, shook hands. It was a cool handshake. But it marked the end of the civil war. Two days later, the last six hostages—the men who had been held in Irbid—were freed.

In the last analysis, what did the skyjackers achieve? One of their avowed purposes was to draw attention to the plight of the Palestinian refugees. In this they were certainly successful, not only with the hostages, who were subjected to constant propaganda, but with the world at large, which followed the skyjackings closely.

Also, following the return of the last hostages, the Western nations lived up to their promise to release Leila Khaled and the six other commandos held by Switzerland and West Germany. They were flown to Cairo. Israel released no Arab prisoners.

Lastly, despite official disapproval of the hijackings, the Popular Front gained status and admiration among some Arabs for the audacity and nerve it displayed in stealing the four aircraft. In an area as volatile as the Middle East, the Front's success may turn out to have as yet unknown effects.

But there is a debit side to the ledger, too. The hijackings served as a warning to the Western nations that they had better take stronger steps to safeguard their airplanes. As early as September 11, President Nixon announced that armed plainclothes guards would be aboard many United States flights. Other precautions would also be taken. In the future, the odds are high that aerial hijackers will be apprehended or—as in the case of Leila Khaled's accomplice—fatally wounded.

The risk to the lives of innocent people was enormous. Fortunately, none of the hostages was injured, but in the civil war, which the hijackings helped to trigger, the death and devastation were catastrophic. Estimates of the number of casualties have ranged from 5000 to 20,000, and nobody knows how many women and children from the Palestinian refugee camps were among them.

Undoubtedly, President Nasser was himself a victim of the crisis. His efforts to conciliate the warring factions had been strenuous, and at the close of the negotiations on September 27 he said, "All I want now is sleep!"

The following day, at 6:15 P.M., Nasser died at his home in a suburb of Cairo. Because he had agreed to the American plan for peace in the Middle East and was even then working toward implementing it, he was considered merely another of the Popular Front's many enemies. But for the millions of Arabs who mourned Nasser from the Atlantic coast of Africa to the Persian Gulf, his loss was incalculable.

Finally, despite the propaganda value of the skyjackings, the reaction around the world was strongly condemnatory. U Thant, Secretary General of the United Nations, labeled them "savage and inhuman acts," and called for "prompt and effective measures to put a stop to this return to the law of the jungle." Pope Paul said, "These outrageous acts of piracy must never be repeated."

Though the guerrillas may have drawn attention to their cause, they lost much of the world's sympathy in doing it.

27

Patrolling the Deadly Streets of Belfast

Peter Lennon

After its final defeat in 1923, the Irish Republican Army contin- ued to sputter like a damp fuse. When Eamon de Valera became Prime Minister of Eire in 1932, he suppressed his former com- rades-in-arms with a firm hand. By 1949 the Dublin Brigade of the IRA was down to forty members.

In the year 1949 the Irish Free State became a republic and took itself out of the British Commonwealth. It looked as if the IRA had become rebels without a cause. But the six counties in the north known as Ulster remained tied to England, and pos- sessed their own Protestant-dominated Parliament. Here was a continuing cause! For Ireland could not be truly free—so the IRA argued—until all Ireland was rid of the British yoke.

The fact that the Catholic minority in the north was denied jobs, segregated and in general treated like second-class citizens, was reason enough to make trouble. From 1949 to 1968 the IRA waged a spasmodic campaign of border raids and terror to help the northern Catholics. But it was not until 1968 that the Catholics showed any real appreciation of this help. In that year, they began to demonstrate—peaceably enough—for better homes and jobs and a place in the government. The demonstrations soon led to bloody rioting, as the Protestants reacted harshly to what seemed a threat to their control.

Soon there were British troops in Ulster to keep the peace. And scores of IRA operators, representing the more violent faction of that shadowy organization, were drifting in to make trouble and to train their Catholic comrades in the ways of clandestine warfare.

Sniping, looting and burning became the order of the days and nights. Up to now, more than five hundred lives have been lost. One of the most terrible days came on January 30, 1972, during a Catholic march in Londonderry. Goaded and perhaps shot at by the marchers, British troops opened fire. Thirteen Catholic civilians were killed and many more wounded, as "Bloody Sunday" went into the sad history of Ulster.

More vividly than anything else I have read, the following article describes the climate of fear and violence of life in Belfast, Ulster's capital city. The time is the grim winter of 1970–71, and the writer, Peter Lennon, is a reporter for The London Sunday Times. *As vantage point, he takes a young British soldier with no special ax to grind, just trying to do his job and get out alive. But there are overtones here that affect us all. For Ulster is a microcosm—if an extreme one—of the world of violence in which we all live.*

PRIVATE GEORGE FERGUSON, perched on the back of the hooded Land-Rover as it sped into the center of Belfast, stared in disbelief at a sign outside a British store: BOMB DAMAGE SALE. A queue of typically British housewives were in line outside, hoping for bargains—war-soiled dresses or smoke-damaged handbags.

The stores—Marks and Spencer, Woolworths—the red telephone booths, spacious streets and low buildings were just like those in any large provincial town in Britain. It was only when the vehicle came out of Royal Avenue in full view of the city hall that Ferguson had the first hint he was in a town with a colonial history. It was a white, palatial, grandiose building, so unlike the modest, squat, red-brick city halls he was used to at home.

Ferguson, aged twenty-five, married, with one six-year-old daughter back in Balham, outside London, was late following his regiment to Belfast. A minor ulcer operation had saved him thirty days of his four-month tour of duty. A sincere, slow young man, he had been an apprentice butcher, then joined the army to "get security" while he made up his mind what trade he would follow. There was a vague motive of outdoing his father. "He was always going on about his six years in the RAF," George told his buddies. "So I said, 'Right! I'll do six years in the army.'" But he had now decided that when he got out he would be a plumber. "You hardly ever hear of them going on strike," he explained.

A boot nudged his foot: "You're dreamin', mate," his companion McKinley said. "Snap out of it or it may be your last dream."

Caught in a sharp, wintry light, even the prosperous center of this city of half a million people looked maimed. Almost every street seemed to have office windows fresh-patched with plywood. A short string of three shops was boarded up. By the railway station they passed a sporting-goods store which was now nothing more than a base of rubble and a hollow, ragged shaft tunneling up to a pierced roof. Two hotels on the main street had FOR SALE signs.

When they swung past the new Belfast Europa Hotel and headed up wide, shabby Grosvenor Road toward the Falls Road section, the sense of desolation became intense. At intersections along Falls Road paving stones had been ripped up and thrown by demonstrators, leaving black, pitted gullies for the rain. In one blasted storefront some children sat chatting on what had been the shelf space. A pub was gutted. On the fronts of houses petrol bombs had left black scorches like giant smudged finger-prints pointing up to bedroom windows. And when the Land-Rover came into a new housing estate of neat, semi-detached houses, the roads were littered with stones and glittered with slivers of glass. It was not like a bombed city so much as a depressed city suffering from some kind of eczema of boils and bursts and blemishes. Since the British had resorted to internment without trial a month or more ago, terrorist bombing, commando attacks on the army and mob rioting had occurred night and day.

A four-year-old child waddled out of a front garden and clumsily heaved a small stone at the Land-Rover.

"I heard it was bad," Ferguson said bitterly, "but this is ridiculous."

Ferguson was already uneasy. He had never been under fire. The regiment's last assignment had been guarding Windsor Castle. "We're keeping an eye on the Queen's cutlery," they told the girls in town. Before that there had been three pleasantly monotonous years on the Rhine, and ten weeks of pointless jungle maneuvers in Ghana.

They were within a few minutes of the barracks. They took a sharp turn into a long narrow street of terraced houses. A woman was pushing a baby carriage and dragging a stumbling child after her. Ferguson was half conscious of a man beginning to walk rapidly across the road as they passed. When the man got to the center of the road he did a curious kind of dancing side-step, a shot rang out and Ferguson watched in a stupor as blood gushed from McKinley's arm. The second shot brought him to his senses. He leapt from the skidding Land-Rover, nerves blurring his vision, and flattened himself against one of the houses. "Don't ever throw yourself flat," the sergeant had warned, "or they'll drop a petrol bomb on you and roast you for supper. And remember, the IRA can run into any door on the street, but *you'd* better know what's behind it before you run in."

While the driver frantically applied a tourniquet to the wounded man, Ferguson crouched nearby and swung his rifle slowly over the faces of the quiet houses. People came to the doors and watched with vague interest. There was a sticker on a window near his shoulder: RELEASE THE INTERNEES.

He felt he was being made a fool of, standing armed and alert in a street full of indifferent women, children and old men. It was as shocking to him as if a crowd in England had decided not to come to the aid of someone hurt in a road accident. At a signal from the driver he sprang into the Land-Rover and they took off at top speed. A single voice called out: "G'wan ye bastards!" and the shout was taken up by teenagers on street corners farther up the road. Ferguson was enraged.

"The houses were so alike I didn't even see which one he ran into," Ferguson said nervously to the commanding officer.

"Not to worry," said the major briskly. "In Falls Road Ballymurphy they could run into almost any house. That is one of our difficulties—to win over the moderates so that they can be trusted not to give shelter to the gunmen. I think we could safely say we have succeeded in winning over 80 per cent of the moderates here," the major said absent-mindedly.

Packing away his gear with Sandy, the quartermaster, Ferguson asked: "Is it true that 80 per cent are moderates around here?"

"If 80 per cent are moderates I wouldn't like to meet a bloody militant," Sandy said. "Come on and I'll give you the guided tour."

The Henry Taggart barracks was a converted assembly hall set on a slope. Alongside, deep in the sandbagged and barbed-wire area, was a school, and below the school was a corrugated hall used as a dormitory for the soldiers. The small complex also contained a police substation.

"So we are a prime target," Sandy said cheerfully. "If there is anything those Fenian bastards hate more than the army it's the Royal Ulster Constabulary. See how nicely we're fixed?" He pointed up the slope to a deserted twelve-story apartment house. "Snipers creep in there at night and try to pick us off. By the time we surround it they've vanished." Ferguson noticed that the moment Sandy stepped into the open—despite the sentries and sandbagged gates—he had drawn his revolver. Now he waved it down the hill toward a vast stretch of semi-detached houses. "That's the petrol-bomb and stone-throwing area. At night they sometimes come right up to the gates." They stepped inside again. "This is where you'll bunk," Sandy said. The corrugated hall was pitted with several hundred bullet holes. "We were warned," said Sandy, "that being an intervention company we would probably be hard hit. Just this week we've had three injured, and young Scott got picked off by a sniper up there." He pointed to a heavily sandbagged, elevated sentry post in which Ferguson could just make out the lower half of the sentry's face. "Got him in the neck and hit the spine. He's in the Royal Victoria now, paralyzed from the neck down. Only twenty, poor bastard."

"Are there any good pubs?" Ferguson asked to change the subject.

"You must be joking," Sandy said. "The last one of our lot went to a pub in civvies they took him out and blew his head off up a lane. You can't even get parcels from home—they might be bombs. I tell you, the only fresh air you're going to get is out on foot patrol, and even though you're liable to lose your noggin you'll soon be glad of that. I think sometimes I'm going crackers down in this sandbagged tomb." Sandy gave the corrugated structure a sharp kick.

Of the next seventy-two hours, Ferguson was only between the sheets for ten. The regulation was four hours on and eight hours off, but even when he was technically off duty he still had to sleep in full kit and be ready to move at a moment's notice. At first it was cordoning off streets while the bomb-disposal squad worked against time to dismantle bombs which the IRA had left in office blocks or official buildings. Since the IRA generally warned people to clear out a few moments in advance, the army had only five or ten minutes—if that—to do the job. Some of the gelignite bombs did not go off, but when they did they shattered glass for half a block.

The only strip club in town had been blasted weeks before. It was the one place the soldiers could get women—all imported from England. Although the people were friendly in the Protestant areas . . . the troops could no longer move around the city with any kind of freedom. . . . On the Catholic side the girls were afraid to talk to them. Those who went out even briefly with a soldier often ended up with their heads shaven.

"They say that when we first came, after the riots of '69, the Catholics came out and cheered us," Sandy said one night as they sat polishing their gear. "Now you're lucky if you only get stoned. It's a mess. The more we wait for the politicians to make up their minds, the more troops we have to have. Seventeen hundred came in last week. That brings us up to just about 14,000 in Ulster alone. Not to mention a few thousand local troopers and the police. We can't even act like soldiers, either—we're like some kind of bleedin' police. When you go out there facing a mob of women and children you have to be careful not to shoot the kids."

"Why?" demanded a lean sergeant named Harrison who had been in Cyprus. "They're only a lot of animals."

Ferguson found it depressing in the long, cluttered room packed tightly with bunks. It reminded him of the hold of a troopship. The windows were all blacked out with heavy blue curtains or sandbagged to within two inches of the top of the glass. They sat around for hours listlessly turning the pages of girlie magazines or talking about home. Sometimes they would run a film on the projector: *Soldier Blue* or some other Western.

After three days Ferguson had his first turn at night foot patrol. "It might not sound like it, mate, but it's the best way," Sandy said. "Our chaps got ambushed four times in a week in the Land-Rovers, and when you get stuck you're just a sitting target. They blew the front wheel off a pig (armored car) a couple of weeks ago and dropped petrol bombs on the men as they climbed out. On foot patrol all the men are at the ready all the time. Funny thing is *we* can't patrol much in cars, but the police daren't show themselves on foot. They're a poor lot."

Sergeant Harrison had chosen a flak jacket for Ferguson. " 'Ere," he said. "A beauty for you." He dangled the jacket in front of Ferguson. There was a tear in it like an exclamation mark: a hole and a split.

"Belonged to one of our blokes," Harrison said. "He was riding in a reinforced Land-Rover the other week and a sniper got him. Right through the wall of the Rover, through the back of his jacket and out the front. High-velocity rifle. They've only got half a dozen good snipers, but when they come around you're in trouble. You wear it, mate," Harrison said, tossing the jacket to Ferguson. "On the principle that no sniper is good enough to strike twice through the same hole."

They marched down the narrow corridor past the mess and the faintly nauseating smell of stale shepherd's pie. At the gate the sergeant checked on the radio code and they set off, well-spaced, down into the Protestant area. The sergeant carried a rifle with a telescopic night lens. He was an official sniper. The corporal had a gas gun and one of the men carried a pistol adapted for firing fat, 5½-inch rubber bullets. "It's like getting a whack with a cricket ball right in the kisser at double the speed of the fastest man who ever bowled for England," Sandy had said. "Once one of the men shot it into a rioter at close range and it pierced his stomach."

The streets of the Protestant working class were as cheerless and dank as those in the Catholic quarter, but few were damaged. People in the low doorways greeted them in murmurs and once or twice girls joked with them for a moment. But the sergeant was tense and impatient.

As they filed down a road toward the corrugated barricade which marked the end of the Protestant street and the beginning of the Catholic area, they were followed by children asking for badges. . . .

The sergeant, irritated, told them to shove off.

Ferguson was in the Catholic area before he realized it. The houses and poorly lit streets were identical, but here the people in the streets—young couples or silent older men and women—

passed the soldiers without a word. A woman dragging two children behind her zig-zagged through the soldiers as if they did not exist. George felt he was in a dream, carrying the painless wound of his flak jacket through a town where everyone was mute. The patrol began to walk up Farringdon Gardens. A double row of two-hundred terraced houses had been burned. They walked up the spectral street, the gutted houses with their roofs silhouetted in blackened, twisted patterns against a wintry sky. It was just like the street Ferguson lived on in London, only here the houses looked as if they were giant, scorched twigs of brown paper that had been used to light some monster's pipe.

"The area used to be mixed," Sandy said. "The Protestants burned their own houses so that the Catholics couldn't get at them. The Catholics did the same thing. And some did a bit of both."

"They must be crazy," Ferguson said. "I'm a Catholic, but religion doesn't make me daft. Of course I hardly ever go to church."

"It's religion and politics and unemployment and God knows what else," Sandy said. "Forty per cent of the bastards in this area are unemployed. So they have all day to think up mischief."

"What do you do with an IRA man when we catch him?" Ferguson asked.

"What do you fancy?" Sandy asked.

At 4:45 the next morning Ferguson was roughly awakened by a push from a sergeant. He sprang from his bunk. All around him the men were blackening their faces. "We got a tip a couple of IRA men are back visiting their old mums in Ballymurphy, so we're going to back up the paratroops when they pick 'em up. Look out for trouble," the sergeant said.

They ran full tilt behind the paras down into the housing estate. When they came to a double row of quiet houses by a church the men filtered into the front gardens and crouched under each window in the darkness. They had hardly come to a halt when there was a shout. Then from behind a house close to Ferguson someone began to clatter a dustbin lid. In a moment the street was a pandemonium of rhythmically clattering dustbin lids and flying stones, warning the IRA men of the presence of the army. From the depths of a narrow lane a milk bottle came swinging up in the air and crashed at Ferguson's feet. He had to leap aside to avoid the stream of flaming liquid. A soldier swung on his heel and fired into the lane.

The paras had already gone in. They leaped from the gardens and smashed the windows of the houses. From the center of the road a marksman aimed at a door and shouted, "Come out, you Fenian bastard." The door opened and a pale young man in shirt and trousers stood there. A soldier fired a rubber bullet at his chest, knocking him back into the hall. Other troops had moved into the houses, crashing through the doors. Babies were screaming and women protesting shrilly. Ferguson saw a gray-haired man being dragged out of a house in vest and trousers, his feet bare. He was clutching at his trousers to keep them up and trying to walk gingerly along the path strewn with glass. The soldier pulled him along. The man's feet were bleeding.

When Ferguson went into one house he saw that all the floor boards had been ripped up in a search for arms. A woman sat weeping in a chair and beside her a girl of about nine stood staring at him fearfully. Both her hands were wrapped in dirty bandages from a previous riot.

Within half an hour they had pulled back to barracks, and then the rioting started. From the darkness across the road men, women and children appeared, throwing stones and lobbing home-made petrol bombs. From different points in the darkness gunfire rang out, but few of the shots hit the barracks. For hours, until dawn broke clearly, there was a muddled mass of shouting, stoning and intermittent shooting from the darkness. There was something pointless and hopeless about the skirmishing. Ferguson was jumpy from lack of sleep, and when something cracked near him he instinctively swung and fired into the darkness. He suddenly realized that he'd fired where a bunch of kids had been standing. Sickened, he peered hard to see if he had hit anyone, but he couldn't make out anything but restless shrieking shadows.

As Ferguson tried to drop off to sleep in his bunk that night, his whole body would tense up at intervals with apprehension when he thought that his bullet might have struck a child. He wondered what his wife would think. He had mentioned it to one of the other men as they had filed back into the corrugated hut, but the man had just shrugged indifferently. Ferguson noticed that some of the men, particularly those who had served in Cyprus or Aden, referred to the people simply as "the natives." He got the impression that Sergeant Harrison was itching to shoot one of them. He had himself felt a burst of indiscriminate rage as he chased the mob in the darkness and remembered young Scott, only twenty years old and paralyzed from the neck down for the rest of his life. He was already prepared to kill a sniper if he spotted one. In the brawling darkness, his uncertain image of what an IRA man looked like began to expand until he found himself half-consciously including twelve-year-old stone-throwers.

Patrolling Ballymurphy in the clear light of the following afternoon, he was even more confused. This was what the newspapers called a "Catholic ghetto," but the well-spaced houses with their once-neat front gardens, set on slopes, bore no resemblance to his idea of a ghetto. It was a shade more attractive than his own home back in England. It had a pleasant shopping center, spoiled now by a litter of stones, broken glass and abandoned dustbin lids.

He had first looked with some sympathy at the stout mothers gathered around the shopfronts and had smiled at the cheeky, smudged faces asking for badges. But after his experience with the shrieking mob, he now looked at them with growing resentment and fear. It was suddenly clear to him that at any moment of the day or night, in the most innocent surroundings, he faced death, and that these people were indifferent to his death. And they were Catholics like himself. He had said it once, peevish and exasperated, to a woman, "I'm an RC just like you," but she clearly hadn't believed him. It seemed too late now for any British soldier to win their confidence. They seemed to take religion much more seriously than he did. A lot of the tough young men gathered in the streets reminded him more of sullen, hostile coal miners after a pit collapse.

When his three months' tour of duty was up he would go home. But probably he'd be back. Some of the men had been here three times. Next time he might be guarding prisoners. Would he have to watch them being tortured?

Sergeant Harrison had said that the army was doing a job now of rounding up the IRA; the internees were starting to sing, and sing well.

There was a lot of talk about the interrogation centers in the internment camp. When they brought in a suspect they put a thick sack over his head and kept it there for five or six days. The rumor was that they had learned the trick from the Russian secret police. The suspects completely lost track of what time it was, where they were, or who was talking to them, threatening them.

They even took suspects up in a helicopter, flew around for a few minutes so the suspect would think they had gained altitude, and then dropped them out from about twenty feet up. The prisoners were interrogated for days by people whose faces they never saw. Sandy said you could go mad with a sack on your head like that. Ferguson thought for a moment of living for days in suffocating darkness, surrounded by hostile voices, and felt he would not be able to stand up to it for more than a few hours.

The police were supposedly doing the interrogating but it was the army that was rounding up the men and handing them over. He knew that some of the soldiers didn't care who they picked up. If they couldn't get the right IRA man, one of his family would do. "How many IRA men did we pick up?" George asked the sergeant.

"Oh, none of those people were IRA men," the sergeant said. Even the old man Ferguson had seen dragged over the broken glass had been let go. The raid had been for nothing—they hadn't picked up any real suspects. It was a mess.

Walking in the fresh breeze through Ballymurphy, his rifle tensely at the ready, he felt apprehensive of the future. A little girl carrying a full milk bottle walked past him. They would probably be filling it with petrol before dark, he thought bitterly.

Afterword

So here are the saboteurs—famous and infamous—of the present century. What strange bedfellows they make! Nimble Schellenberg, double-faced Dasch and torpid, sullen Van der Lubbe; Prince Borghese and Captain von Rintelen, those two *beau saboteurs;* the gallant Poles and the hard-bitten Norwegians . . .

What lesson can we learn from all this undercover violence by men of good will and of bad?

Perhaps no composite picture emerges of what makes a saboteur. But one thing is very clear as the century grows older: sabotage today is justified *only* in wartime or when one's own country is occupied by the enemy. No aura of romance, no shred of nobility clings to it today. It has become a dirty, brutal business, so dangerous now that every precaution must be taken, every scrap of understanding brought to bear on the *whys* and the *wherefores*.

By land, sea and air sabotage has become a dread and virulent threat to our survival. Take a look at these current headlines, picked at random:

SWISS AMBASSADOR KIDNAPPED IN RIO . . . SABOTAGE SUSPECTED AS DUTCH SHIP BURNS IN NORTH SEA . . . PALESTINE GUERRILLAS KILL JORDAN PRIME MINISTER IN CAIRO . . . CANADIAN TERRORISTS SIEZE BRITISH DIPLOMAT. Think of the hemorrhage of Ulster, the tinder box of the Middle East as a whole, the dark and terrible fate of the eleven Israeli athletes and coaches at the 1972 Olympic Games in Munich. And, nearer home, the hijacking of planes and—more terrifying still —the placing of time bombs in them. There is no sense in hoping that these forms of violence will just go away, because they won't.

There will always be people who like to blow things up by night and stealth. And as long as there are lines of battle, military or political, there will be behind-the-lines activity. Wherever there are four columns in uniform, there will be a Fifth Column within the camp or city of the foe. The recognition of this fact, and some knowledge of the forms that sabotage can take, will help to make it less of a terror unknown.

My last selection of all has some bearing on these harsh facts. It is called "First Patrol." It was written by J. Bryan, III for Es- quire *in the 1950s, but its message is timeless:*

CROUCHED there in the sweaty dark, waiting, waiting for the signal, the young soldier tried again to make his mind go blank. It still wouldn't, so he counted a thousand by fives. Then he ordered his first meal when he'd get back home, and that made him think of the girl who helped out at the bakery, and he counted another thousand. But always his imagination squirmed loose and ran ahead, to the shock and the scream, the torn flesh and the—the hot gush—

Five! *Ten!* Fifteen! Twenty, twenty-five, thirty . . .

He was into the six hundreds when he realized that his left arm had gone to sleep. Slowly he began to ease his weight off it, slowly, carefully, as the captain had told them, so that their buckles wouldn't scrape or their straps creak; slowly, carefully, in the dead quiet. His numb arm suddenly jerked free, and his bracelet rapped against Red's helmet: *clink!*

God! He bit off his breath and listened, cowering from the alarm that had to follow. Now? *Now?* Now? Not a sound. Nothing. Nothing but his heart pounding. *What was that?* His eyes strained into the blackness. Nothing. You're *sure?* Listen! Nothing. His pulse slackened. Still nothing: no shouts, no trampling feet, nothing. He drew a shallow breath, and another. Presently he drew a deep one. . . . What was all the panic about? The enemy couldn't have heard *that* little noise, not through these thick planks! Especially since they'd all pulled back, most probably, to wait for dawn. No, they hadn't heard it. They *couldn't* have. You were right on top of it, and you'd heard it only because noises always sound louder in the dark. That's it. Chances were, nobody else in here had heard a thing.

Oh, no? Not even the sergeant, that big bastard up there, big as a skinned mule and twice as ugly? Trust his big flapping ears to catch everything! As soon as this patrol is over, he'll run right to the captain and tell him you made more noise, the big bastard, than a—than a pack horse falling down a mountain. Serve him right if he got his tonight, the—

Hold on, there! Hold *on* a minute! Who made the noise, you or the sergeant? The sergeant's certainly big and he's certainly ugly, but he didn't make sergeant just for that. He made it because he's proved he's a good man in a fight.

And speaking of such, how about *you?* Are *you* good in there, too? Not dock fighting or alley fighting, but *fighting.* Have you been at it long yourself? Oh, so this is your first time out! Then no wonder you clatter around like a holiday drunk! Keep that up, and this first fight will be your—Don't believe it! You'll live through it. Plenty of other men have. Shorty did, and look at him when they brought him home: arm gone, hole in his belly you could. . . . No! No! *Don't!*

. . . Why, what's the matter? Mother's boy doesn't like to think about getting hurt? A little scared, maybe? No? So that's beer trickling down your neck and the back of your knees? Or is it that hot in here? Just remember: whatever happens, don't say they didn't warn you. Father warned you, Shorty warned you, they all warned you: never volunteer. They said they'd learned it the hard way, but that even if the general asks for help in eating his dinner, *nev-er vol-un-teer*. They warned you, but you knew better. Fresh at the front, hardly got your land legs yet, and you volunteer. There wouldn't be enough glory to go around: you had to get your share before it gave out. And look at you now!

Well, you hadn't *exactly* volunteered. . . .

Just before the noon meal today—that is, yesterday—the sergeant had said, "There's one coming up tonight I never heard the like of, and I've been in this army a long, long time. I wouldn't lie to you. All I can say is, if we pull it off, it'll be one for the records. The captain will tell you the rest. All right: volunteers?"

The whole outfit stepped forward, so you stepped with them.

The sergeant said, "I can use about half of you. High-dice it out," and he threw down a pair.

Lefty rolled high, then you, then Red, then the rest.

When the captain told them what the job was, they couldn't believe it. The general must be crazy! Hazily, you heard the captain finish, "Drink as little as possible this afternoon. We'll be in there most of the night. No rations. We can't risk the slightest sound. Don't forget that, you men: *no noise!* Everything clear now? Any questions? Dis-*miss!*"

The captain was still shaky from his last attack of malaria, but he'd be there with them. The men were glad to hear it. They liked to say, "The general will get us in, and the captain will get us out." He was the kind of officer who, when you did wrong, gave you hell in his tent, but when you used your head, praised you in front of everybody. You couldn't let the captain down, even if this *was* going to be that thing you dreaded and hated, the thing that haunted you, a—a—(spit it out!) a knife fight, a knife fight in the *dark,* with wrestling and ripping, and hot, wet, red. . . .

The youngster shut his eyes tight and tried to shake the picture from his mind. Easy! Careful of that helmet! He slumped back, panting. After a moment, he made himself slide the knife from its sheath at his belt, and heft it, and run his thumb along the blade. It was a *man's* knife. A knife like this, and you—

Somebody was pinching his shoulder. He leaned toward it. Red whispered, "Get set! Pass the word!" He had to swallow before he could speak. He settled his helmet and belt, shifted his chin strap and settled his helmet and belt again. Suddenly he began to yawn and couldn't stop. There was a faint light: the captain had opened the hatch. He was gone at once, and Lefty took his place. Then Red took Lefty's. The youngster hitched forward, still yawning. Red was gone. The youngster touched his holy medal as the sergeant pointed to him: *now!*

He clutched the sides of the hatch, and swung down, and dropped from the belly of the wooden horse into the streets of Troy.